Employee-Driven Systems for Safe Behavior

Employee-Driven Systems for Safe Behavior

Integrating Behavioral and Statistical Methodologies

Thomas R. Krause, Ph.D.
Co-Founder and President
Behavioral Science Technology, Inc.

 VAN NOSTRAND REINHOLD
IⓉP™ A Division of International Thomson Publishing Inc.

New York • Albany • Bonn • Boston • Detroit • London • Madrid • Melbourne
Mexico City • Paris • San Francisco • Singapore • Tokyo • Toronto

Back cover photo courtesy of Andrew Gilman
Cover design: Martin Mellein

Van Nostrand Reinhold Staff
Editor: Jane Kinney
Production Editor: Barbara Mathieu
Production Manager: Jim Forbin

I⏇P™ Van Nostrand Reinhold is a division of International Thomson Publishing, Inc.
The ITP logo is a trademark under license

Printed in the United States of America
For more information, contact:

Van Nostrand Reinhold
115 Fifth Avenue
New York, NY 10003

Chapman & Hall GmbH
Pappelallee 3
69469 Weinheim
Germany

Chapman & Hall
2-6 Boundary Row
London
SE1 8HN
United Kingdom

International Thomson Publishing Asia
221 Henderson Road #05-10
Henderson Building
Singapore 0315

Thomas Nelson Australia
102 Dodds Street
South Melbourne, 3205
Victoria, Australia

International Thomson Publishing Japan
Hirakawacho Kyowa Building, 3F
2-2-1 Hirakawacho
Chiyoda-ku, 102 Tokyo
Japan

Nelson Canada
1120 Birchmount Road
Scarborough, Ontario
Canada M1K 5G4

International Thomson Editores
Seneca 53
Col. Polanco
11560 Mexico D.F. Mexico

4 5 6 7 8 9 10 BBR 01 00 99 98 97

Library of Congress Cataloging-in-Publication Data
Krause, Thomas R.
    Employee-driven systems for sare behavior : integrating behavioral and statistical methodologies / Thomas R. Krause.
        p.   cm.
    Includes bibliographical references and index.
    ISBN 0-442-01671-9 (hc.)
    1. Industrial safety.   2. Industrial safety—Statistical methods.
3. Total quality management.   I. Title.
T55.K75   1995
658.3'82—dc20   95-5189
                                                                   CIP

Contents

Preface

QUALITY-BASED SAFETY = BEHAVIOR-BASED SAFETY

Process approaches to quality and safety are so complementary that, when they are both at work in a facility, they tend to reinforce each other. The safety effort gains strength from the quality effort, and vice versa. The close match between these two methods also means that a facility using the employee-driven process approach in either safety or quality, but not both, runs the risk of sending an inconsistent message to the workforce, thereby losing effectiveness from the process approach where it is working.

It is noteworthy that companies applying behavior-based safety extensively have discovered that its long-term effects are often more profound than those following quality improvement. Perhaps this is due to the "natural motive" for safety improvement found almost universally in first-level employees. In any case, this "priority" of safety over quality bears looking into. More than one company has reported that it "learned more about quality from behavior-based safety than from quality."

This linkage of these two methods is no accident. Deming and others showed industry how to use statistical methods to identify, track, and manage the upstream production factors that are the final common pathway to quality. This approach to quality necessarily means involving employees who are close to the production process. In workplace safety, this same approach combines statistical methods with behavioral science methods to track and manage the upstream factor that is the final common pathway of safety performance. That safety factor is behavior itself. The two essential components of "quality-based" safety are

- behavioral science methods
- statistical methods familiar to in-depth users of total quality management (TQM)

The behavioral science component provides the theoretical understanding of behavior, along with a practical method for measuring the incidence of identified

ix

critical behaviors. The statistical component is used to record and interpret the ongoing behavior measurement and to properly manage the downstream results measured by incident frequency rates.

Quality and Safety

In some ways the topic of this book is not new. Many observers have speculated that it should be possible "somehow" to apply quality methods to safety. In the late 1980s, safety magazines and journals published a number of articles offering general "safety translations" of Deming's famous 14 Points. The authors of those articles were primarily concerned with the message that safety was *not yet* using the Deming approach. That message was a necessary first step pointing beyond the old safety programs. The theme of those articles was that the reliance of traditional safety on games and posters as well as on incidence rates was the same as the older quality emphasis on defect management. Deming had shown the way beyond defect management by focusing on system improvement. He did this by teaching quality improvement teams how to identify, measure, and manage the upstream predictors of quality. In recent years safety professionals have looked for positive, practical ways to "apply quality" to safety. The crucial question for safety is: Exactly which factors are the upstream predictors of safety performance?

The central theme of this book is that the incidence of site-specific at-risk behaviors is the single most reliable upstream predictor of safety performance. Following from that central theme, the book presents background information on the basic concepts of behavioral science (Chapters 3 and 4) and on the close tie between those concepts and the basic quality issues of measurement and employee involvement (Chapters 1, 2, and 5). Part II of the book opens with an overview of measurement issues and of statistical process control (SPC). Chapters 8 and 9 present the continuous improvement applications of various instruments and procedures of behavioral science. Part III addresses management issues in safety, ranging from incident investigation to ergonomics, and Part IV discusses illustrative case histories of sites using employee-driven safety to manage continuous improvement.

SCIENTIFIC METHOD—THE CORE OF QUALITY AND OF BEHAVIOR-BASED SAFETY

Behavioral science incorporates the same statistical principles used in TQM. This is not because of Deming or the quality movement, but because the quality methods are the methods at the basis of scientific research. Scientific research uses statistical methods as a tool, and behavioral research is no exception. To apply behavioral science to safety necessarily involves the use of statistical tools. TQM and behavioral safety initiatives have two main elements—statistical methodology and employee involvement.

Statistical Methodology

The use of statistical methods (including experimental design) allows us to answer questions such as:

- Which variables are predictors of performance?
- What is the best way to define and measure those variables?
- Which tools are best for analyzing the accumulating data?
- Which tools are best for determining when, how, and to what degree variables are related?

In TQM initiatives, the answers to these and related questions take the form of run charts for tracking and managing upstream factors of production (or service) performance. In behavior-based safety initiatives, these questions are answered by operationally defining critical behaviors, sampling them through observation, and using the resulting data for problem solving.

Employee Involvement

In both quality and safety, the effective use of these statistical methods requires floor-level employee involvement. From the outset of any continuous improvement initiative, involvement at this level is necessary because those employees are closest to the work at issue. They have the most detailed views of what actually goes on at the site, and their initial buy-in is critical to a successful launch.

After the developmental phases of the initiative, employee involvement is central in various ways to the goal of continuous improvement. Involvement brings ownership of the ongoing safety process and thus long-term engagement in its maintenance. This connection is so strong that, in effect, behavior-based safety is the same thing as employee-driven safety, and vice versa. Consequently throughout this book the terms "behavior-based" and "employee-driven" are used interchangeably.

It Ain't as Easy as It Looks

The ideas presented in this book are straightforward. Experienced managers often respond to this material with statements such as, "This isn't anything new in particular, but the configuration is different—it brings many important pieces together in one approach." For their part, on the other hand, when behavioral scientists read of this application to safety, they often say, "Why of course there is a natural fit," without realizing how many organizational realities need to be dealt with in the course of this "natural" fit.

In fact, it is very difficult to implement any significant behavioral and cultural change initiative. All of the systems that produce injuries are stable, with their roots firmly embedded in the culture. Change is not easy, and it is resisted with vigor and even ingenuity. Relations between labor and management often have an implicit rule prohibiting change. One of the primary purposes of culture is to provide stability by avoiding change—even otherwise admittedly "good" change. Most sites have a history of failed change efforts, failures which create skepticism and even cynicism. Furthermore, a business climate of cutbacks and downsizing does not help matters. Managers don't have time for change efforts.

Difficulties abound, and yet the author's experience is that success occurs at a high frequency when the proper guidance is given. As implementation begins, this guidance, which encourages leadership at the site level, needs to be given by someone outside of the site organization. The guidance can come from a consultant within the company or from an outside consultant who has had experience with multiple implementations. Psychologists, for instance, can be effective consultants, but in the author's experience it is easier to train experienced managers in behavioral science than to train psychologists in the realities of organizational life.

Acknowledgments

This book is the result of a collaborative effort. Foremost among its contributors are John Hidley, M.D., co-originator with the author of the behavior-based approach to safety, and Kim Sloat, Ph.D., a long-time associate of the author. The author is also grateful for the contributions of other members of his firm: Don Groover, CIH, CSP; Jim Spigener; Jim Marcombe; Garnett Langston, Ph.D.; Larry Russell, CSP; and Kristen Van Zee. In addition, Marty Mellein designed the cover art; Andrew Gilman provided the graphic work in the charts, figures, and tables; and Stan Hodson's editorial assistance is present throughout the book.

This book is also richer for including the experiences of some remarkable people from industry. They are company representatives who have nurtured employee-driven safety performance at their sites, making solid progress toward continuous improvement. Notable among them are: Paul Villane and Glen Reddish of Monsanto Company; Tom Durbin and Roger Corley of PPG Industries Inc.; Jeff Johnston, Curtis Modisette, and John Ellis of Eastman Chemical Company; Bob Jones, Ron Griffin, Terry Ward, and Eddie Rhea of Boise Cascade; Carl Pederson, Randall Dover, Jerry Flynt, Sid Thomas, Jimmy Snow, and Ray Ward of the Chevron Pascagoula Refinery; Marc Swartz, Jackie Vanderpool, and Jim Mendenhall of Hill's Pet Nutrition; and Manfred Kling and Ron Walts of the Canadian Department of National Defence.

Employee-Driven Systems for Safe Behavior

Part I

Employee-Driven Systems for Safe Behavior

Integrating Behavioral and Statistical Methodologies

1

The Driving Mechanism of Continuous Improvement in Safety

The driving mechanism for continuous improvement in safety is the proper use of modern scientific method coupled with employee involvement. Establishing this mechanism is more easily said than done, however. Management is faced with a daunting challenge, how to maintain in an organization the *focus of effort* that is required for continuous improvement. All kinds of change are stressful to people, even changes that bring improvement. Because of this, resistance to change is a natural thing. This hard fact of life is true in every management field, but is more emphatic in those fields that do not have very well established mechanisms for the basic structures that support the improvement effort: measurement, feedback, continuous training, cultural values and systems. Until recent developments, safety was a prime example of a field handicapped by a lack of adequate structure (see Chapter 3 in *The Behavior-Based Safety Process.*)

In a market economy it is not difficult to maintain a focus on production. The culture in any manufacturing plant supports this focus. Managers and supervisors at all levels support it. Measurement systems are in place to provide frequent, often daily, feedback on small variations in production performance. Everyone understands the priority of production. However, safety is a performance area for which it is much more difficult to maintain a focus. In most companies the cultural and systems support are lacking.

Because of this lack, managers have traditionally attributed variations in safety performance to variations in "awareness." Of course over the years, engineering, facilities, and maintenance have received attention and have provided some safety improvement. But any supervisor or team leader knows that incidents

Don Groover, CIH, CSP, contributed to the development of this chapter.

3

come primarily from the "human element." When workforce safety responsiveness is high, accidents are lower. One sees this in the risk-level of workers who are neither "novices" nor "old hands." Both new and seasoned employees are at-risk for injuries because both are low in responsiveness to safety challenges—the novice through lack of job experience and the old hand through familiarity and complacency. The workers least at risk of injury are those who are familiar with critical task-related behaviors, but who have not yet become set in their ways. This optimal training phase of adaptive readiness to safety is very much a human element but merely identifying it is not enough. The management question is how to maximize this level of readiness for the workforce as a whole. This is another form of the question about how to minimize variability of performance. Lack of effective answers to these questions has led to variable performance—to the Accident/Safety Cycle (see Fig. 1.1).

In business and manufacturing, the concept of variability first became a subject for management in relation to the quality of goods and services. With the advent of the Quality movement a new field has been sketched. The field aims to understand and manage variation by involving employees in teams that problem-solve for continuous improvement. The science and statistics at the core of total quality management (TQM) are solid and dependable, but implementation itself has met with variable success. The reason is that the cultural and feedback mechanisms for quality are not securely in place. In the last analysis, the success or failure of Quality initiatives does not depend on the brilliance or truth of the insights of Deming, Juran, and others. Whether in safety or in quality, the ultimate success of these methods rests with leadership.

The critical test in industry now is how well managers are able to engage and sustain employee involvement in this new kind of applied science. Such ongoing engagement by the workforce is the driving mechanism of continuous improvement.

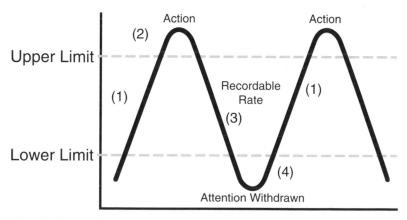

FIGURE 1.1 The accident cycle.

This book presents applied scientific methods successfully adapted in North American business and manufacturing since the early 1980s—scientific methods for the management of safety performance. The disciplines from which the basic knowledge is drawn are behavioral science and statistics. Integrated or fused in the employee-driven approach to safety improvement, these two applied sciences make up the subject of this book. Part I offers an overview of the field, presenting in Chapters 3 and 4 the basic concepts of behavioral science as applied to safety, and in Chapter 5 the overlap between safety and quality. Subsequent parts of the book expand upon each in turn.

Employee Involvement + Scientific Method = Continuous Improvement

The driving mechanism for continuous improvement in safety is the proper use of behavioral and statistical science coupled with employee involvement. The total quality of our scientific knowledge of the world has improved continuously for the past 300 years. The success of science as an institution is very instructive. Like other institutions such as education, finance, and government, science has goals and vision statements. However, most observers agree that the improvement achieved by those other institutions is not continuous. A key factor here is that even the experts in these fields have not established objective standards of improvement, let alone ongoing systems for measurement and feedback—and employee involvement has hardly been considered.

For too long, the field of safety management has labored in this same way— trapped in the swings of the accident cycle, or stalled on a performance plateau (Fig. 1.2). This is not to be wondered at. Think what would happen at most facilities if the line organization viewed production in the same way they have typically viewed safety. The result would be a production nightmare bordering on the strangeness of the command economy of the former Soviet Union.

Seeing this, safety management at some leading companies is becoming more scientific, and not only in the field of engineering solutions. The trend in engineering improvement is, of course, solid and welcome. Quite obviously, however, good engineering alone is not enough. In spite of undeniable safety gains in equipment and procedures, we have seen safety performance variability continue, both within locations and between them. What is needed now is the proper application of scientific method to manage safety performance.

The proper use of these methods to manage safety hinges on two factors:

1. scientific measurement and management of all employee levels of workplace behavior
2. the involvement of all employees in this ongoing feedback and problem-solving process

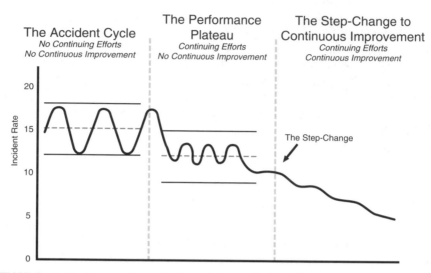

FIGURE 1.2 The three paradigms of safety performance: Accident Cycle, Performance Plateau, and Continuous Improvement.

The reason to focus on behavior is that when an incident occurs, behavior is the crucial final common pathway that brings other factors together in an adverse outcome. Therefore, ongoing, upstream measurement of the sheer mass of these critical at-risk behaviors provides the most significant indicator of workplace safety. And the only satisfactory mechanism to drive this activity is employee involvement.

The foundation of continuous improvement is measurement, of course, and for over a century now statistical methods have provided the basis of scientific measurement. Scientists view statisticians and their methods as critical partners. W. Edwards Deming and others pioneered techniques of statistical process control (SPC) in industry, giving rise to scientifically grounded continuous improvement in quality. A large part of their success is in their emphasis on what should be measured—the upstream factors of the production process.

This book reports on the work of a number of companies who have effectively engaged and sustained employee involvement in this kind of applied science, producing a step-change in their safety performance.

BACKGROUND ON CONTINUOUS IMPROVEMENT

The Spring 1991 issue of the *Sloan Management Review* includes an article that is related to the topic, "America's Most Successful Export to Japan: Continuous Improvement Programs." In addition to showing a flair for a catchy title, the authors, Dean M. Schroeder and Alan G. Robinson, present a concise history of continuous improvement programs, or CIPs. According to the authors, CIPs were developed and widely used in the United States many years before they were "exported" to Japan by U.S. trainers working for the post-WWII occupation authorities. The view that continuous improvement is alien to the North American workforce may indeed be misguided.

Schroeder and Robinson indicate the right direction. Continuous improvement is natural to the can-do spirit of North American enterprise. And where better to pursue continuous improvement vigorously than in safety? Everyone can be involved in safety. In safety, everyone benefits. And the benefits, both direct and indirect, are of tremendous significance.

MANAGING INVOLVEMENT FOR AN INJURY-FREE WORKPLACE

We have observed three stages that companies go through in their safety performance: the accident cycle, the performance plateau, and the step-change to continuous improvement (see Fig. 1.2 and Table 1.1).

The Accident Cycle

In the accident cycle, (1) rising incident rates trigger → (2) increased attention to safety after which → (3) performance improves whereupon → (4) resources move elsewhere and → (1) there follows yet another period of rising incident rates. Although the accident cycle leads to frustration and sometimes to superstition, at least it offers a reason for rising injury rates. Ignorance of the accident cycle itself is a worse position to be in, with no understanding of the reason for rising injury rates. However, although a system that is running through the accident cycle is relatively stable in the long term, it does not produce continuous improvement. Moreover, because it is "injury driven," it usually produces short-term rather than long-term solutions. There is nothing inherently wrong with being "reactive," of having quick reflexes, so to speak. The problem is that reactive improvement efforts are oftentimes not very far-sighted. On the reactive model, the good news is that the fire is put out. The bad news is that there is no thought given to preventing future fires.

The Performance Plateau

Getting free of the accident cycle is a genuine and noteworthy achievement for an organization because it represents constancy of both purpose and practice in relation to safety. However, what most frequently follows is that safety performance levels-off at a plateau—continuing effort does not bring continuous

TABLE 1.1 Checklist for the Three Paradigms of Safety Performance

The Accident Cycle *No Continuous Improvement* *No Continuous Improvement*	The Performance Plateau *Continuing Efforts* *No Continuous Improvement*	The Step-Change to Continuous Improvement *Continuing Efforts* *Continuous Improvement*
☐ Safety performance continually varies in the accident cycle	☐ Good improvement at first, but in spite of continuing efforts, performance levels off and plateaus	☐ Performance improves continuously
☐ Management is inconsistent in its support of safety	☐ Management support for safety is more consistent	☐ Management support for safety is consistent and committed to accident prevention
☐ Lack of agreement on safety between levels of management and wage-roll	☐ Lack of agreement on safety between levels of management and wage-roll	☐ All levels of management and workers agree that safety is important
☐ The safety effort is reactive and crisis driven	☐ The safety "pressure" is constant and numbers driven	☐ Safety initiative is focused continually on upstream measures, prior to incidents
☐ Safety Department responsible for safety	☐ Line supervisors held accountable for safety numbers	☐ Meaningful employee involvement and performance accountability at all levels
☐ Special meetings for reactive training	☐ Training, meetings, programs, incentives committees — using descriptive statistics in an undirected way	☐ Ongoing data-driven problem solving and action planning by workgroups in regular safety meetings
☐ Arbitrary numerical goals	☐ Sporadic, department-specific accident focus	☐ Proper use of statistical methods (SPC) to evaluate results and direct site-wide activities
☐ A history of programs	☐ A history of programs	☐ Site-specific adaption of a process approach
☐ Reliance on Games / Incentives	☐ Reliance on Posters / Announcements / signs	☐ Reliance on an inventory of objectively defined critical safety-related behaviors
☐ Inconsistent use of disciplinary action	☐ Accident investigations tend to focus on fault-finding and assignment of blame	☐ Accident investigations use multi-level participation and are oriented to data-gathering, establishing mechanisms to sum results for directed problem solving
☐ Accident investigations are adversarial, "Whose fault was it?"		

improvement. Attempting to address this challenge, companies often try many things to increase safety awareness and modify people's attitudes, such as give-aways and poster contests, pep rallies and training sessions, and a host of off-the-shelf safety programs. In this stage, incident rates are often respectably low by most standards, but they are slow to improve. What is needed is a systematic process or mechanism for continuous improvement. Continuing effort alone is not enough. The effort must be directed where it can make a difference—to the systems that "produce" injuries.

The Step-Change to Continuous Improvement

Companies achieve the step-change to continuous improvement when they develop methods to measure, track, and improve their performance of site-specific critical safety-related behaviors. For an overview of the key concepts of this task-related approach to workforce behavior, see Chapters 3 and 4.

SAFETY AND QUALITY—TWO SIDES OF THE SAME COIN

In many seminars and consulting sessions over the years, safety leaders familiar with quality initiatives have told the author and his colleagues that employee-driven safety performance reminded them of TQM applied to safety. They were responding to an important relationship—safety and quality are two sides of the same coin.

The physical and managerial processes of a given workplace make a production system. Its intended products are goods and/or services. All too often it also "produces" a certain number of injuries. Many forward-looking managers are drawing the conclusion that if the basic nature of a company's operation is responsible for the production of injuries and illnesses, reactive, add-on safety programs stand little chance of long-term success.

This insight is an important breakthrough. Once managers see a company as a system that unintentionally produces injury and illness, safety becomes a systems issue, concerned with barriers to safe work that are a function of the systems of the organization.

APPLYING SCIENTIFIC METHODS TO SAFETY

This systems insight is the same one that Deming and others brought to the field of quality. Safety management before continuous improvement looks a great deal like traditional quality control. Discovering through statistical measurement whether a system is in control is the first step to system improvement. As a downstream statistical measurement, injury rates can indeed be a sign that the system is in control. Of course, analysis of injury frequency rates alone is not the best way to bring continuous improvement to bear on the safety *system*. In SPC terms, injuries are defects and a defect-driven quality process necessarily turns into defect management. In the same way, an injury-driven safety effort is going to sustain injuries. The best that an injury-driven safety effort can achieve is frustrating re-runs of the accident cycle. The challenge for safety, as with quality, is to resist the obvious temptations of defect management and to identify critical factors that are both upstream *and* measurable with statistical validity.

As familiar as this concept of upstream measurement may seem to many of us now, it was not always so. The work of decades, by Deming and others, is largely responsible for our sense of familiarity about the effectiveness of statistical measurement of upstream factors.

UPSTREAM SAFETY FACTORS

In most areas of performance, activities both precede and produce outcomes. Common examples of this relation are found wherever practice is encouraged as the prerequisite of skill (practice makes perfect), or research and development as the source of new products, or hard work as the route to better pay. In SPC terms, the processes (activities) are upstream (practice, research, hard work), and their results are downstream (skill, new product, better pay.)

In the case of quality improvement, management is not guided by product defects (downstream factors) but by measurements of upstream factors of production that are predictive of defects. The same methodology applies to the management of continuous improvement in safety performance. In the terms of this approach, accident frequency rates represent downstream indicators. Accident prevention relies instead on sampling the sheer mass of safety-related behaviors that lie upstream and that precede any particular incident.

This basic fact about safety bears repeating. A great deal of exposure to risk and hazard has already occurred before any given injury or accident occurs. Each particular incident is precipitated out of a mass of preceding at-risk behaviors. Furthermore, the vast majority of exposures occur with no noticeable downstream results. In other words, there is a demonstrable but indirect relation between the frequency of at-risk behavior upstream and the frequency of accidents downstream. The indirectness of this relation makes it confusing and hard to grasp, let alone to pursue long-term in an undistracted way. It is this basic fact which causes most of the problems in poorly focused and ineffective safety efforts (witness the accident cycle.) In part because the linkage is indirect between the upstream and downstream factors of safety performance, management does not know what to pay attention to and, therefore, tends to overreact to random variability in accident rates.

COMMON MANAGEMENT ERRORS

Figure 1.3 shows the difficulties that safety presents to downstream management efforts. Cultural factors give rise to various aspects of management systems. Management systems, in turn, either create or eliminate exposure to risk and hazards. Finally, emerging from the patterns of exposure there are incident rates.

Where in this overall system should measurement occur? The traditional approach focuses measurement exclusively on the end point of the process, and the resultant measure is the accident frequency rate. However, this is at best a limited indicator of real performance and it provides no information at all about upstream factors such as exposure, management systems, or culture. Suppose, for instance, that accident frequency is down for one quarter. Does this mean that the system should be given a clean bill of health? Practices and procedures that are prejudicial to sustained high safety performance may still be present in the system, and these must be considered along with incident rates.

To ignore this fact and proceed on the basis of incident rates alone is analogous to defining the physical health of an individual as the absence of disease. This is not good diagnostic practice even when the doctor as health manager does not yet know much about the patient. It is especially poor practice when the physician knows that the individual smokes cigarettes, is overweight, does not exercise, has elevated blood pressure, eats a poor diet, and suffers from high stress. Managers, supervisors, and wage-roll employees almost always know it when their facility has bad safety habits. Though they often disagree about the precise nature of the

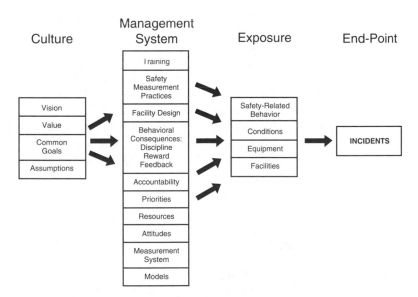

FIGURE 1.3 Incidents are downstream—not upstream.

safety problem, they know when they receive undeservedly high grades for low accident rates.

Blaming the Employee

Along with confusion about accident frequency, the other common error of management is to blame the employee for accidents that are perceived as arising from "stupid" or careless actions of employees. This reaction, as understandable as it may be at times, is a mistake on two counts. In the most basic human terms it is counterproductive to blame employees as though they got hurt intentionally or as a result of simple negligence. This approach puts the employee in the position of resentment and resistance. And, equally important to management effectiveness, blame is also a mistake because it fails to take into account how the overall management system influences employee behavior.

When an injury results from at-risk behavior, what is the probability that the implicated behavior has been performed on numerous previous occasions? It is a near certainty. This is another aspect of the linkage described above—many exposures occur prior to any injury. For instance, when an employee is injured while reaching into moving equipment to clear a jam, it is tempting for the frustrated supervisor to react in terms such as, *What's wrong with my people? These guys are stupid!* However, the underlying and very pertinent questions are:

- How do management systems influence this critical behavior?
- What consequences are in place that *favor* the action of reaching into moving machinery?
- Who is responsible for the consequences?

Knowing that the management system has either implicitly or explicitly accepted this behavior in the past, the investigative question becomes, How can we successfully modify the systems that influence this behavior?

Employees are justifiably resentful in cases where their at-risk behavior is an accepted part of the system until an injury occurs, and then they are not only injured but subjected to disciplinary action as well. Of course, disciplinary action for real safety violations has its proper place; however, it is the responsibility of management to establish and maintain systems that consistently produce safe behavior.

Going for Short-Term Results

It is always tempting to seek out the quick fix. Managers are trained to do this and they are appropriately oriented toward action and results. This is an important virtue to keep. But it is misguided to think that a system embedded in a culture can be influenced in the short term without long-term efforts. This would be like relying on exhortations and slogans to improve the traffic flow in a busy city. After more than a decade of safety consulting, countless managers have asked the author, "How long will it take?" This is one of the first questions that safety leaders and managers ask when they are considering new safety initiatives. What they mean, and what they sometimes say, is, "We need results *now.*" In part this is a function of their being in a reactive posture. Since they are reacting after the fact, usually by the time they ask the question, "How long will it take?" they are already in a predicament. They need relief and they want it sooner rather than later. There are of course things that can be done in safety to produce short-term results. The real danger is in relying on such quick fixes whenever a problem occurs, thereby postponing the initiatives that produce long-term improvement of accident prevention. It is hopelessly naive to think that the safety system can be improved in any meaningful way in the short term. In addition, the short-term focus also takes a serious toll on an organization's safety measurement system— the topic of Chapter 6.

How far Upstream is Best?

In the opposite direction from looking for quick fixes too far downstream, there is a growing interest in applying TQM principles directly to the safety culture of a site. This direction was perhaps reflected in the "TQM and Safety" theme of the June 1994 issue of *Professional Safety* magazine. From the point of view of establishing employee-driven safety performance, there is a drawback in the position of many theorists. Most articles on TQM and safety are primarily concerned with "shoulds, coulds, and woulds." That is, although the articles convey many good ideas, they very rarely report the results of actual safety/TQM initiatives. This means although the authors are writing about possible applications of science, their articles do not report the use of scientific methods.

One reason for the scarcity of reported results is that most companies do not actually apply TQM principles in their safety efforts, even when they have identified it as a valuable thing to do. There is a reason that many of the current treatments of TQM and safety seem to miss the mark when it comes to focus—they don't know the best place upstream to apply scientific methods in an industrial setting. In terms of the sequence shown in Fig. 1.3, it is as if many commentators want to jump from their old focus on the end-point of incidents all the way upstream to culture.

Management Systems and Exposure Levels

The refocus away from incidents is good, but to jump all the way to the "head of the line" does not really work in practice. Companies who try this approach almost always waste valuable resources on "woulds, coulds, and shoulds" because that is the way that culture expresses itself—rather than more productively attending to vision statements, goals, values. The problem here, and it is an old problem, is that as much as a change in safety culture may be desirable, in most real-world situations it is almost impossible to manage such a change directly. What does such a change effort measure, track, and steer by? The common experience is that change efforts focusing directly on culture do not develop structures of accountable employee involvement.

THE ANSWER TO EMPLOYEE INVOLVEMENT

To achieve employee involvement in applied scientific methods, the proper upstream focus implements new management systems to identify, measure, track, and improve the overall levels of exposure. That is the formula for employee-driven safety performance, and companies using this approach (see Chapter 17) have demonstrated an important fact about culture change. Namely, the best, and perhaps only, way to achieve a change in safety culture (attitude) is first to change the safety management system (behavior) and related levels of exposure (behavior). This is another important case where behavior change *leads* attitude change rather than vice versa (Chapters 3 and 4). In numerous implementations across industries and regions of the U.S. and Canada this sequence has been borne out. After a site begins to establish its new dual focus mid-way upstream on management systems and exposure levels, the company culture changes naturally, expressing its new safety values and assumptions in new vision statements and common goals.

The difference in this kind of culture change is crucial. Instead of aiming directly at culture change and trying to make it happen through vision statements and other appeals to "right attitude," genuine culture change grows out of solid procedural changes on the ground. Employee-driven safety performance has a much better chance of "making believers" out of a workforce because this behavior-based approach is also data-driven. For their own problem solving needs, workgroups have data collected during ongoing peer-to-peer observation. It is this management system change that allows the workforce to monitor its own progress and plan for accident prevention. Once this continuous improvement mechanism is in place, the idea of achieving an injury-free culture can begin to sound like more than just a fine slogan; it can begin to be a real vision statement. Chapter 2 presents an overview of the problem-solving mechanism that lies at the heart of employee-driven safety and sustains it for continuous improvement.

2

Using Behavioral Data to Sustain Continuous Improvement in Safety

At the heart of employee-driven safety performance is the ongoing collection and analysis by the workforce of its own behavioral data. This is the mechanism that achieves results (Chapter 16) and sustains a safety initiative for the long term (see Chapter 17 on case histories.) Behavioral data is very different from accident data. To get from traditional accident data to behavioral data takes a giant step, and making that step is a precondition of making continuous improvement a reality. It is management's responsibility to take this giant step by defining for their organizations the meaning of behavioral data. In leading companies management has already done a good job of defining accident data—when an injury occurs, employees know that something important has happened. The event gets attention and it stimulates action. It moves the heart and mind and causes behavior. This reaction is not a bad thing. It would be a bad situation if an injury passed without notice and *did not* motivate people in any way. The trouble with being reactive is that it is insufficient for continuous improvement. The important point here is that given a sole reliance on accident data, the best an organization can be is reactive. In the field of safety the only way to be proactive is to manage by indicators that lead accident data. Those indicators are behavioral data, and proactive managers have learned to give them the same meaning and importance that they used to give to accident data. Management's job is to create an organizational context in which at-risk behavior has the same importance as injury.

The data of behavioral observation provides the means to refocus an organization in this way. Effective managers take the giant step and create the importance surrounding behavioral data. Managers still caught in the older approach receive

---

Kim Sloat, Ph.D., contributed to the development of this chapter.

the data but do not use it. The author has seen this pattern at various sites. For example, while doing a re-assessment of an ongoing employee-driven initiative, the author found the site in a high pitch of excitement—of alarm, almost—over a lost-time accident. A man had tripped on a protruding piece of metal and had broken his foot. Managers were meeting in tremendous consternation, "How could this have happened?" They were shocked and dismayed. However, the telling point is that that very hazard had been there for the past seven months and had been noted explicitly four times during the site's behavioral observations. At that site, however, that data did not have the necessary meaning to move people to action. In the strictest sense, the injury was no surprise. It was predictable based on known facts.

Ongoing behavioral data analysis is essential because it

- closes the improvement loop
- helps identify and correct equipment and design barriers to safety
- establishes proactive and systematic solutions versus reactive and ad hoc "bandaids"
- improves the safety culture through group problem solving and action-planning

Closing the Improvement Loop

Data collection for its own sake is a barren exercise. The whole point of expending resources on upstream measurement is to establish an ongoing data base as the foundation for accurate correction and improvement. This is also part of the continual education that Deming makes one of his points. The data needs to get back to the shop floor so employee involvement can be solution oriented. The safety data base described in this book allows for exactly this kind of accountable employee involvement. The charted feedback lets the workgroup know how it is doing measured against the site's inventory. The data is used to identify areas that need attention.

Correcting Equipment and Design Barriers

In most contemporary industry, the large majority of causes of injury are behavioral in nature. Some at-risk situations arise because of equipment or design considerations, and there is a strong interaction between conditions and behaviors. Identifying and correcting these conditions is a natural outgrowth of behavioral analysis. A group that scores low on the use of personal protective equipment (PPE), for instance, might discover from behavior analysis that one of the important antecedents of its poor performance had to do with the poor availability of PPE. An action plan to correct this condition would include both improved PPE availability and a higher rate of behavioral observation and feedback for PPE use. Taken together, this twofold approach improves the antecedent (better PPE availability) and improves the consequences of PPE use (positive verbal feedback and increased rates of measured performance). This is the most effective way to discover and remove barriers to performance improvement.

Being Truly Proactive and Systematic

In the absence of ongoing, data-driven problem solving it is hard to see how safety initiatives can be anything other than reactive and ad hoc. Although it will always be true that crisis tends to focus the mind, the whole point of management is to prevent a crisis wherever possible. The kind of focus that comes with crisis is the wrong kind. In addition to being unsustainable it is reactive and unsystematic. The cost of crisis management most often cited is that it waits to respond until after an accident has occurred. Less often mentioned but perhaps equally important is the fact that reactive solutions also tend not to be systematic. In fact, sometimes the reactive "solution" is so ad hoc or specific that the only accident it is likely to prevent "next time" is one exactly like the last one. However, accidents usually do not repeat each other this exactly. The proactive solution needs to be systematic enough to prevent entire categories of incidents. The behavioral data base encourages this sort of problem solving and so helps the workgroup move away from reactive, ad hoc strategies. In many companies this change toward a constant safety focus amounts to a change in the safety culture itself. The behavioral approach offers an important aid here, too.

Improving the Entire Safety Culture Itself

The culture of an organization is the assumptions, values, and practices that people share. Some parts of the culture are "hidden"—people take some things for granted, and are not even aware of it. Improving safety often requires improving the culture. The things that people take for granted need to be identified. People have to change their assumptions, values, and practices. Since culture is shared by groups of people, changes in the culture need to be achieved at the group level. The behavioral approach uses group problem solving to improve the safety culture itself. At its most basic level this kind of change happens when people begin to see that there is an effective alternative to their customary way of doing things. Oftentimes cultural change is blocked for the simple lack of any group acquaintance with an alternative. If crisis management is all that a workgroup has ever known, they are going to need more than good intentions, slogans, and feel-good pep rallies to improve their performance. What they need is a chance to *make a difference* by actually *doing something different*. Data-driven, workgroup problem solving makes believers of people at all levels of an organization.

Steps of Data-Driven Workgroup Problem Solving

1. Identifying a Problem

The first step is to decide what to work on. There are usually several things that could improve. Effective groups don't work on everything at once, though. Their selection is guided by two important criteria. They are looking for

    a. action items with the most potential for reducing exposure to injury
    b. action items they can do something about

Many of the most common reactive strategies (move a valve, post a slogan, improve people's attitude about safety) fail one or both of these criteria. Although it is true that moving a valve or posting a slogan is (b) something that the workgroup can do, it is often very unclear that such "actions" have much impact on reducing exposure to injury. And as for "improving people's safety attitude," there is no direct way that anyone can do that but even if it were possible, it is not clear that such a general attitude adjustment would reduce exposure to injury. Workers with a very "good attitude" are very easily injured if they do not know and practice the critical safety-related behaviors of their tasks.

    The key to this step is using data. The group has data from observations in the form of tables, comment reports, and graphs. They may also have injury or incident reports. They have the impressions of the observers, and others in the workgroup, on potential problems, and they may do specialized data collection.

2. Identifying Root Causes

Having identified a problem to work on, they figure. out why the problem exists. That is, they identify the root causes of the problem. The root causes are the basic things that need to be changed to eliminate the problem. Root causes are discovered through behavior analysis and fishbone diagramming. A common mistake in problem solving is to identify a problem, and then jump to developing solutions. When a group doesn't understand the causes of the problem, their solutions may miss the mark.

3. Generating Potential Actions

There are usually many various actions that can improve a situation. The group thinks of as many things as possible. A group working together usually can come up with more ideas, and better ideas, than people working alone. Not all things will be equally effective but the more ideas the group has the more likely it is that they will come up with a good solution.

4. Evaluating Possible Actions

Once they have a list of potential actions, the group evaluates them. Perhaps they cannot do all of them right now. They may not have the resources to do some of them. They might decide that some of the potential actions won't really help. The group may want to test some of the actions. If an action requires a lot of money or effort, it can help to try it out with a small group first.

5. Developing an Action Plan

From the list of possible actions, the group selects the ones they can do now. Each action and deadline is assigned to someone. This list constitutes the action plan.

6. Follow-Up: Measure and Evaluate

The items in the action plan may not be the right ones to solve the problem. They may not be implemented well. So the group follows up on its action plan. They check to see whether all the action items were done. They also review ongoing behavioral observation measurements to see whether the problem they were trying to solve has actually improved. If the problem has not improved, the group may need to revise their action plan.

WORKGROUP PROBLEM SOLVING

The group decides what to work on to improve safety. There are usually many opportunities for doing this, and effective groups select a problem based on data. Allowing for opinions and pet peeves, the group focuses on its best opportunities for reducing potential for injury. To identify these opportunities, they review all available data:

- previous action plans
- observation data
- injury/incident reports
- other data

Previous Action Plans

With the initial use of the safety improvement process, there aren't any previous action plans. After a short time, however, there may be several plans at various stages. If an action item has not been completed, the group then considers whether it is still needed. The group may find that the problem has not improved, even though all the steps in the action plan are complete. This may mean that they did not identify the true causes of the problem. In this case they re-analyze the problem. Another possibility is that the actions in the plan were not adequate to change things. The group may need to identify other things they can do to improve the situation.

Observation Data

Observation data is the source of information for identifying potential problems. The group looks at summaries of observation data. Observations are samples of the level of safety in the workplace (see Chapter 9). The quality of this information directly determines the potential quality of the action plan. Any particular sample may not be representative. Of course, the group takes action right away on serious immediate problems identified during an observation. Software used to analyze the data needs to provide two kinds of summary data, reports and graphs.

Tabular Reports

Tabular reports list the categories and items from the group's inventory of critical behaviors. For each item the report shows:

- how many times the item was marked *safe*
- how many times the item was marked *at-risk*
- the percentage safe (%safe)
- the number of data sheets on which the item was marked
- the percentage of sheets on which the item was marked

The observations included in a report can cover any date range. Monthly summaries are common. Tabular reports can summarize data for selected locations. (A "location" is the lowest organizational level at which observations are identified.) For instance, a report could be for an individual workgroup (if locations have been set up down to the workgroup level), a department, or the whole plant.

Comment Reports

These reports list the comments written by observers by behavioral inventory item number. Comment reports can be for selected dates, and locations. Usually the comment reports cover the same dates and locations as the tabular reports.

Variable Reports

Variables are factors that might influence the level of safety. They are identified by each facility. Examples of variables are

- shift
- weather conditions
- operating conditions: normal, upset, turnaround
- overtime/straight time

Proper behavioral analysis requires software that can generate a summary report for each variable. For instance, if shift is a variable, the report will have an entry for each shift. For each element, the report shows:

- the number of safes that were marked
- the number of at-risks that were marked
- overall %safe
- the number of sheets on which the element was marked

Graphs

Graphs are useful for looking at changes over time. Change in some behavioral inventory items may take place gradually, over months. As Chapter 7 shows, it can be difficult if not impossible to notice the change by looking at tabular reports. But on a graph the trends in the data may be clear at a glance.

Analyzing Injury/Incident Reports

Injury and incident reports are an important source of information about opportunities for improvement. Such reports identify situations in which people have been injured. The group reviews reports of all injuries or incidents that have happened in their area since the previous problem solving session. The group might also look at injuries that have occurred in groups doing work similar to theirs. For instance, a group from Shipping Day-Shift would also probably look at injuries that had occurred on the other shifts in Shipping.

Identifying Critical Behaviors

The group identifies the behaviors that are critical to preventing the injuries they are reviewing. If the accident investigation process at their facility has been coordinated with the behavioral process, the accident report will list critical behaviors (see Chapter 11). If the report does not list critical behaviors, the group needs to identify them. This process is possible because an inventory of critical behaviors has already been developed. (See Chapter 8 on the development of the inventory of critical behaviors.)

Other Data

There may be other data for the group to consider in identifying possible focus areas.

Specialized Data Collection

Sometimes a group collects information in addition to observations. For instance, they may have observers interview people. Or they may do specialized observations. They may have observers focus on only a few Items, or have them observe something not on the behavioral inventory.

Informal Observation

Observers, supervisors, and others may have valuable information based on their informal observations in the course of work. For instance, someone may have seen or been part of a serious near-miss. The near-miss may not have been documented.

Audits

The facility or company may have an internal or external auditing program. Audits may identify problem areas to which the safety improvement process can be applied.

Selecting a Focus Area

After they have identified possible focus areas, the group selects one to work on. Sometimes the focus area is very obvious. Other times it is not as clear (see Fig. 2.1). The key idea is to work on something that will reduce exposure to injury.

Degree of Risk.   In general, the group selects as a focus those things that represent the greatest potential for serious injury.

Amount of Exposure.   They concentrate on the situations in which there is the most exposure. For instance, they work on the Items with low %safe.

Potential for Improvement.   They may make the most progress in the long run by first selecting things on which they can make rapid improvement. The group wants to achieve success, and to demonstrate results. This is more important in the early stages of the safety improvement process.

Guidelines for selecting a focus

First Choice:

Low %safe • high-risk/high-exposure behaviors • involved in recent injuries.
(Note: Where accident investigations have already resulted in action plans, groups don't duplicate the effort.)

Second Choice:

High %safe • high-risk/high-exposure behaviors • involved in recent injuries; or low %safe • high-risk/high-exposure behaviors • not involved in recent injuries

Third Choice:

Low %safe • lower-risk/lower exposure behaviors • not involved in recent injuries

FIGURE 2.1   Guidelines for selecting a critical behaviors focus.

Frequency/Severity Analysis

The more often an at-risk situation occurs, the more likely it is that someone will be injured. If the potential severity of every item were the same, the group would probably work on improving the behavior that happened most often. In the example shown in Fig. 2.2, using cheater bars is more common than failure to lock out equipment. The potential severity of injury from not locking out is considered much higher, however. Working on locking out, or not climbing on pipes would have the highest potential for benefit.

Drafting a Problem Statement

After selecting a problem to work on, the group writes a problem statement that is:

- Based on data relevant to the group: the problem affects the safety of the group, the data is from the group.
- Measurable: the group works on something that they can measure in order to be able to tell if things have improved. Attitudes or awareness are not easily measured, for instance.
- Something that they can influence: they work on something that they can influence. Factors out of their control are referred to management for appropriate action. Also passed on to management are observer comments and reports on observation frequency of the hazard or hazards.

Frequency. For each item on their list, the group assigns a number that represents their estimate of how often this behavior happens. These numbers are estimates. What they are interested in is the relative frequency of at-risk behavior. Here is a 5-point rating scheme:

1 = %Safe is high. Behavior has not been a factor in recent injuries. No other evidence that the behavior is a major issue at this time.

2 = between 1 and 3

3 = %Safe is not the lowest of all the items on the behavioral inventory, but is not high. Behavior has been involved in some recent injuries.

4 = between 3 and 4

5 = %Safe is low, or is lower than other items. Behavior has been in factor in a number of recent injuries.

Severity. The group has a similar analysis for the injury severity of the items on their list. The possible consequences of some behaviors are much more severe than others. Here is a sample rating scheme for severity:

1 = Severity potential for this behavior is low. An injury is very unlikely to be more than minor (such as a small contusion or abrasion).

2 = Severity between 1 and 3

3 = This behavior could easily lead to a moderately severe injury (such as strain, laceration, significant burn). Or, this behavior is very likely to result in at least a minor injury.

4 = Severity between 3 and 5

5 = This behavior could result in severe injury (fall, serious burn, major lacerations). Or this behavior has an extremely high probability of resulting in moderate injury.

Combining frequency and severity. After assigning ratings for frequency and severity, the group multiplies the two numbers together. The higher the number, the more serious the problem. The table below gives an example of some potential focus areas, ratings for frequency and severity, and overall rating number.

Item	Frequency	Severity	Overall
Not locking out	3	5	15
Climbing on pipes	2	5	10
Using cheater	4	2	8
No hearing protection	3	2	6

FIGURE 2.2 Analyzing for frequency and severity combined.

- Formulated in specifics: the problem statement is specific. It includes information about who is involved, what the problem is, when and where it happens.
- Reason for selection: the problem statement includes the reason that this problem was selected, and some measure of the problem how often it happens.

The following are typical behavioral problem statements drafted in accordance with the foregoing criteria.

Statement of the Problem

Operators in Unit 3, all shifts, are climbing on pipes and handrails to reach valves. There is potential for very serious injury from falls of over 10 feet in height. In the last three months, combined behavioral observations for Unit 3 record a %safe level of 65 percent for at-risk climbing. This item on the site's inventory of critical behaviors has one of the lowest %safes for Unit 3 (high frequency at-risk behavior). It is lower than any other in the inventory category of Body Use and Position. There have been two incidents in Unit 3 in the last three months where people climbing on pipes slipped but did not fall (near-miss). There was a serious injury in Unit 4 two months ago resulting from standing on a handrail (another Unit, same at-risk behavior).

Identifying Root Causes

Once a group has written a problem statement, they avoid the temptation of jumping right into action planning. First they do behavior analysis. Behavior does not exist in a vacuum. When people work safely, it is not by chance but because there are forces in the workplace that encourage safe work. When people are working at-risk, this too is not by chance. There are specific forces at work that produce at-risk behavior. To make improvement, to reduce the chances of injury, the things that produce at-risk behavior must be identified.

Behavior Analysis

Behavior analysis is one of the basic tools of the employee-driven safety process. (See Chapters 3 and 4 for a more in-depth treatment of behavior analysis.) Most safety problems involve someone's behavior. Behavior is controlled by antecedents (things that trigger behavior), and by consequences (the things that both follow from behavior and influence it).

Step 1. Analyzing the At-Risk Behavior

Step 1.1 of behavior analysis is to describe the at-risk behavior in strictly observable terms:

climbing on pipes and handrails to reach valves

Step 1.2 is to identify the antecedents by listing the things that trigger the at-risk behavior. The group concentrates on the antecedents that actually occur. The question for the group is, "What are the things that are triggering us to do this?" In the case of this at-risk behavior, the workgroup might list such antecedents as:

1. The crew has a heavy workload and is typically pressed for time.
2. Poor scheduling of the lifts that we do have.
3. There are not enough lifts and ladders available for the crew's work load.
4. The crew members share a macho attitude about "toughing it out" and "hustling."
5. No one can remember ever having received training on lifts and ladders, or on the severity of falls.

Antecedents are carefully listed because an effective action plan (Step 3) addresses both the antecedents and the consequences of the at-risk behavior.

Step 1.3 identifies the consequences of the behavior—the things that follow the behavior in question and influence its future occurrence. Consequences that are simultaneously soon, certain, and positive are the most influential in reinforcing a behavior. In this case, when the group lists consequences of "climbing on pipes and handrails to reach valves" they might produce the following set:

1. When they don't worry about locating lifts and ladders, the crew completes its entire work assignment during its shift (soon-certain-positive).
2. By hurrying on without the lifts and ladders, the crew gets a longer break (soon-certain-positive).
3. Sometimes people fall and are injured (soon-uncertain-negative).
4. Working without lifts and ladders, crew members feel very resourceful and competent (soon-certain-positive).
5. They avoid the boredom of waiting around for scarce, poorly scheduled lifts or ladders (soon-certain-positive).
6. They avoid production pressure from Supervisors (note: avoiding a sure negative = receiving a certain positive).

As is usually the case with "naturally occurring" at-risk behaviors, a consideration of the existing consequences shows that the most influential consequences (soon-certain-positive) favor the at-risk behavior of climbing on pipes and handrails to reach valves. Conventional wisdom is misguided in expecting the likelihood of a fall to deter this at-risk behavior. Of the six listed consequences, the possibility of a fall is the weakest of the lot. Although the worker experiences the pain soon after a fall, the consequence is not certain to occur and even when it does it is negative. A soon-uncertain-negative consequence will lose out to soon-certain-positive consequences every day of the week. All other factors being equal, that is why a safety initiative that counts on the threat of falls to motivate people to use lifts and ladders is a safety initiative that is going to sustain falls. Therefore it is up to the workgroup not to leave all other factors equal but to intervene with an action plan that addresses both the antecedents and the consequences of the identified at-risk behavior.

Step 2. Analyzing the Safe Behavior

Step 2.1 identifies the safe behavior in observable terms:

using proper lifts or ladders to reach valves

Step 2.2 lists new antecedents that trigger or elicit the safe behavior:

1. Schedule available equipment better.
2. Acquire enough equipment to handle the workload of Unit 3 operators on all shifts.
3. Institute training on the equipment.
4. Institute training on the potential severity of falls.

Step 2.3 lists new consequences to be delivered for the identified safe behavior:

1. Standardize the length of breaks so that Unit 3 operators do not feel rewarded for rushing or taking shortcuts.
2. Increase observation rates for these shifts for this behavior.
3. Increase supervisor feedback for the safe behavior.

Step 3. Drafting the Behavioral Action Plan

The behavioral action plan amplifies Step 2 by assigning responsibilities and deadlines for each item on the action list. As illustrated in Exhibit 2.1, the action plan has three parts:

- focus statement
- action list
- follow-up

SUMMARY

For targeting new levels of achievement, the accumulating behavioral observation data is one of the most important sources of information for continuous improvement. Another source used by highly functioning organizations is the behavior-based accident investigation, which is the topic of Chapter 13 in Part 3 on Current Issues in Employee-Driven Safety.

Exhibit 2.1 Sample Behavioral Action Plan

Focus Statement

Focus: Compliance with policy when working with high valves.
- The problem is that operators in Unit 3 rarely use lifts or ladders to reach high valves.
- Behavior percentages are holding steady at about 65 percent Safe.

Patterns: According to behavioral observation data, operator compliance is equally lacking on all shifts in Unit 3.

Action List

- Equipment dispatcher to make sure that areas with either no work or light work to dispatch lifts and ladders to Unit 3. Monitor for two weeks starting date: _____.
  —(Antecedent intervention 1 and 2)
  —Department Manager
- Equipment dispatcher monitors new assignment of lifts and ladders to see whether additional equipment is needed for Unit 3. If the answer is yes, requisition additional equipment. (Antecedent intervention 3)
  —To be completed in four weeks
  —Department Manager
- Training department to conduct training on lifts and ladders for all shifts. To be completed in two weeks.
  —(Antecedent intervention 5)
  —Department Manager
- Within next two weeks, operations supervisors to show all shifts the video on potential severity of falls. Express clear and firm expectation of compliance with policy.
  —(Antecedent intervention 5)
  —Department Manager
- Standardize breaks so that operators do not feel they are being rewarded for rushing or taking shortcuts.
  —(Consequence intervention 1)
  —Supervisor
- Increase observer coverage of all shifts of Unit 3 for one month, to start in two weeks on date: _____; remember to provide positive feedback for improvement.
  —(Consequence intervention 2)
  —Observers
- Instruct all observers to discuss potential severity of falls with any operator who is seen not using lifts or ladders when working on high valves.
  —(Consequence intervention 2)
  —Supervisor
- Supervisors to rotate coverage of all shifts in this area for one month, to start in two weeks. They will approach each operator with appropriate positive or negative consequences.
  (Consequence intervention 3)
  —Department Manager

Action Plan Follow-Up

In one month, observation data will be reviewed for compliance with lifting policy. (Consequence intervention)

3

Foundation Concepts of Behavior-Based Safety Management

Employee-driven safety management uses the principles of behavioral science in all three phases of an initiative: assessment, implementation, and continuous performance improvement. During the assessment, behavioral methods (interview techniques, behavior analysis, surveys) are used to analyze the strengths and weaknesses of existing safety measures and of safety culture. This allows a company to target the most important opportunities for improvement. During the implementation phase, behavioral principles are used to develop an inventory of behaviors that are critical to safety at the facility. The subsequent sampling and charting of the facility's performance of this set of critical behaviors establishes a baseline measure of the existing levels of %safe behavior. The instruments and procedures for measuring %safe and %at-risk are discussed in Chapters 8 and 9. After implementation is complete, new critical safety-related behaviors are identified, tracked, and managed as part of an ongoing process.

In the same way that Deming and others have applied scientific research methodology to the improvement of quality (operational definitions, measurement, feedback), the behavioral approach to performance applies the same methodology to a variety of behavioral issues—in this case the issue of safety performance. This similarity of origin accounts for the strong parallel between employee-driven safety management and the quality improvement process. See Chapter 5 for more on the parallels between quality and behavior-based safety.

This chapter ranges over some of the basic concepts and practices of the behavioral process. The discussion then turns in Chapter 4 to the important topics of how to improve safety culture by focusing on the relationship between behavior and attitude, and how to ensure employee involvement in the safety process.

Portions of this chapter were written by Kim Sloat, Ph.D.

THE CRITICAL-MASS APPROACH TO AT-RISK BEHAVIOR

At the outset, the most important thing to understand about the employee-driven safety is that this approach focuses on the sheer mass of at-risk behaviors at a facility. The at-risk behaviors in question are the work practices of the facility. At-risk behavior is the final common pathway in accident causation. This statement emphatically does not mean to say that the injury is the employee's fault. Nor does this statement contradict the message of quality improvement methods that 80 percent of the problems with quality are due to poor management practices. Wherever it appears in this book, the statement that accidents are *caused* by at-risk behavior refers to a very specific kind of cause known as the *final common pathway*.

For example, a worker may be feeling pressured by the production schedule he is trying to meet, and at the same time perhaps he is preoccupied with an illness in his family. However, if he gets hurt during this time it is almost always because he *does something at-risk* in response to his situation—some action such as trying to clear jammed equipment without first turning it off, for instance. In other words, the worker's anxiety about production pressures and family worries are understandable facts of daily life. However, the concern here is not with them but with the observable behavior of reaching into moving equipment. This behavior may be commonplace at a given site. It may be necessary to keep the equipment running. Nevertheless it is behavior that puts the employee at risk of injury. This behavior is a *critical behavior*—so-called because in this case it is a behavior that makes a critical difference in whether or not a worker gets injured while using the equipment in question.

Data from the work environment make it clear that a very large number of at-risk behaviors precede every accident. To use an image, this swarm of pre-existing at-risk behaviors and conditions is in the air, like water vapor just waiting to precipitate out as a thunder shower, or like the avalanche primed to happen. Focusing on behavior is crucial because an instance of at-risk worker behavior is like the small sound that touches off the avalanche. These small causes that precipitate large effects are causes that provide a final common pathway for many preceding causes to come together. This is the kind of cause that employee behavior represents. In accident causation, employee behavior provides the last link and common pathway for an accident to happen. However, the at-risk behavior at issue is a part of the management system, implicitly either encouraged or condoned by management. Therefore, to blame employees is counterproductive. It is management's responsibility to develop systems that promote safe behavior.

The effective approach identifies critical safety-related behaviors, measures the sheer mass of them, and manages their levels so that accidents stop occurring. This concept is new in safety circles but it has been known and used in science for many years now. In order to picture the linkage between at-risk behavior and injuries, it is helpful to think of the relationship between the critical mass of a radioactive substance and its explosiveness. For instance, in the case of a piece of uranium of critical mass, no one has any idea precisely which unstable atom is going to touch off the chain reaction resulting in an explosion. Just as there is a randomness or unpredictability about individual atoms in a mass of radioactive uranium, so there is a randomness and unpredictability about individual employee behaviors at a particular facility. On the other hand, the activity of the whole mass of uranium is *statistically* very predictable. And in the same way, the overall safety performance of an entire facility is statistically very predictable—at a given level of at-risk behavior there will be explosive events—accidents are going to follow.

Given what physical science knows about radioactive uranium, the people who manage it are very careful to store it in quantities well below its critical mass threshold. Given what behavioral science knows about behavior, managers responsible for safety do something similar. In this way, sites that start out concerned with lost-time accidents (LTAs) manage their performance to the point that they have no more LTAs to measure. They then move on to first-aids and near-misses. At each level of continuous improvement the method is the same. Site personnel identify the relevant accident threshold (the critical mass) of their facilities by using behavior analysis to identify critical behaviors. Once they have identified the critical behaviors, they measure performance through observation and they provide feedback for immediate improvement. Data gathered from observations is analyzed to develop targets for system improvements. This core linkage—facility safe behavior percentage up, facility accident frequency down—has been demonstrated in a variety of business and industrial applications. The first two graphs shown here, from a nylon producing facility, illustrate the inverse relation between %safe levels and accident frequency. These results are typical of behavior-based efforts (see Figs. 3.1 and 3.2).

In each facility the rise and fall in the level of safe behavior is a function of various factors: management system, workforce, physical plant, machinery and processes of production, the product itself, and so on. As the frequency of at-risk behaviors increases, the likelihood that injuries will occur increases. Many first aid injuries generally occur prior to a more serious injury, and so forth up to fatalities, as shown in Fig. 3.3.

The challenge is to determine the accident thresholds of a particular facility and then to track and manage worker behavior at levels well below even the first threshold. This proactive management of safety performance steers by indicators in advance of even first aid accidents. To steer by injury levels even as relatively benign as first aid accidents is to give up management control and to invite the fluctuations of the accident cycle, as discussed in Chapters 1 and 6. The accident cycle is a familiar fact of organizational life where an organization's safety effort

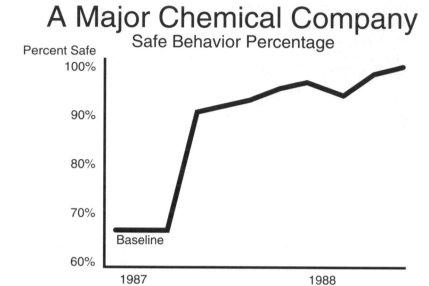

FIGURE 3.1 As %safe levels rose at this major chemical company, accident frequency fell (see Fig. 3.2).

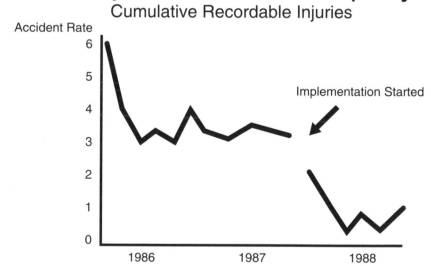

FIGURE 3.2 As %safe levels rose at this major chemical company (see Fig. 3.1), accident frequency fell.

Behavior
A Leading Indicator for Safety

FIGURE 3.3 At-risk behavior is the base of the accident triangle.

is based on response to injuries. That approach is reactive rather than proactive, and it produces an intermittent, marginal solution to the problem. By waiting for recordable accidents or injuries to trigger its response, the reactive approach proceeds as though continuous improvement were impossible.

Whether hidden or explicit, the premise of reactive safety management is that staying even is all that is possible. The employee-driven approach focuses on the strategic, long-term needs of a company by perceiving safety as a long-term product of the organizational system rather than as an accidental by-product of unknown origin. It is also important to distinguish the behavioral approach from other approaches that emphasize attitude change over behavioral change. As its name implies, the behavior-based approach improves safety culture by identifying and then managing a change in the behaviors that are critical to safety in a given facility.

Behavior versus Attitude

Chapter 4 presents attitude-behavior linkage in greater depth. The most basic point, however, is that in most traditional safety "programs" attitude is a distractor. Because attitude can affect behavior, it is tempting to focus on attitude first. The goal is to change safety-related behavior, so companies post slogans and hold meetings urging people to have a change of heart about safety. Behavioral science points out that when a change of behavior is the goal, there is good news—companies can, and should, start with behavior. It turns out that there is a two-way street between attitude and behavior, and behavior has the power to change attitude, too. And in a business or industrial setting there are two powerful reasons to focus on behavior first:

1. Behavior can be measured and therefore managed, whereas attitude presents measurement problems.
2. Changes in behavior can lead to a changes in attitude.

Although programs emphasizing attitude change make a strong appeal, such programs are flawed because they overlook these two points. Everyone agrees that a good safety attitude is important. The problem with trying to manage change by focusing on attitudes is that attitudes are internal events that are difficult to measure on a daily basis. Given the importance of measurement in the management process, it follows that focusing on attitude is not an efficient method. To actually manage a process of continuous safety performance improvement solely by means of attitude change would require some form of attitude monitoring and control. This is not feasible even if it were desirable. In actual practice, attempts at changing safety culture by changing attitude invariably suffer from a lack of precision and control.

The key here is that culture cannot be *systematically* changed by focusing on attitude change. For instance, to the question, "What are we doing to improve safety attitude, and how do we know whether it works?" a prudent manager would be hard pressed to say anything more than, "We try many things—it's hard to tell what works and what doesn't." But to the question, "Is the incidence of at-risk body placement on the increase or the decrease at our plant?" a behavior-based safety management process can give a definite answer, indicating by how many percentage points the incidence of the specified behavior is up or down over the last measurement period. The objectively observable character of behavior makes it amenable to both measurement and management, addressing the first weakness of attitude-focused programs. The second strength of the behavioral approach is that changed behavior can cause a change in the attitude of the workforce.

Although conventional wisdom is not usually aware that changed behavior can change attitude, this effect of behavior on attitude is also a common fact of life. A recent example of this behavior-to-attitude change in American life has to do with the use of seat belts in automobiles. As recently as the 1960s, seat belts were something of a rarity in cars. When seat belts were first introduced into cars, many people had driven for years without them. In the early days, drivers polled by researchers about seat belt use said that they didn't use (behavior) seat belts because they felt uncomfortable (attitude) wearing them, and they worried (attitude) that the belt would somehow trap them in their cars in the event of an accident. In other words, many drivers had a negative attitude or feeling about seat belts and this was reflected in their behavior—they didn't voluntarily install seat belts in their cars, nor did they use seat belts even when they were already installed in their cars. Over the years seat belt use has changed from being a novelty, to being a recommended option, to being required by many businesses, municipalities, and state highway patrols. In other words, people have been encouraged to change their habits (behavior) no matter what they might think (attitude) about seat belts. After only a short time of regular seat belt use, research showed that many of the same drivers polled earlier said they now felt uncomfortable when they *didn't* use seat belts. Their attitudes about seat belt safety had changed completely around. This is a classic instance of the way that a change in behavior can cause a change in attitude.

This same principle has been demonstrated in the workplace on numerous occasions. For instance, during a safety assessment effort at one facility, behavior analysis of incident data revealed that one of the behaviors associated with a significant number of accidents and/or injuries was at-risk body placement in relation to task. This behavior was a prime candidate, one that could be part of an inventory of behaviors targeted as a leading indicators of how safe or at-risk the work place is, in advance of any accidents at all. The rationale is straightforward—the more times workers use *at-risk body placement in relation to task,* such as standing in the line of fire, the more likely it is that an accident is going to happen. Conversely, other factors being equal, the fewer times that somebody stands in the line of fire, the less likely it is that an accident is going to happen. Using a data-sheet that incorporates the operational definitions of such critical behaviors, trained observers make random samples of work place behavior, producing a measure of the facility's level of safety performance.

At the facility in question, a common sequence of events took place. Work crews typically take their at-risk behavior for granted. Within the safety culture of that facility there was the unspoken assumption that at-risk body placement was simply part of being an efficient worker, a team player with hustle. Within six to eight months of experience with the employee-driven process, however, their behavior and their attitude changed dramatically. The workers came to understand the basic concepts of the process. They saw that the observers were careful to keep their observations objective and accurate. They saw that management was careful not to distort the observations with disciplinary action or punitive measures. In other words, the workers saw that their performance was being tracked against standards that *they and their peers* helped to define during the development of the facility's inventory of critical behaviors. This is the constant message of the behavior-based process. The result is that the same workers who used to think of standing in the line of fire as an acceptable thing to do come to regard it, and related at-risk body placement, as inappropriate behavior that is improper in a mature team player.

GETTING AN INTUITIVE HANDLE ON CONSEQUENCES: A CRASH COURSE IN BEHAVIORAL SCIENCE

An antecedent is anything that precedes and elicits a given behavior. A consequence is anything that follows from a given behavior. When the telephone rings (antecedent) we answer it (behavior) to find out (consequence) who is calling.

Trick question: Does the ringing bell cause people to answer the phone?

That question is a trick question because it plays into our old, unexamined paradigm about behavior. The scientific and far-reaching answer to the trick question turns out to be:

Yes, people respond to the bell by answering the phone, but

No, the bell does not cause them to answer the phone.

The insight of behavioral science is this: people respond (behavior) to the bell (antecedent) because it *predicts a consequence*—someone to talk to on the phone. It is this predicted consequence that moves people to answer the phone. The bell merely serves to signal the presence of a caller. When a phone malfunctions and rings repeatedly though there is no one on the line, people stop responding to the bell. The bell has not changed. What has changed is that the bell no longer reliably predicts a consequence of interest.

Behavioral science has shown these relationships among antecedents, behaviors, and consequences:

- Both antecedents and consequences influence behavior, but
- They do so very differently.
- Consequences control behavior powerfully and directly, and
- Antecedents influence behavior indirectly, primarily serving to predict consequences.

Expecting Too Much from Attitude Alone

Prior to the employee-driven approach, traditional safety management tried to accomplish performance improvement by appeal to attitude. On that model the following scenario often took place.

Bob Smith is a model employee, and he just got hurt on the job. Our facility had completed almost two million work hours without a recordable injury—until Bob's. Bob led the safety meeting last month and talked about his personal commitment to safety. He is known to be a good worker. What gives?

When experienced employees who are reliable, productive, positive workers talk about their commitment to safety, companies want new employees to hear them. It looks like a perfect opportunity to transmit the safety culture that the company wants to encourage. Then, however, it turns out that those same seasoned employees do not always follow good safety practices. They are injured, or they are involved in an incident or in at-risk behavior. Something doesn't seem to add up. It leaves us perplexed about the right course of action:

> How can our best workers have such good safety attitudes on the one hand, and on the other hand engage in at-risk behavior?

This combination of good attitude and bad practice does not seem to make sense. Companies justifiably wonder what is going on here.

Part of what is going on is that this approach relies on conventional wisdom to explain the linkage between attitude and behavior. Conventional wisdom assumes that a good safety attitude is a reliable predictor of safe behavior. Pursuing this unexamined assumption, safety efforts often spend a significant proportion of available resources on what could be termed attitude adjustment measures—contests, posters, slogans, meetings, motivational training, and other similar efforts designed to improve attitudes and to increase awareness.

In other words, conventional wisdom talks and acts as though the linkage between attitude and behavior were very direct. On this view of things, to assure what people will do about safety, say, companies just have to be sure that their safety attitudes are correct. This is one of those cases where conventional wisdom is misguided. People's *general attitudes* about safety *do not reliably predict* what those same people will do when faced with *specific safety situations*.

Consider the example of safe driving behavior. Most people are familiar with this behavior and with their personal relation to it. Suppose that in general my attitude about driving safety is positive. This means that I not only think that driving safety is important, but that it should be important for everyone in general. In this case I have a "good attitude" but how well does it predict that I will drive safely? That is, how predictive is my general belief in the importance of driving safety? Does my general attitude predict that I will obey speed limits, or that I will avoid alcohol before driving, or that I will keep my eyes on the road? No, general attitudes are not very predictive of particular behaviors. In the first place, who does not believe in safe driving? Drunk drivers *believe* in safe driving. The important sequence of questions then goes not to belief but to issues like the following:

1. Do I have a conscious intention to perform safe driving behaviors including those listed above?
2. If yes, is it within my control to perform the behaviors?
3. If yes, do I perceive these behaviors to be within the norms of my group?

4. And finally, and of most importance, what consequences follow for me when I perform (or fail to perform) these safe driving behaviors?

Expecting too much from attitudes alone is an old paradigm that is all the more stubborn for being so familiar. By their nature, old paradigms do not fade away just because they don't work. An old paradigm gives way only when it is matched by a new and more effective paradigm. The new and more effective paradigm offered here is the behavior-based approach to managing continuous improvement in safety performance. Using ongoing soon-certain-positive consequences to focus attitudes on identified critical behaviors is the effective way to assure that workforce safety attitudes reliably predict safe behaviors.

THE SECONDARY ROLE OF ATTITUDE AS AN ANTECEDENT OF BEHAVIOR

For leadership purposes the important use of the attitude-behavior linkage is as follows:

1. The consequences of behaviors are significantly more powerful than the antecedents—including attitudes, which are internal antecedents.
2. Behaviors can be measured and therefore managed, whereas trying to change attitudes is a murky business.
3. Furthermore, attitude is only one of the antecedents of behavior (see Fig. 3.4).

The point of item 3, above, is that although an antecedent attitude is important, it remains only one of several kinds of significant antecedents of behavior.

Three things are important:

1. Recognizing the power of consequences over antecedents, leadership action plans are directed to developing soon-certain-positive consequences for improved safety performance.
2. The primary focus of improvement is behavior—which can be measured and managed—versus attitude.
3. Assessments of existing antecedents take into account their full range, giving safety attitude its proper due as one of the antecedents of safety-related behavior.

The Behavior Analysis Closed-Loop Flow Chart, Fig. 3.5, shows the place of attitudes in the overall scheme of workplace safety. By way of example, other factors shown here as antecedents are Skills, Facility Conditions, and Availability of PPE. To represent the closed loop using only two dimensions, Fig. 3.5 shows

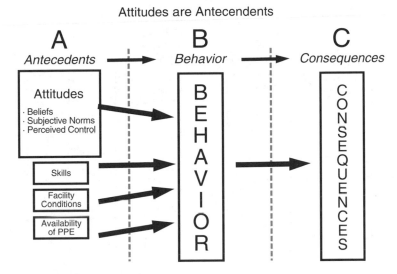

FIGURE 3.4 Attitudes are antecedents—not consequences.

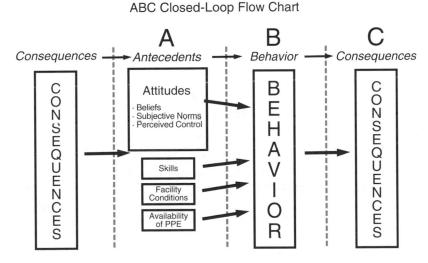

FIGURE 3.5 Consequences form a closed loop with antecedents.

consequences in both the first and the last columns of the flow chart, reflecting the way that consequences both follow from behaviors and, subsequently, modify attitudes (Fig. 3.6). In other words, attitudes are of secondary significance in the closed loop of previous consequences, antecedents (among which are attitudes), behavior, and new consequences.

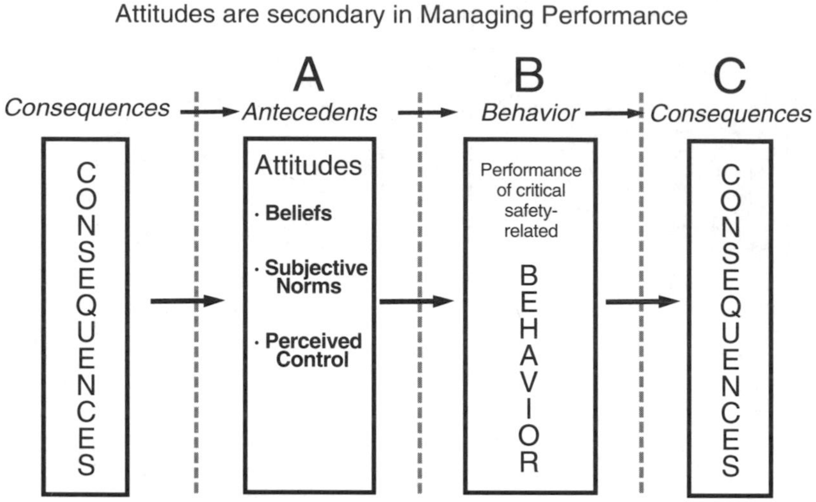

Attitudes are secondary in Managing Performance

FIGURE 3.6 Antecedents are secondary to consequences in managing performance.

In spite of its demonstrated effectiveness at explaining and predicting behavior, the behavior-based paradigm is not yet widely understood. Recent studies on the inherent biases in human judgment go a long way toward explaining how even trained professionals tend to make mistakes when they are required to work with a new paradigm (Kuhn; Kahneman, and Tversky; Nisbett; and Bazerman).

Consequences are the Best Predictors
of Behavior

Science has been surprising people since its beginnings. Science surprises even scientists, requiring them to change their established ways of seeing things, and of arriving at reliable descriptions, judgments, and predictions of events. Behavioral science requires a new rule of judgment too, one that "demotes" antecedents on the one hand, and recognizes consequences as the best predictors of behavior.

Consider the example of the pioneering astronomer Copernicus. In the centuries before Copernicus, people consistently misjudged the relations of the earth and the sun. In the same way, until this century everyone—experts included—misjudged the relations between antecedents, behavior, and consequences. Almost everyone made the unexamined assumption that since antecedents *come before* behavior, antecedents must be the *best predictors* of behavior. Behavioral science examined this assumption carefully and discovered that consequences, not antecedents, are the best predictors of behavior.

This new paradigm takes getting used to. At first it even seems contradictory:

How can something that follows behavior determine behavior?

This is similar to the puzzle that Copernicus posed:

How can something as still and immense as the earth rotate on its axis daily?

It took astronomers some decades to get used to "seeing" the earth differently. Because the community of managers is still in the early phases of reorienting their thinking about behavior, even highly trained managers can have trouble incorporating the behavioral paradigm into their rules of judgment.

In the field of safety management this confusion gives rise to the disproportionate attention and resources spent on the antecedents of the desired behavioral improvement—attitude change, slogans, posters, pep rallies, and so on. Typically these efforts are short-lived, if not stillborn. They mean to change behavior by changing the causes of behavior, and that much is correct. It is right to manage behavior by managing its causes—the error here is to think of antecedents as the causes of behavior. The lesson from the history of science is that although the confusion of antecedents with causes is natural, as a paradigm it is also counterproductive.

Once You See It—You See It Everywhere

Although the relationship between behavior and consequence seems peculiar at first, once people begin to see it they suddenly see it everywhere—another well known mark of paradigm shift. Some examples follow.

Threats

A threat (antecedent) is only as powerful as the consequences that it predicts. A threat of no consequence is an empty threat, a bluff. The antecedent may remain the same—same words, same tone of voice, same list of penalties, but people respond to it very differently when it no longer predicts threatening consequences. Clearly the power was not in the antecedent.

Promises

A promise (antecedent) is only as powerful as the consequences it predicts. People will accept (behavior) someone's word as his bond as long as he keeps (consequence) his promise (antecedent).

Resolutions

A resolution (antecedent) is only as effective as the result (consequence) that it achieves. Resolutions are promises that people make to themselves. Such promises, like good intentions, are notoriously hard to act on (behavior). The reason is that resolutions, and good intentions or good attitudes often remain just free-floating antecedents ungrounded in powerful consequences. More about this later in Chapter 4. The point here for private individuals and safety leaders alike is to resist the distractor of free-floating antecedents and to focus on effective consequences.

Many well intended safety efforts fail because they rely too much on antecedents—safety rules, training on attitude, procedures, meetings, and the like—that have no effective consequences backing them up.

The Most Effective Consequences for Managing Performance Improvement

Having established that consequences are more powerful than antecedents, it is also very important to take stock of the different kinds of consequences.

Soon-Certain-Positive

Some consequences are more powerful than others. For sustained performance improvement the most effective consequence is one that is simultaneously soon, certain, and positive.

Timing

A consequence that follows soon after a behavior is more effective than a consequence that occurs later.

Consistency

A consequence that is certain to follow a behavior is more effective than an unpredictable or uncertain consequence.

Significance

A positive consequence is more effective than a negative consequence.

The consequences that are least effective are late, uncertain, and negative. Many safety efforts are unsuccessful because they rely solely on late-uncertain-negative consequences to make their point. For instance, a hearing-loss prevention effort that depends on warn
ings of possible (uncertain) hearing loss (negative) eventually (late) is an effort that is going to sustain hearing loss. It is also noteworthy that an antecedent approach necessarily has no influence on the system. It must be a "program" because it has no mechanism. If such an approach is effective at all, it will run its course and then die out.

Chapter 4 looks at the effective way to manage the attitude-behavior linkage.

4

Managing the Attitude-Behavior Linkage

Chapter 3 presented a basic introduction to the secondary role of attitude in performance management. To say that the role of attitude is secondary does not mean that attitude is unimportant. Most people acknowledge that attitude is one of the important indicators of shared company culture. The difficulty for most managers is that they do not know what practical measures to take to actually address issues of attitude change. Chapter 4 pursues this matter in greater depth and detail, presenting a twofold strategy for addressing workplace safety attitudes:

1. Achieve a rigorous understanding of the proper role of attitude in the overall scheme of workplace safety, and
2. Implement organizational consequences that focus attitudes into intentions to perform specific, critical, safety-related behaviors.

To supply the background for Step 1, this chapter incorporates elements of a Theory of Planned Behavior (Ajzen). Step 2 is supplied by the behavior-based safety process, applied here as a way of assuring that safety attitudes reliably predict safety-related behavior.

THE LIMITS OF ATTITUDE

Good Attitude and Bad Practice

The Theory of Planned Behavior sheds light on our earlier perplexity (Chapter 3) about good safety attitude and poor safety practice. This model explains how

Portions of this chapter were written by Kim Sloat, Ph.D.

people can say one thing, sometimes truly believing and meaning it, and then do another. When the subject is safety this means that just because workers have and express a strong attitude in favor of safety, it in no way assures that they are going to behave in a safe way. Although this can be very frustrating, it does not mean that expressed safety attitudes are unimportant. The question is not whether to take attitude into account but how to do so in a way that focuses on performance. Psychology offers important knowledge about the conditions under which attitude is a predictor of behavior.

Beliefs, Subjective Norms, and Perceived Control

For safety purposes, the important elements of the Theory of Planned Behavior are as follows: attitude *becomes more predictive* of behavior as *the sum* of a person's attitudes about something forms an "Intention-to-Perform" a *specific behavior.*

Furthermore, the model analyzes this formation of a person's intentions from three sources:

- beliefs
- subjective norms (peer pressure)
- perceived control (support, involvement)

Taken by itself, even an intention-to-perform a specific behavior is not an iron-clad guarantee or predictor that the behavior in question will occur (see Fig. 4.1).

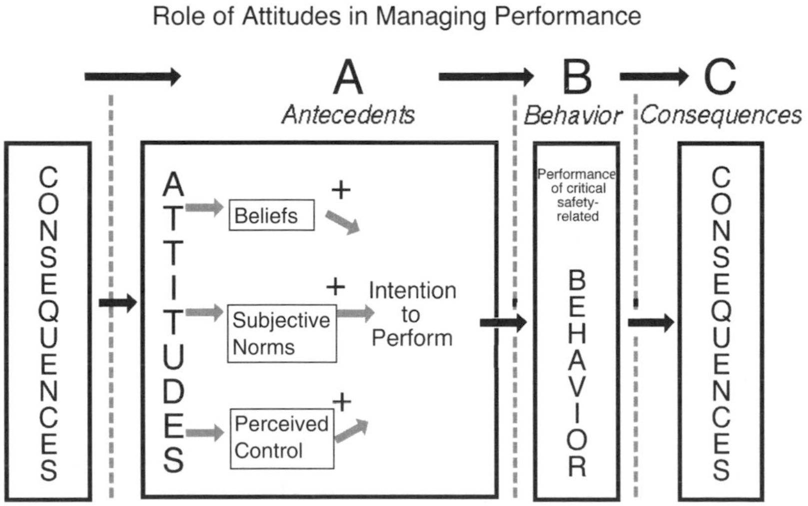

Role of Attitudes in Managing Performance

FIGURE 4.1 A closer look at the role of attitudes in managing performance.

An Ice Cream Illustration of the Limits of Attitude

The following situation from everyday life provides an example of how these three components of attitude work together. Consider a hardworking frequent flyer who is cutting back on the high-fat foods in his diet. As part of his new attitude toward his diet he has formed the following good intention, "I will not eat ice cream." Most of us have wrestled with New Year's resolutions and good intentions like this one. They are notorious for being ineffective much of the time. Why are intentions so unreliable? The model offers an explanation of why belief alone is not enough to activate a behavior (see Fig. 4.2).

Mr. Frequent Flyer is in a difficult situation in spite of his good intention because out of these three components of attitude, he has only belief working for his intention. In this tug-of-war the other two components—subjective norms and perceived control—are working against his intention rather than for it. All three of these components of attitude come together in his statement about his situation.

Belief, *for* intention (+):   Fat is unhealthy, but

Subjective norms, *against* (–):   everybody eats fatty foods, and

Perceived control, *against* (–):   it's all they have for dessert on this plane.

Although he believes that fat is bad for his health, he also knows that the group he is with regards eating fatty foods as normal (subjective norms), and he has a

Belief is not enough to Activate a Good Intention

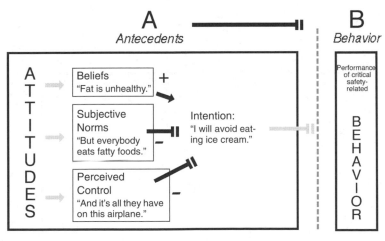

FIGURE 4.2   Belief is not enough to activate a good intention.

limited sense of control over the situation (perceived control.) Just in terms of attitude alone, this man's good intention has two strikes against it.

As it stands now, this man's attitude runs counter to his intention and favors unhealthy eating. Furthermore, in addition to his attitude there are other antecedents at work in his situation and they also favor the unhealthy behavior of eating high-fat foods. This fact can be brought out by doing some behavior analysis of this unhealthy behavior (Fig. 4.3). The strongest consequences here all favor unhealthy eating. These are consequences 1 through 3, they are all soon-certain-positive (SCP). The naturally occurring consequences that do not favor eating high-fat foods are all of the weakest kind—late-uncertain-negative (LUN).

Each of the elements sketched here—the components of attitude, and the role of antecedents and consequences—has important effects in the workplace.

AN INTEGRATED BEHAVIORAL APPROACH TO ALL THREE COMPONENTS OF ATTITUDE

Anyone engaged in workplace improvement efforts can profit from understanding this critical relationship between attitude and behavior (performance). Failure to understand these crucial matters leads to the inefficient improvement efforts and performance frustration experienced by many organizations today. The stage is set for failure whenever safety efforts stop short of developing workforce attitudes into the intention-to-perform specific safety-related behaviors which are

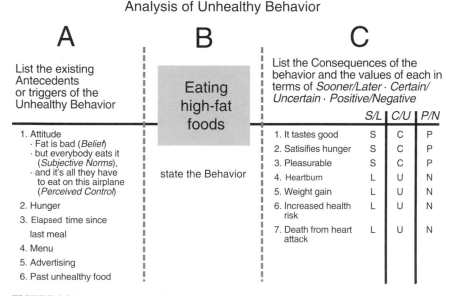

FIGURE 4.3 Behavior analysis of an unhealthy eating behavior.

followed by soon-certain-positive consequences. Furthermore, this development needs to proceed in all three areas of attitude—beliefs, subjective norms, and perceived control.

Successful safety efforts simultaneously address all three of these components of attitude because they

1. focus general beliefs on specific identified behaviors
2. assess and correct peer pressure (subjective norms)
3. address and remedy issues of support and involvement (perceived control)

Failure to achieve ongoing success in all three of these areas stalls overall progress on safety performance issues.

For example, consider the following three scenarios in which first one and then another of these three components goes unaddressed.

No Behavioral Focus. The workforce at Company A is uniformly enthusiastic about a new safety effort they have heard about at a sister site. In other words, peer pressure (component 2, subjective norms) favors the safety initiative. Management is also supportive (component 3, perceived control), providing both resources and permission so that the workforce generally feels that it both can and may get involved in the new safety effort. However, the program in this scenario depends for its entire effect on cheerleading, slogans, posters, and games. It lacks component 1. since it is completely unfocused on specific measures and critical safety-related behaviors. As a result the program is ineffective.

No Employee Involvement. Consider the supervisor audit program at Company B. The program is well focused on (component 1) specific identified behaviors. In addition, (component 3) management support is obvious to the supervisors in the training, time, and other resources provided to them for this audit program. But since the entire effort is top-down in character, it lacks condition (component 2) and workforce buy-in remains weak or unengaged altogether. As a result the program is ineffective.

No Perceived Support. Finally, consider Company C. An inventory has been developed that is (component 1) focused on site-specific critical behaviors. In addition, (component 2) there is widespread wage-roll enthusiasm and ownership of the inventory because it was produced by wage-roll personnel. However, in a well meaning but misguided bid to give the workforce *its own* safety initiative, management has remained so uninvolved that supervisors don't know about the safety effort and don't support it. Company C has failed to satisfy component 3, and the workers feel that they have neither the capacity nor the resources to carry through. As a result, the program is ineffective.

Each of these three scenarios is familiar, and each represents failure because a shortcoming in any one of these three antecedent areas stalls the effort. The challenge therefore is to bring all three of these strands of workforce attitude together into an intention-to-perform identified safety-related behaviors.

The Inventory of Critical Behaviors—Assuring Attitude-to-Behavior linkage

Employee-driven safety establishes and maintains a mechanism for assuring that attitudes reliably predict behaviors. Central to this outcome is the development, review, and ongoing feedback concerning the facility's inventory of critical safety-related behaviors.

A facility's behavioral inventory is developed through behavior analysis of incident reports. Site-wide input from all levels is involved in this preparatory work. The inventory undergoes peer review to sharpen its categories and to introduce it to the workforce. Trained wage-roll observers then use the inventory to establish the facility's %Safe baseline. The charted baseline is then presented to the workforce in kickoff meetings directed to buy-in and ownership of the ongoing safety process.

In the course of the implementation effort, the observers give positive verbal feedback to the workers they observe, and the accumulated observer data is presented as charts to the workforce and is analyzed for problem-solving targets. As workforce performance undergoes improvement, new performance targets are reviewed, added to the facility's behavioral inventory, and brought under ownership in a problem-solving mode that establishes continuous improvement.

This ongoing mechanism offers the best way of assuring that safety attitudes reliably predict safe behaviors. The inventory review, buy-in, feedback, and problem-solving provisions of the process address at the same time all three areas of attitude development.

Bringing Consequences to Bear on Attitudes

Figures 4.4 through 4.8 address the role of attitudes as antecedents. The purpose throughout is to describe the way that these factors interrelate, and to show how the behavioral approach

- develops specific safety-related beliefs (Fig. 4.4)
- corrects subjective norms (peer pressure) (Figs. 4.5 and 4.6)
- addresses issues of perceived control (employee involvement) (Figs. 4.7 and 4.8)

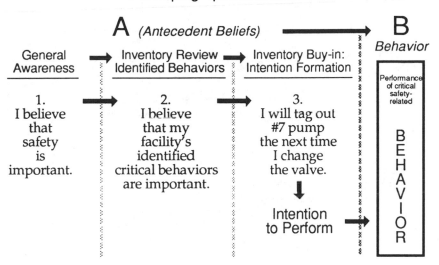

FIGURE 4.4 The sequence for developing beliefs that are specific.

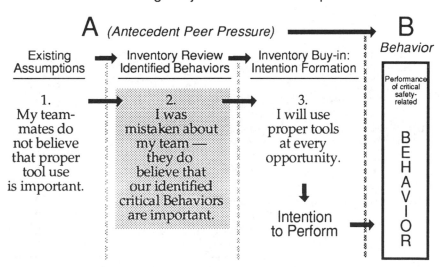

FIGURE 4.5 Correcting subjective norms—Step 1.

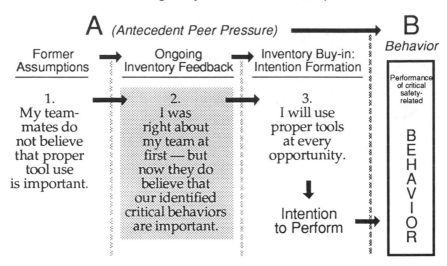

FIGURE 4.6 Correcting subjective norms—Step 2.

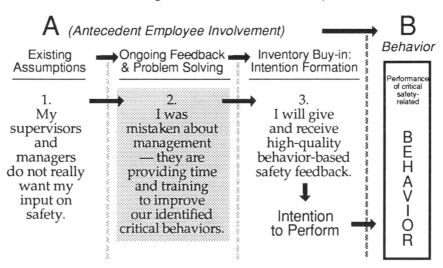

FIGURE 4.7 Correcting perceived control—Step 1.

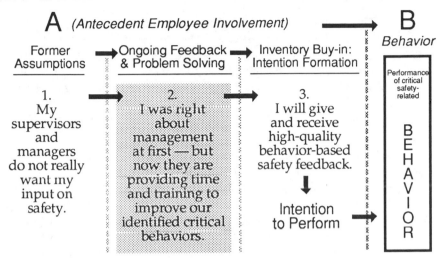

FIGURE 4.8 Correcting perceived control—Step 2.

Developing Specific Safety-Related Beliefs

A linkage between attitudes and behavior needs to be actively established and maintained because while attitudes are often general, behavior is specific.

This fact offers an important clue to how safety assessment efforts fail. We may ask the right *people* about their attitudes toward safety, but if we ask the wrong *questions,* we end up measuring their attitude on a level that is too general to relate to their performance of specific behaviors that are critical to safety at their facility.

Workers may have and express a generally favorable attitude toward safety, and yet they may do things that are clearly hazardous, such as working without the proper protective equipment. Leaders and fellow workers can find this very frustrating. At meetings when the general subject is safety the workers are right there, talking-up safety, but afterwards out on the shop floor there seems to be an inconsistency. The problem may be that the meeting discussion was too general.

The primary point here is that *in the absence of operational definitions of the specific behaviors at issue, the people at a safety meeting can only fall back on their individual interpretations of how to work safely.*

Everyone agrees that safety is important, but each one is agreeing to something different. Such a meeting may achieve agreement in word but it does nothing to correct extreme variation in practice. This situation holds all the way from the bottom to the top of the organization.

Behavioral Inventory: Focusing General Attitudes on Specific Safety-Related Behaviors

Workers need to know which safety-related behaviors actually hold the most potential for incident-free performance. Most workers are already prepared to say, "I believe that safety is important." They need to know which specific, operationally defined behaviors are critical to accident prevention. It is noteworthy that conventional wisdom is not always a reliable guide in these matters. Behavior-based assessments show that individual hunches , anecdotes, and experiences are often misleading about the kinds of behaviors and number of incidents that truly characterize a workgroup.

The best source for a reliable workgroup safety exposure profile is behavioral analysis of relevant data. The critical safety behaviors emerge from this examination (Fig. 4.4). Workers trained to observe those behaviors can track and chart workgroup performance.

It is only at this point that the generally favorable safety attitude can find a worthwhile focus—specific behaviors critical to safety. In this way the individual worker begins to have and express favorable attitudes toward specific safety behaviors—using personal protective equipment, correct tools, and safe body placement in relation to task, and so forth.

Our imaginary safety meeting is now to the point that each worker has not only a generally favorable safety attitude,

> 1. *I believe that safety is important.*

but also some more focused attitudes:

> 2. *I believe that the facility's identified critical behaviors are important.*

Forming an Intention-to-Perform

A worker whose attitudes have been focused on specific safety categories is just a short step from forming an intention. The focused attitude of "I believe that the facility's identified critical behaviors are important" (no. 2 from above) is on the threshold of becoming the stated intention of

> 3. *I will tag-out #7 pump the next time I change the valve.*

As an expression of safety attitude, statement no. 3 offers a far greater degree of predictability about safety behavior than the focused attitude of statement no. 2. For the same reason it offers a much greater degree of predictability than the unfocused, general attitudes that most safety efforts rely on, such as

1. *I believe that safety is important.*

Although they look somewhat the same, they range from general to specific on their way from a belief to an intention-to-perform-a-behavior. Each level of generality/specificity has an important role to play in the workplace. As the most general expression of safety attitude, statement no. 1 is the minimum that is expected of facility personnel. And indeed most people do think that safety is important. As statements of intention, however, both statements no. 1 and no. 2 remain empty or incomplete. Because of their general form they do not commit the worker to a specific action or behavior.

A Related Principle

The Theory of Planned Behavior points out an important related principle to the fact that there is an unreliable linkage between a general attitude and a particular behavior; namely, that there is also only limited linkage between one particular safety-related behavior and another. There is no shortcut here. Each relevant intention-to-perform a specific critical behavior needs to be established in the same way.

ADDRESSING PEER PRESSURE AND SUPPORT FOR SAFETY

In the real world it often happens that the preparatory work of focusing beliefs is accomplished quite well but it falls short of being translated into an intention to perform. The process is arrested at the stage of statements such as, "I believe PPE use is important and I will pay attention to it." In other words, workers are pro-PPE but PPE use rates remain unacceptably low. Putting more effort into focusing beliefs about PPE use would be effort misspent. It is time to look to the status of Subjective Norms and Perceived Control.

Subjective Norms—Peer Pressure

Intention formation is also influenced by subjective norms (Figs. 4.5 and 4.6). A subjective norm is one person's beliefs about the attitudes of other people toward him or her concerning some particular behavior. For instance, a worker may have strong, positive attitudes in favor of proper tool use, and yet subjective norms of the wider workforce could counter or offset the worker's tendency to form an intention to use proper tools. Thus the influence of subjective norms is an important second place to look when behaviors are not being performed. This is where the importance of culture and peer group pressure comes in.

- Safety Belief:
  I believe that proper tool use is important, and I will pay attention to it sometime. However,
- Subjective Norm:
  I also want to feel that I am part of the group; and it seems to me that
- Existing Assumption:
  my team mates do not believe that proper tool use is important.

In this case the subjective norm counterbalances and cancels the formation of an intention to use proper tools at the next opportunity.

Correcting Subjective Norms

Step 1: Check the Accuracy

The best way to strengthen norms toward safety-related behavior is to involve workers in the process of specifying the critical safety-related behaviors of the facility's inventory. This opportunity for involvement allows people to explore whether the workers have an accurate assessment of what the norms of their group really are. Sometimes what is needed to moderate the power of subjective norms is to change the perception of what the norms truly are.

If I have a good attitude about tool use but I haven't yet formed an intention to use proper tools because I have the mistaken idea that my co-workers look down on it, it can be a big load off of my mind to discover that I have read my co-workers wrong (Fig. 4.5). They not only don't mind wearing proper tool use, they may think it is a good idea. This change in my assessment of subjective norms can clear the way for me to form an intention to use proper tools the next time I have an occasion to do so.

Step 2: Reset the Norm

On the other hand, if the original subjective norms are accurate and the crew really is negative about the effort to assure proper tool use, then the challenge is to reset the subjective norms (Fig. 4.6). This is best accomplished through continued focus on the facility's behavioral inventory, and through continuing feedback about performance.

Correcting Perceived Control

Finally, workers beliefs may be well focused on specific behaviors, and their peer group reinforces their focus, but they still do not form an intention to perform the specific safe behaviors critical to continuous improvement in performance. They may be stalled by a third factor that has an impact on intention formation—the factor of perceived control (Figs. 4.7 and 4.8). Perceived control refers to my perception that I am not capable of performing the behavior.

Perceived control has two facets:

1. capacity to perform
2. resources to perform

The first point has to do with the fact that people who do not believe that they can perform the behavior in question are not very likely to form the intention to perform it. "It may not be my ability that I doubt but whether I have the resources to match the task." People who believe that they do not have adequate resources, tools, time, and so on, are less likely to form an intention to perform the safe behaviors.

Step 1: Check the Accuracy

The best way to strengthen workforce perceived control toward safety-related behavior is to involve workers in the process of inventory development, observation, and follow-up problem solving. This opportunity for involvement allows people to test their perceptions of control when it comes to safety (Fig. 4.7). Perhaps workforce perceived control is not accurate. A worker might underrate his ability to perform well under behavioral observation. Many workers resist being observed only to find out that they get consistently good feedback from observers on their performance. Or perhaps workers feel that management is not really committed enough to safety to allocate sufficient resources to make the employee-driven process work. During inventory development or problem-solving meetings the workers get a chance to see that management means business about safety.

- Supervisors receive training in the process and are careful to preserve its nondisciplinary character.
- Adequate time and training are provided for the observers and for the workforce at large.
- Problem-solving efforts actually result in remedies that are themselves incorporated into the facility inventory for continued tracking and improvement.

Step 2: Address the Issues

These and related developments change the way that workers perceive their control of their overall safety situation. To the degree that workforce perceived control is accurate about areas where management commitment to safety could improve (Fig. 4.8), there is no better forum for working in improvement than during the ongoing problem-solving meetings of the behavior-based approach. These functions then have the effect of addressing and correcting Perceived Control.

ASSURING THAT ATTITUDES PREDICT BEHAVIOR

The employee-driven approach to safety offers the most effective way to assure that safety attitude reliably predicts safe behavior.

- Free-floating general safety beliefs are directed to specific safe behaviors.
- Peer pressure is checked for accuracy, and is reset in favor of the intention to perform identified critical behaviors.
- Workforce perceptions of support and involvement are also checked for accuracy. Whatever issues exist here are addressed in the course of ongoing problem-solving, and workforce perceptions of control are reset in favor of performance of critical safety-related behaviors.

Observation and feedback provide ongoing soon-certain-positive consequences for specific identified behaviors that are critical a facility's continuous performance improvement. By not relying on attitude alone, the behavioral emphasis strengthens safety attitude.

Chapter 5 presents the significant common ground between the behavioral approach and Deming's approach to quality.

5

Shared Principles of Safety and Quality Improvement

Since the late 1980s a number of academic, and professional observers have recognized that there should be a connection between the fields of quality, and safety. In this spirit a number of loosely parallel translations of Deming's famous 14 Quality Points were published in the safety literature. But where Deming formulated his 14 Points after decades of single-minded dedication to applied science, it seems that many of his safety "translators" are starting with impressive sounding points, and hoping that the applied safety science will invent itself somehow or other. More wish list than action list, those well intended translations can only be loose because they lack for safety the combination of core elements that effective quality initiatives are founded on:

1. continuous improvement *through*
2. statistical tracking *of*
3. objectively defined
4. upstream predictors of excellent performance

The behavioral sciences bring the necessary technology to complete the task for safety. Fortunately the heart of safety performance, like any type of performance, is behavior, and behavior satisfies the criteria above.

Quality-Based Safety is Behavior-Based Safety

Long before quality became something of a fad, there was serious work underway in safety, developing for safety the four key elements listed above. Those researchers, and safety professionals were working in the field of applied behavioral science. The reason that behavioral science proved so fruitful for this work is that when it is approached scientifically, human behavior satisfies the criteria of the "quality" checklist. Since (3) behavior can be defined objectively, (2) it can be measured, and tracked statistically, and since (4) certain skills-related, site-specific behaviors are the best upstream predictors of excellence at a facility, by managing the levels of those behaviors a site can achieve (1) continuous improvement in safety performance. This chapter presents the basic "Quality Principles" as they are shared by employee-driven safety. The following is a consideration of a combined list of some of Deming's Points, Diseases, and Obstacles found at the core of his landmark book *Out of the Crisis*.

Create Constancy of Purpose—Long-Term versus Short-Term

Resist "instant pudding." This is all the more important because short-term thinking is so natural to people—consequences that happen sooner are more influential than those that happen later. The trouble is that the long term is where people live, and work. Our own cognitive bias in favor of "instant pudding" is therefore the most significant obstacle to creating constancy of purpose. Lack of constancy of purpose contributes to the accident cycle (see Fig. 1.1). When a company's injury rates go up, the organization focuses on safety. When their rates are high, they want to do something. But when their incident rate falls, they lose safety focus.

Constancy of purpose is degraded as organizations turn from one approach to another—the "program" mentality. Constancy of purpose is undermined by management turnover, and it is a rampant problem in safety. When constancy of purpose is a problem for an organization, it starts at the top, and filters downward. In organizations lacking constancy of purpose it is inadvisable to try behavioral safety. By its nature, the employee-driven approach requires constancy of purpose. If an organization has this quality, behavioral safety is an ideal way to communicate that fact throughout the workforce.

Build in Quality

Cease dependence on inspection. For safety this means cease sole reliance on injury rates with all of the associated dislocations of the safety effort (see Chapter 6 on management errors).

The effective place to manage a process approach to safety performance is upstream, not downstream with the incidents. Accident prevention is the goal, not better, and quicker accident reaction. Everyone realizes that injury rates are not leading indicators. People get stuck with injury rates when they feel that they have nothing else to go by. The challenge is to look at safety performance in the same way that Deming, and others have taught us to look at production, and service—to rethink safety as a "product." On this view, the leading indicators of safety are frequency rates of identified behaviors critical to safety at a particular facility.

Continuously Improve the System

Improve constantly, and forever the system that produces safety-related behaviors, thus constantly reducing the costs of safety-related rework. Eliminate downstream targets (injury rates) on the factory floor, and focus on process improvement upstream (behavior rates). At their best, downstream targets are counterproductive. Usually, however, numerical targets do not bring out the best in an organization. Managing the numbers is an altogether too common practice where downstream targets drive the safety effort. But even where management resists the temptation of managing the numbers, incident frequency management is reactive, trapping the organization in hindsight rather than fostering problem-solving, and foresight.

Drive Out Fear

Drive out fear, and fault-finding in safety. Stop hectoring the workforce for zero injuries, and new levels of safety achievement. Such treatment creates adversarial relationships since the majority of the consequences favoring at-risk behavior belong to the system, and thus lie beyond the authority of the workforce.

Fear is engendered by the safety effort when the atmosphere is punitive. Workers fear that an injury will result in loss of pay or even loss of a job. These fears are usually stretched beyond reality, but they easily follow from a few mismanaged cases of disciplinary action for safety violations. This is not to say that disciplinary action is inappropriate for safety violations. The positive point is that such action needs to be managed carefully to avoid creating an atmosphere of fear and intimidation.

Driving out fear means that management follows fair policies about safety rules, and regulations, involves employees in safety, practices good communication across levels, and departments, and recognizes that controlling behavior through fear is a losing strategy.

Eliminate Slogans, Exhortations, Targets, Quotas

Eliminate reliance on attitude adjustment. Deming's observations about the ineffectiveness of productivity, and quality pep rallies also applies to safety. Hectoring the workforce for zero injuries, and new levels of safety achievement only creates adversarial relationships since the majority of the consequences favoring at-risk behavior belong to the system, and thus lie beyond the authority of the workforce. It is the role of management to institute changes within the facility's system of behavior.

What is wrong with pep rallies, posters, and exhortations? They are directed to the wrong audience. These strategies arise from management's idea that production workers could, simply by changing their safety attitude, accomplish a zero recordable rate. The posters, and slogans take no account of the fact that injuries come from the system. Exercises in attitude adjustment generate frustration, and even resentment because they indicate to the workforce that management is unaware of the barriers to safety that characterize the facility's safety culture.

Attempts at attitude adjustment are primary examples of the short-term approach, the quick-fix program. The immediate effect of these approaches may indeed be some short-term improvement in the safety numbers. However, over time these gains disappear or even reverse. The latest safety effort is recognized as "just another program." The remedy is for management to accept the central responsibility for improving their facility's system of safety-related behaviors and, along the way, to remove both the special and common causes that are detected by statistical sampling of workforce performance of the identified critical behaviors.

Remove Barriers to Pride of Workmanship (Involvement)

Pride of workmanship is a logical consequence that sustains high performance in a mature individual. In effect, such workers give themselves their own incentives for high performance. Younger or less mature workers often need leadership to provide the initial soon-certain-positive consequences for long-term development of their own pride in safe workmanship. Although good work is its own reward, at first younger or less mature workers may need an external source of soon-certain-positive consequences to show them the significance of good work.

When leaders set up such a framework, the workforce develops a wonderful feeling of pride in the "intelligence" of their own problem solving and work. This is the mark of an "intelligent" organization, one that institutes soon-certain-positive consequences that favor the development of long-term commitments to safety, and mature workers for whom good work is finally its own most effective soon-certain-positive reward.

Remove barriers that rob people of their pride, and involvement in effective upstream safety initiatives. Esprit de corps can be organized around a variety of goals. When production is number one, everybody knows it. Leaders are being short-sighted when they praise or otherwise reward a crew for their hustle, and productivity even though the leaders saw the workgroup taking safety shortcuts, and engaging in at-risk behaviors. This message is even more counterproductive when the workforce knows that their unsafe behavior was witnessed but overlooked.

The concept of internal customers and vendors has very good application to safety performance. In their relations with each other the members of a workforce—from top to bottom—are "vendors" of safe behavior, and they are each other's "safety customers." Supervisors who reward their crews for working unsafely may think that they are rewarding them for working "cheap." They are awarding them business—continued wages at the facility—on the basis of a lower price tag, in this case "cut-rate" safety practices. Deming is right, however—cheap is not inexpensive. The true cost of injuries is hard to measure, but on almost any measure these days the cost of injuries is a burden that smart organizations avoid. The safety culture that slights safety in favor of shortcuts and habitual risk-taking is a culture that promotes not only injuries but the anxiety and stress associated with them, along with high turnover and absenteeism, and the related training and makeup costs. In other words, rework—personnel rework.

It is not hard to find barriers to pride of safety workmanship. Whenever safety systems encourage at-risk behaviors, fail to provide realistic or viable opportunities for involvement, or send contradictory messages, their effect is to block the natural pride that follows good safety work.

Reward Performance Based on System Improvements, Not on Downstream Results

Eliminate downstream targets (injury rates) on the factory floor, and focus on process improvement (behavior rates).

The safety paradigm is changing. The behavior-based safety paradigm is a turn away from the reactive approach to safety that is so frustrating for everyone concerned. Effective management of safety performance presents a uniquely complex set of organizational challenges. The human stakes of health and well-being, the necessary interface with productivity—these and other important factors can make safety one of those volatile issues that brings out adversarial tensions in an organization. Workers blame conditions, and workers in turn get blamed for their injuries.

It is easy to reward performance through peer observation, positive verbal feedback, and improvement action plans. This type of reward is appreciated by the workforce; it improves safety-related behavior; and it creates a positive atmosphere.

Don't Manage the Numbers

Eliminate management by injury rates. Substitute leadership of the safety process. Wanting to do more than manage the numbers is not enough, however. They need integrated instruments, and procedures that let them measure progress in safety. Safety-related behaviors can be operationally defined, observed, and tracked (Chapters 8 and 9).

Good management depends on good measurement. Where human performance is an issue—as it is in safety, and quality—the difficulty of measurement has been an area of frustration, and concern. The answer is to bring the scientific principles to bear on performance issues.

Encourage Teamwork

Implement structures, and procedures that put everybody in the company to work to accomplish the transformation in safety performance. Managing involvement for an injury-free culture is everybody's job. Veteran wage-roll employees are often the best resources a facility has when the challenge is to extract critical safety-related behaviors from accident reports. Teamwork at all levels is necessary to make the employee-driven process work properly. It is encouraged by the behavioral system itself, which calls for active participation, and problem solving across levels.

Employ Leadership, Not New Gadgets or Gimmicks

Eliminate safety incentive programs. This may have to be done gradually as better methods are integrated, but it is a worthwhile change to make. More often than not, safety incentive programs are harmful to real improvement efforts. Hold supervisors responsible—appropriately—for activities that precede reduced exposure.

Equipment, and administrative fixes. The role of leadership is to facilitate continuous improvement in safety. Leaders do this first by making sure that the facility's designated observers or samplers have time, and permission to get adequate training. Subsequently supervisors, and leaders support the trained observers while they fulfill their various duties.

In addition, supervisors, and leaders themselves take the training in behavioral observation. This makes them knowledgeable, if not fluent, in the facility's inventory of operational definitions, and its related data sheet. It also gives them a healthy respect for both the rigors of behavioral observation, and the high level communication skills necessary for giving good verbal feedback. Possessed of this knowledge supervisors, and leaders can be very effective in their ongoing support of the observer teams for whom they are responsible.

Don't Blame the Workforce

Management's acceptance of responsibility for safety goes a long way toward driving out fear and fault finding. In the most basic human terms it is counterproductive to blame employees as though their injuries occurred independently of management systems. Blame is also a mistake because it ignores the way that the overall management system influences employee behavior. The leader versed in behavior-based techniques knows for certain that when an injury results from an at-risk behavior, the implicated behavior has been performed on numerous previous occasions. Therefore the responsibility for this behavior, and its frequency lies with the management system as well as with the employee.

Nothing impresses, and assures employees more than a no-fault accident investigation process. No-fault does not mean do-nothing. The value in an accident is in learning how to avoid it in the future. With that goal in mind, effective accident investigation teams include the injured employee. By using behavior analysis on the accident, this team is able to incorporate their findings into the facility's inventory of critical behaviors. In this way the observers can include it on the data sheet, and give the workforce feedback about the newly identified behavior/s.

Institute a Vigorous Program of Training

Management literacy = statistical literacy. DuPont has a saying that safety is a condition of employment. Well, in the behavioral safety paradigm,

Understanding variation is a condition for being a manager.

A company would not hire a manager who could not add and subtract. These days companies do well to hire leaders who understand variation and consequences.

Along with the emphasis on SPC techniques as they apply to safety data, the implementation and maintenance of this new safety paradigm hinges on training in investigative interviewing, managing resistance to change, behavioral observation, and listening and verbal feedback skills. Since the training model involves coaching for skills development in key roles of the safety process itself, training transfer is assured from the outset. Consequently, although this behavior-based training concentrates on many so-called "soft skills," both the quality of the training and its application on the shop floor are much more like training on a new piece of machinery. These central skills of the safety process are not only nice to know someday—they are necessary.

Furthermore, since it is common for wage-roll employees to serve on steering teams, and for management personnel to take training in every role of the safety process, the message goes out that safety is a place where training is for everyone, and it is ongoing.

SUMMARY

So much by way of background. Part II begins with the basic Quality Tools as they apply to safety.

Part II

Methods for Continuous Improvement in Safety

6

Measurement of Safety Performance

OBJECTIVES OF PERFORMANCE MEASUREMENT

The Standard Incident Frequency Rate is a Mixed Blessing

One of the distinct advantages of safety as a target for performance improvement is that, relative to other human resources improvement activities, safety has a clear outcome measure. This clear outcome measure is lacking in most other activities undertaken in the area of human resources development and improvement in industry. For example, when managers allocate resources for soft-skills training, they usually cross their fingers and hope that something good will follow. More often than not, there is no way of knowing for certain whether or not the training was effective. In this field of instruction—for supervisory skills, or diversity training, for instance, there is nothing comparable to the industry-wide safety standard of the incident frequency rate (number of recordable incidents per 200,000 labor-hours per year). Accident frequency rates are treated below.

We can only manage what we can measure. Compared to human resources initiatives, this fact about measurement makes safety performance stand out as an area where management is possible. There is a downside to this story, however. Although the incident frequency rate is helpful as a clear, "wholesale" measure, so to speak, there are a number of limitations associated with its use, and some ways in which it is seriously detrimental. First the limitations

1. The performance outcome it measures is so far downstream that it is unsuited for proactive monthly or even quarterly performance management, let alone day-to-day use. And, as every employee knows, safety performance happens daily, hourly, minute by minute.

2. The greater the emphasis on incident frequency rates, the more unreliable they become as people learn how to "make the numbers come out right."
3. Because the incident frequency rate is susceptible to being distorted, the rewards, and punishments based on it come to be seen as capricious and unjust.

So although at first the widespread acceptance of accident frequency rates makes safety seem ideal from the standpoint of measurement, it turns out that the rates need very careful managing. Used incorrectly, accident rates can be quite counterproductive, and it is an exceptional organization that uses the rates correctly. Overall, the proper objective in measuring safety performance is to have an indicator of how the safety system is functioning.

PERFORMANCE MEASUREMENT

There are three specific reasons for measuring safety performance.

An Indicator

We want to know whether we are improving. We have the notion that we should improve. We're doing the same work; we ought to be learning along the way how to do that better. We rely on whatever the measurement system we have to tell us whether we are improving. Another consideration is benchmarking. How do we compare to other people in our industry? How do we compare to other plants in our division or company? How does department A compare to department B within a plant.

Accountability

The second objective of measurement is accountability. Performance measurement of an activity allows for accountability to occur. When the performance indicator is safety, that accountability should be evident at all levels from the CEO to the hourly employee.

At first glance, accident frequency rates seem an ideal way to hold people accountable for safety. "It's your job to see that people don't get hurt. We can measure that, and we'll hold you accountable for it." Usually this translates into making the supervisor's performance appraisal contingent on accident frequency rates. This appears to be good management practice at all levels of the organization. Unfortunately, this idea is almost always wrong. Accountability is a good thing. However, for all of the reasons presented in this chapter, using accident frequency rates as the measure is usually ineffective.

Feedback

The third objective of performance measurement is to provide a feedback mechanism. A feedback mechanism has tremendous value. It reinforces good performance, and it corrects performance that is lacking. Where performance is inadequate, very frequently the fault is an inadequate feedback mechanism. One could go so far as to say that the naturally occurring areas of good performance exist because there are natural feedback mechanisms in place that reinforce, and strengthen the performance. False feedback, on the other hand, impairs performance. Many organizations give false feedback about safety—such as the misuse of accident frequency rates. False feedback in an organization acts as a barrier to continuous improvement in safety.

Feedback improves performance when it accurately reflects the behaviors that are critical to success at a task. Feedback that tries to address the large issue of safety performance without addressing such site-specific behaviors, risks being false feedback. False feedback does not improve performance because it does not accurately reflect the behaviors that are critical to performance excellence. However, such misleading safety feedback is often given unknowingly by an organization that is fixated on its accident frequency rates. Over time, the effect of false feedback is impaired performance and what scientists refer to as "superstition"— the false generalization or reasoning about causes.

Experimental studies have intentionally used false feedback to test the effectiveness of real feedback as a performance improvement mechanism. For example, to determine the effect of feedback on the performance of a work task, scientists would compare two groups. One group would receive real feedback, feedback on behaviors critical to excellence of performance. The other group would receive extraneous information or false feedback, feedback on factors not critical to success. By comparing the performance results of the two groups it is possible to measure the degree of effectiveness of real feedback. Many such studies have been conducted over the years, and the overwhelming conclusion is that not only does real feedback enhance performance improvement but that false feedback severely compromises performance. As one might expect, false feedback not only does not help improve performance, it degrades performance by confusing the performers, and encouraging them to draw "superstitious" conclusions about why their performance does or does not work.

In most organizations, from the CEO's office to the shop floor, most people are confused by false feedback about safety. The result is an organization characterized by safety superstition. "Our quarterly injury frequency rate is up. This is unacceptable. The last time we had a situation like this, what did we do? Whatever it was, do it again quick—we need to drive these numbers down now, or I'll be looking for a new job." Why is this false feedback? Anyone who can answer this question has properly absorbed an idea that most North American managers have yet to understand in connection with safety performance. Interestingly, many of those same managers do understand this concept when it is applied to quality. Somehow this crucial idea does not generalize easily from quality to safety. The cause of this confusion or poor generalization is the topic for another book, one which spells out the natural source of biases in human judgment. To answer the question posed above, the reason that reliance on incidence rates amounts to false feedback is that the outcome measure itself (this quarterly frequency rate) does not necessarily correspond with real improvement in performance (reduction of exposure). As things stand now, managers and their groups are regularly rewarded or punished on the basis of random variations in their performance.

TRADITIONAL SAFETY MEASUREMENT METHODS CURRENT IN INDUSTRY

The traditional measurement system used by most companies has three loosely related components:

1. accident frequency rates
2. audits
3. informal knowledge

The Proper Use of Accident Frequency Rates

The annual accident frequency rate is a standard calculation in the U.S. The measure most frequently used is

number of incidents × 200,000/total hours worked

Taking as its standardized unit of measurement a workgroup consisting of 100 people, each of whom works on average a 40-hour week for 50 weeks of a year, the calculation gives an incident rate for the unit of 200,000 person-hours of exposure to workplace hazards. Recapitulating the numbers, 100 workers × 40 hours a week × 50 weeks per year = 200,000 personhours per year.

Although the calculation is straightforward, and in wide use throughout industry, it is nonetheless quite easy for managers to lose sight of just what their frequency rates actually mean for their safety efforts. When a period of time passes with no injuries, it is tempting to think that safety performance is good, or even improving. Conversely, when several accidents occur within a short period, it is easy to conclude that performance must be down or declining. Either of these conclusions could be wrong.

The true significance of either of these results can only be determined statistically by comparing these outcomes to the predicted random outcome for the facility in question. In other words, *a stable system will produce a variable number of injury events.*

Take the example of a work group of 100 employees that has just completed the first quarter of their current safety measurement year. For the preceding twelve-month period, the work group had a recordable rate of 2.0. In the three-month period just completed, however, the recordable rate has risen to 4.0. At first glance it appears that safety performance has declined significantly, but what the quarterly number actually tells us is that one injury has occurred within the past three-month period.

Given the work group size, the apparent quarterly increase to 4.0 does not represent significant variability (special cause). Although taking account of random variability is standard procedure using statistical process control in the quality improvement process, an awareness of random variability remains rare in safety management. In the field of safety, many reward systems and performance appraisals are based on numerical goals and measures that are untested for random variability. For the supervisors of this hypothetical work group, this could well mean receiving a bad performance rating that is undeserved.

On the other hand, the unclearness of this concept in safety also means that work groups often get good safety ratings when they do not deserve them. For instance, suppose a work group with the same past-year frequency rate of 2.0 but a first quarter in which no recordable injuries have occurred for a three-month frequency of zero. This apparent improvement in their safety performance is also just that, merely apparent. For a work group of 100 with an annual rate of 2.0, a quarterly range of frequencies from 0.0 to 4.0 has *no statistical significance.* This range of random variability of outcome is typical of a stable system in which there is *no change* in the ratio of safe to at-risk behaviors.

To take another example, examine Fig. 6.1. Suppose an organization has 1000 employees and a recordable incident rate of 2.0. The numbers for this hypothetical case describe a facility in which we expect 20 injuries in a 12-month period, or fewer than 2 per month. This is an extremely low number of events for a population of 1000 people exposed daily for a one-year period.

On average at this frequency rate in this population, an individual would experience one injury for every 50 years that he or she worked. This is another way of saying that the rate is one injury per 50 person-years of work. Because accidents at this frequency level are such rare events, a very large number of hours worked must be logged before this method of measurement achieves statistical validity.

How many worker-hours are needed for statistical validity? Of course this depends on the incident frequency rate, and the amount of variability present. The higher the frequency rate, and the lower the variability, the fewer the hours needed for validity. Standard SPC techniques work nicely with injury data, and the usual statistical guidelines provide an accurate answer for questions of validity.

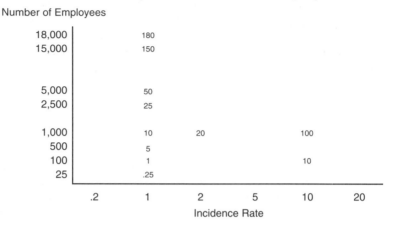

FIGURE 6.1 Number of injuries per year by incidence rate and number of employees.

For the typical facility these statistical methods mean that the injury frequency rate is a measure that is accumulating validity as time goes by, but that these frequencies are of no predictive value to safety management on a monthly or even quarterly basis, let alone a weekly or day-to-day basis. On the contrary, given the misplaced trust that people accord to frequency rates, these numbers not only do not help the safety effort, they are an outright hindrance to proactive safety management. Reliance on such incomplete statistics as the primary indicator of safety performance gives rise to the accident cycle (Fig. 1.1).

This graph of the accident cycle shows the relationship between a facility's thresholds of acceptable injury rates and management's changing response to the rates. When the recordable rate goes above a facility's upper limit, management acts to drive the rate down. When the rate falls below the acceptability limit, attention is withdrawn from safety, and the recordable rate rises again. In this cycle the management action for improvement follows fluctuations in the accident frequency.

This means that companies who respond to the accident cycle and work very diligently to push down their accident rates, make a new problem for themselves. Since they are triggering their intervention off of a downstream measure, they lose their focus when rates are low. They may want to work on safety because they know that when they don't, their accident rates will rise again. Some high-performing companies beat the safety cycle by working on safety no matter how low their accident rates go. However, although their rates no longer cycle, they usually reach a point beyond which they do not improve, either. By achieving a low but unfortunately stable rate, the company beats the accident cycle only to stall on a safety performance plateau. Additional effort achieves very little added benefit.

The Audit

In the safety audit someone (usually from outside the location) visits the facility to evaluate a predetermined set of criteria thought to be important to safety performance. The audit is usually conducted by interviewing employees, looking at records, and observing the work place. From these the auditors try to judge whether the desired systems, measures, and procedures are in place. On the basis of information gathered, the auditors attempt to discover how many of the safety systems that are supposed to be in place actually are in place. External safety audits at the site level are often done by the corporate group. A client of long-standing from a chemical company told the author that when the auditors from his company's corporate office show up, they always say the same thing: They are there to help, they don't want to get in the way, and they won't take very long. He believes none of the above to be true and, in fact, they do just the opposite in all aspects. Seriously, the common perception at the plant level is that the corporate auditors are more evaluative than helpful, and that it's kind of a game of trying to appear to be doing a good job and obscuring the real issues.

The result of the audit is usually a rating. Different companies have different rating systems, but it is usually a numerical index that tells the extent to which certain activities or systems are in place. Third-party vendors have also developed audit systems. Unfortunately, whether conducted by the parent corporate office or a third party, it is unclear whether audit systems actually measure anything that is predictive of accident frequency rates or of real safety performance. The audit is often seen as a paper trail, the suggestion being that what is actually audited is whether documents exist. The implication is that the relationship of those documents to reality is not necessarily one-to-one.

Some organizations have instituted self-audits. In this method the site outlines specific criteria that constitute excellence in safety systems. Then an on-site team is assigned the task of determining the extent to which they meet those criteria. Usually the internal auditors also summarize their findings in a numerical fashion. Carried out with due regard for local conditions at a given site, the internal audit has potential to be more useful than either the third-party or the corporate external audit. The usefulness of audits is to answer the basic question, "Does this site have the necessary systems in place for excellent safety performance?" The more difficult question, often left unanswered, is whether the existing safety systems promote continuous improvement. In the absence of consistent measures of exposure, this latter question is nearly impossible to answer.

Informal Knowledge

The third method currently used is what could be called informal knowledge. Most facilities have a reputation within a company for being good, bad, or mediocre in safety performance. Most of the managers within a company will be aware of that reputation. For example, a corporate safety manager who has responsibility for five locations can rank sites A through E. Asked about plant A's safety performance, the manager will say, "They are pretty good; they have given safety a lot of emphasis; they don't have a lot of labor conflict; they have good supervisory involvement; their safety manager is very effective; they have a plant manager who gives a lot of emphasis to safety, and they have evolved, and developed pretty good safety systems." Within the company that reputation is taken quite seriously as an indicator of how the location is doing. In fact, however, the informal rating may be false feedback because it is independent of actual safety performance. This state of affairs often accounts for the statement that one hears about the site later, "They were doing great for several years, and then wham, they were hit with . . . I don't know what happened."

It is important to note that it is not always useful to compare locations by accident frequency rates because different plants do different kinds of incident classification, and reporting. In actual practice, the seemingly universal measures of incident frequency rate are not universal. In spite of the issue described here, informal knowledge is not to be ignored. In fact, it may be in some sense one of the best indicators that most companies have.

PROBLEMS OF THE TRADITIONAL SAFETY MEASUREMENT METHODS

Reporting Problems

The traditional safety measurement methods presented above have several quite severe problems. The first problem is the reporting of accident frequency itself. Obviously if incidents are not reported, then the measurement system breaks down immediately. In assessments carried out since 1980 across industries, and regions of the United States, and Canada, the author, and his associates have found that first aid injuries are almost always underreported. In some cases as few as 10 percent are actually reported, and with a reporting range of 50 to 60 percent, even the best companies do not have a system that inspires confidence in first aid numbers.

This section discusses reporting issues for several classifications of injuries, starting with the most minor. Note that companies just starting to make improvements in safety have little or no regard for lesser injuries, focusing on lost-time injuries. However, companies that have improved a great deal necessarily pay attention to all injuries.

Why classify injuries at all? Why not just report on total incident frequency? The reason is that the distinctions are intended to add value to the overall measure. Companies A and B from the same industry have total incident rates of about 20. But Company A has zero lost-time injuries and a recordable rate of 1.0, while Company B has a lost-time rate of 3.0 and a recordable rate of 5.0. Which company has better safety performance?

If you selected either A or B, you answered too soon. In order to answer this question properly we have to know the duration over which the measure occurred, the size of each workforce, the recording, and classification procedures of each, and we have to perform some statistical analysis, perhaps plotting the data on a statistical process control (SPC) chart. Having done that, the classification of injuries will help us determine which company had better safety performance, even though their total injuries are about the same. Only then can we say appropriately whether Company A or B is better.

Which is the best single indicator to look at? Assuming correct reporting, and classification, the all injury frequency rate is usually the best overall indicator because it is the farthest upstream, and the highest number. This means that it is subject to the least amount of random variation, and will therefore be the easiest to work with using SPC techniques.

First Aid Injuries

Companies that are safety leaders are aware of this important flaw in the reporting system, and they have begun to correct it. Such companies push hard to have incidents, even minor ones, reported. They know that a minor incident has the potential of being a major incident. For example, a person might slip, fall, and sustain a minor bruise or cut, but could have broken a bone from the same fall, resulting in a lost-time injury. By reporting all injuries, even minor ones, the system gets information about exposures, and consequently has opportunities to solve problems. This very good idea is often compromised in practice. Most organizations provide negative consequences for reporting injuries. A worker who is down at the first aid station frequently, may develop a reputation as a person who is accident prone. Workers who go into the first aid station with a very minor injury are often given the following negative consequences. People are displeased to see that the workers have hurt themselves, and this expression of displeasure has a chilling effect. The injured workers are often required to fill out extensive paperwork even for something really trivial like a slight cut to the finger that requires a only a small bandage. This paperwork drudgery is a consequence that provides reinforcement for the behavior of not going to the first aid station.

Part of the problem is that in their zeal for exhaustive data collection, companies lose sight of their real objective. What is needed is an effective distinction between those minor injuries that the organization would like to get data on, and those minor injuries on which the organization really doesn't need data. Most safety professionals regard this as heresy. They fear that by opening the door at all, designating some kinds of first aids as unimportant, they will be right back where they started with a major under-reporting problem. As under-standable as this overreaction may be, it represents a new kind of drain on the data-gathering activity of an organization. Functionally, however, it is counter-productive to encourage people to report injuries that *have no meaning* in either direction.

On the other hand, there definitely are minor injuries that need to be included in any accurate reporting system. This is true because such data analysis is the only way to discover whether there is an incident pattern that needs to be addressed. In SPC terms this pattern might be a common cause at work in the facility—something that puts people at risk.

The reporting requirement is all the more suitable in the case of workers who happen only to bruise their toes when a three-ton piece of equipment falls on their feet. That is information that needs to be in the safety data base. Getting this information into the data base does not necessarily mean requiring that every bruised toe be reported to the first aid station. The important thing is to establish a data-gathering mechanism that is distinct from first aid reports.

For many companies the difficulty here is that a worker who neglects a small injury may allow it to develop into a more serious infection, one that ends up requiring medical treatment and therefore qualifies as a "recordable injury." The recordability of this emerging incident is a function of neglected treatment, not of factors within the operating system of the facility. Often it is because companies are trying to rule out this scenario that they make rules about reporting all injuries no matter now trivial. While admitting that there is a real, and ongoing difficulty here, it nonetheless bears noting that at such companies most people ignore the rule anyway—cancelling the intended treatment benefit. At the same time the safety data-gathering function gets a bad name—weakening an important ele-ment of any attempt at continuous improvement. Clearly, overreacting is not a solution.

Recordable Injuries

Beyond the level of first aid, even more serious injuries are often not reported. The severity of underreporting varies a great deal from plant to plant, and from company to company. Ironically, it is sometimes the company with the best repu-tation for safety that has the worst reporting. Usually this is accompanied by an atmosphere of fear, and intimidation.

The author and an associate were recently asked to sit in on a client company's safety seminar for senior managers conducted by a consulting firm favoring the traditional top-down approach. When the issue of underreporting was raised, one participant asked, "Suppose an employee who is generally a good, and safe worker fails to report an injury—what should we do?" The consultant's reply was, "Our advice is to *get* that employee, because underreporting cannot be tolerated." The questioner then said, "But what if his supervisor knows about it?" The answer? "*Get him too.*" This approach may have some advantages, however, driving out fear is not one of them. Clearly this approach is not geared toward creating teamwork, nor empowering employees to become involved, nor developing measures of real safety performance as part of a continuous improvement mechanism. This is management by fear, and intimidation, and it is not unusual in some companies who are high-performers in safety.

In surveys conducted by the author and his associates at such companies, respondents say that if they can get away with it they frequently do not report recordable injuries. They say, "There is pressure from management not to have injuries—so if you can hide it, you do." In the classification system a recordable injury is basically one that would require medical treatment. There are complex rules specifying this class in more detail—the kind of medical treatment, and so on. However, the upshot is that workers may have to exert themselves to hide an injury that is really recordable. The fact is that most organizations are set up in such a way that the effort of hiding a recordable injury is less onerous for workers than the effort of reporting such an injury!

At many plants the safety system is such that, in effect, workers are given many incentives to avoid reporting injuries and to have them treated "outside the fence" (off site). Reporting the injury will make them look bad; it will be embarrassing; it will have negative consequences on the people who work there. Common considerations of this kind amount to very strong pressure not to report recordable injuries. The result is that a substantial proportion are not reported.

Lost-Time Injuries

It is harder to hide an injury that would be classified as lost-time if it were reported. Generally, the more serious the injury, the higher the percentage of reporting. Even in those cases, employees have been very ingenious about hiding injuries. Take the example of a severe bruise. Employees have been known to conceal severe bruises until they can leave the plant to consult a private doctor to see whether they have suffered a broken bone. When the answer is yes, they may call in and take vacation time immediately so that the cast can be put on later that day. They are counting on the break healing well enough in two weeks that they can return to work without the cast.

All of this comes from the wrong kind of pressure to avoid injuries. In each of the cases where the injury is not reported, the activity that is hidden has already happened. What the injured person is trying to hide is the result of the actual system as it exists. This kind of under-reporting is a form of denial, and irresponsibility, and it provides false feedback to the organization about its safety performance. It is in no way productive of safety improvement—just the opposite. It means that the natural feedback mechanisms that keep workers from injury are subverted in order not to cause the organization embarrassment or to make people look bad.

Classification Problems

Another related problem with the existing system is classification. The pressure of false feedback from managers is to look good, and the emphasis is definitely on *look good* rather than *be good*. The system pressure here is to manipulate the numbers so that the workgroup appears to be doing a good job in safety. This pressure is often very intense. One way of dealing with this pressure is to classify injuries "creatively," which is to say incorrectly. If people can figure out a way to classify a recordable injury as a first aid, or a lost-time injury as a restricted work day, or a restricted work day as a recordable, then they can make the numbers look better than the system actually is. The actual classification system is not usually the problem. Relatively clear operational definitions exist that inform the objective safety professional how to classify an injury. Why is there such pressure to classify injuries incorrectly? Again, the pressure is there because the emphasis is on appearance rather than actuality. The premium on appearance over reality has profound negative effects, not the least of which is to undermine the credibility of the safety commitment of the organization. The emphasis on appearance provides fuel for the fire of adversarial relations between workers and management, and it strengthens the false feedback devil.

Suppose someone enters a supervisor's office and says that John Jones was injured. In many companies the supervisor's first question will be, "Is it recordable?" This common first question shows the wrong motive where safety is concerned, and the usual answer to the supervisor's question is, "We don't know yet." Translation—"We are looking at classification alternatives." Some companies have created a restricted-day classification. To the wage-roll employee it may appear that the sole purpose of this classification is to reduce the number of events that would otherwise go in the company's lost-time injury category. Now there is a legitimate purpose for a restricted-day case category that requires employees to stay in the workplace and do restricted work rather than sitting home losing time. This helps employees avoid the psychological syndrome associated with being out of work. There is good medical evidence to suggest that this syndrome is harmful to injured employees and lengthens their recovery time.

However, it appears to employees that some locations abuse the restricted-day case category as a way to hide a lost-time injury by reclassifying it, and in some cases this is probably true. It is not unheard of that a worker who suffers a broken leg, say, and who has a doctor's order to stay home and off of their cast is pressured to show up for work anyway to be put on a restricted-day basis. This kind of activity occurred much more frequently in years past than it does today. In some cases in the past this strategy of creative classification even included ridiculous antics like having company executives go to the doctor's office to discuss the medical treatment regimen for the injured worker, to influence the doctor's strategy so that the injury could be recorded into the desirable category. There are numerous stories of people being brought into the workplace in ambulances and in various conditions where they obviously should be at home, and all in order to avoid taking a lost-time injury. The other side of this coin is that workers can feel that if they do have a serious accident, the supervisor will be there with their walking papers before they hit the ground.

Incentive Programs

Incentive programs often contribute to these abuses. These problems are accentuated by incentive programs that are contingent on having no injuries for a certain period of time, or that distribute company prizes and awards for going X numbers of hours without an injury of a certain kind. In theory such an incentive program is supposed to be beneficial. The theory goes as follows. As the company develops a record of no injuries for a certain period, awareness increases among the workforce, and the result of that increased awareness is more safe behavior. Peer pressure develops to do the job safely because no one wants to get hurt, and because no one wants to ruin the company record. However, in fact it is really unclear how that awareness mechanism translates to the lack of exposure. At best, awareness is increased temporarily (see the section on adaptive readiness), and this affects those safety-related behaviors over which the worker has direct control. On the other hand it is absolutely clear how that mechanism translates to the misclassification, and underreporting of injuries.

It is interesting and instructive to observe the degree to which industry has been influenced by the effects of inadequate measurement. In the perceptions of many managers, the cost of having to "take" a lost-time injury is exaggerated. In many safety cultures, saying that location X had to take a number of lost-time injuries is like saying that half of the plant burned down. In the case of fatalities, that kind of response makes sense. But in the case of lost-time injuries where the actual source can range from the nearly trivial (infected finger) to very important (broken leg), managers are responding inappropriately to a classification artifact blown out of all proportion, an artifact that provides false feedback about the real safety system we are trying to measure.

An example occurred during the opening get-acquainted session at a seminar conducted by the author. A representative from a pharmaceutical company introduced himself by saying that his location of 2000 employees had been a company and industry safety leader for some time. Then this fellow hung his head, looked ashamed, and said that he was nonetheless very unhappy to report that on that very morning his facility had "taken" a lost-time injury. It had been three years since they had such an event, and the man took on a somber tone, acting as if he were talking about something of tragic proportions. He then described what had actually occurred.

An employee had experienced a back sprain. It was minor, but the employee was sent to the hospital for a diagnostic procedure. While in the hospital the employee contracted an infection. The infection had *nothing whatever* to do with the workplace. However, one thing had led to another, and the employee ended up having to stay in the hospital overnight. As a result of this, the plant had to "take" a lost-time injury. Truly the classification gods are capricious and destructive beings! In this case a classification artifact gave the location a black eye, a bad record, tarnishing overnight their prized safety standing within their company and, by implication, the company's standing within the industry. This very common situation would be laughable if it did not have such serious consequences for real safety performance. In such cases, instead of being an aid to management, the classification system is driving the management system. The measurement system is a remedy with serious negative side effects. The negative side effects arise primarily because

1. Managers and regulatory officials are not literate in statistical methods.
2. In an effort to create accountability through performance measurement, the resulting system of measurement has lost its proper place—it has become an end in itself rather than a means to an end. The result is an accounting system that has been stretched to create paper profits. Safety looks good because the books have been cooked, but performance is not really good.

Statistical Literacy

Incident frequency rates are characterized by random variation. Improperly understood, this information can give false feedback to the organization about their performance.

Assume that 10,000 exposure events occur on average for each injury event. In month 1 the 10,000 exposure events result in one injury. In month 2 the same number of exposure events results in two injuries, and in month 3, zero injuries. In fact, real safety has not changed in months 1, 2, and 3, but accident frequency rates have changed quite dramatically. In a small employee group, they may have changed astronomically. If accident frequency rate is the primary indicator of performance, then it is providing false feedback about months 1, 2, and 3. Further, it is not giving us day-to-day, week-to-week information that we need for management. Often random variation is misread in both directions. The solution to all of this is to do control charting with accident data, and not to overreact to changes in either a positive or a negative direction. That requires understanding statistical variation as applied to safety, and most managers do not.

Suppose that a company wants to hold its first-line supervisors accountable for safety, and so it adopts the following policy: at year-end the supervisor's performance evaluation will be based on safety performance as measured by recordable injuries, and the rating is as follows:

Outstanding performance = no injuries in supervisor's workgroup

Good performance = 1 injury

Fair performance = 2 injuries

Poor performance = 3 injuries

Is this a good system? Or is it a system that provides false feedback? This system will be accurate only 50 percent of the time, and 50 percent accuracy means false feedback half the time. If each supervisor has 25 employees, and the plant has a recordable rate of 8.0, the normal random distribution of accident frequency rates by supervisor will range from zero to 3 injuries. The entire range from good to poor is within the limits of normal variation for this system, and this means that there is no significant difference among those numbers—they all fall within control limits of this SPC chart.

Once, the author was giving a presentation to a group of vice presidents of a large chemical company. Before the presentation the senior vice president said to the group, "As you all know, we just got our report on safety for the year, including the last month (June). We had hoped that our performance would improve in June. In fact, it has gotten worse. Our goal for the current year is an incident frequency rate of 1.3, and through May we were at 1.38. In June that has deteriorated to 1.49 and, gentlemen, we need to take some action to reverse this. The trend is going in the wrong direction, and we're currently on a path to failure in relation to our goal. We had better do some things to make sure that we achieve this goal." This is an example of the misuse of the accident frequency data. In fact, the distinction between 1.3, 1.38, and 1.49 is utterly meaningless. Senior management pushes on that number, but that pushing on the number has nothing to do with actual improvement in the system. Lower-down managers understand this; some senior managers do; most do not.

Chapter 7 takes up this topic of statistical illiteracy along with some of its effects. The first step toward statistical literacy for many managers has come in the area of quality. As Chapter 5 shows, there is a natural overlap between TQM approach to defect prevention, and the behavior-based approach to accident prevention.

7

Using Statistical Techniques with Incident Data

A proviso is in order here. This book is not a textbook nor even a primer on total quality management (TQM). Many such books are available. For a solid introduction, readers unfamiliar with the quality literature are encouraged to make the acquaintance of the works of Deming, Juran, and others. The purpose of this book is to draw the connection between the two well established disciplines of quality management, and behavior-based safety. To that end, this book assumes some level of familiarity with the basic principles of statistics that are common to both disciplines.

MANAGERIAL LITERACY = STATISTICAL LITERACY

Picture the safety manager of a new facility with 500 employees. As part of the planning for resources necessary to do the job successfully, the manager needs an idea of how many injuries are likely to occur on a monthly basis, given the kind of exposures the facility has. He consults with an expert about this problem—someone who is very familiar with the kinds of injuries and exposures that occur within the manager's industry. The safety manager asks the expert, how many injuries to expect to have per month. The manager tells the consultant the nature of work that the employees are going to do, and the fact that there are 500 of them. The consultant studies the site design layout, training plan, safety program, rules, and regulations, managerial style, span of control, and so on, and replies that on average the safety manager can expect to have two injuries per month.

The plant opens—with all 500 employees working about the same number of hours each month—and in the first month, the site logs two injuries. At the end of

Kristen Van Zee contributed to the development of this chapter.

the first month having had two injuries, the manager feels fairly confident that the systems he has put in place are appropriate. Table 7.1 shows both the injury count, and the incidence rate for twelve months of operation. In the second month the site has three injuries, and although this is increase over the first month of the operation, the manager still feels relatively confident in the system he has put in place. In the third month the site logs one injury, and he feels that things have improved, and that the employees are getting accustomed to the systems in place. The manager begins to develop a sense of confidence, and then in the fourth month there are four injuries. This makes the second quarter's beginning performance look poor, and causes some concern among fellow managers. As the safety manager takes various steps to make improvements, his concern level is quite high. Then in month 5 he logs five injuries. Now the second quarter performance is more than twice what the first quarter performance was, and the manager is close to pushing the panic button. He re-evaluate his needs. Cursing the expert, and his opinion, the manager hires new people to assist, re-evaluates his budget, spends new money, and asks for additional time.

The new measures take time, however. By the time those activities are getting into place, it is the 20th of the month 6, and so far there have been zero injuries. The safety manager would love to congratulate himself on these efforts, but he has a sense somewhere deep inside that—as much as he would like to think otherwise—it would be impossible for those activities to have had their effect so quickly. Month 6 finishes with zero injuries, and now he faces a dilemma. The manager can take credit and thank people for all of the new resources he has been given to improve safety, or he can feel silly because he asked for them before he really didn't need them.

In month 7 there is one injury, and one in month 8, and zero in month 9. The third quarter is showing a drastic improvement, not only over the second quarter, which was horrible, but also over the first quarter. The safety manager now takes full credit for all of the activities, and resources that have been put in place, and he feels happy to report in the managers' staff meeting about the improvements that have resulted from his efforts. The safety manager even goes so far as to allow production managers, who are needing people, to use some of the people

TABLE 7.1   Sample Accident Data for 12-Month Period

Month	1	2	3	4	5	6	7	8	9	10	11	12
Injuries	2	3	1	4	5	0	1	1	0	4	2	1
Hours worked (thousands)	80	76	76	84	88	72	76	72	76	80	84	79
Incidence rate	5.0	7.89	2.63	9.52	11.36	0.0	2.63	2.78	0.0	10.0	4.76	2.53

For an annual rate of 5.09:
(24 recordable injuries) × (200,000 employee-hours) = 4,800,000
4,800,000/943,000 exposure hours = 5.09

resources that he has recently been allocated, thinking that the problem is fairly well in hand. In month 10 there are four injures, two in month 11, and one in month 12. At this point manager would like to choke the expert. He is confused, and distraught. He feels that his credibility is on the line, and he begins to think about other job opportunities.

What is the most plausible explanation for the scenario just described? Has the expert given poor advice? Is it beyond the control of even the best managers to manage accident frequency? No, what is going on here is normal, expected random variation—changes in the values of a variable that occur for no known specific reason (Fig. 7.1). In the example given above, suppose the safety manager had logged his "ideal" two injuries per month for the first six months of the year. That would have been truly strange, and amazing. In fact, that run of numbers is so unusual that the most likely explanation would be that classification, and reporting of injuries were being done inaccurately. Although the expert's advice is that *on average* the site should expect two injuries per month given the exposure configuration described to him, it is highly unrealistic to expect exactly two injuries each month. According to the principles of statistics, if a site has a long-term average of two injuries per month, the manager should expect that from month to month the injury numbers will range from zero to seven. Monthly variation between zero to seven is to be expected in the normal course of events with a system average of two incidents per month, but what about variation beyond that range?

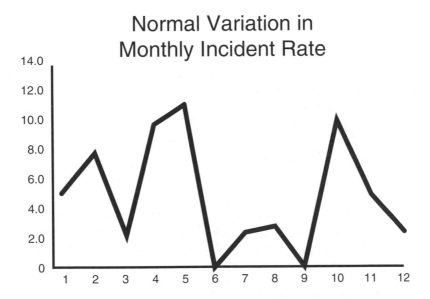

FIGURE 7.1 Normal variation in monthly incident rate.

UNDERSTANDING STATISTICAL PROCESS CONTROL—SPC

Random Variation Happens within Limits

In analyzing safety data, whether it be accident data or behavioral data, the primary question to answer is, "Are changes in frequency rates (either up or down) significant?" That is, do the changes in frequency rates represent changes in the underlying system that produces injuries, or are they simply random variations?

Answering this question accurately is of critical importance to managing the safety effort efficiently. As illustrated by the example given above, if this question is answered incorrectly, the cost can be enormous. An incorrect answer can even undermine the credibility of the entire safety effort. Statistical techniques are designed to assist in answering these very questions. Since occurrence of accidents is affected by random variation, some range of variation is common. However, that does not mean that just any amount of variation is to be expected. Accident frequencies within a certain range are expected; beyond that range they are not. For instance, in a system producing an average of nine injuries per month, a three-month run of 13 injuries per month would not be normal. Nor would a six-month period of ten injuries per month be normal. The purpose of statistical analysis, including statistical process control (SPC), is to distinguish variation that is normal and expected from variation that comes from a source not to be expected. In SPC terms, the normal variation is said to result from common causes. This name implies that the causes of variation are common to the system in question. In contrast, SPC refers to incident counts or rates that lie beyond the range of common cause variation as due to special causes. Special causes represent factors that influence the system unexpectedly or from outside of its naturally occurring variation. Managing for both special causes, and common causes has nothing to do with luck. Instead it requires charting the relevant variables to identify and remove special causes of variation, and then to manage improvement in the common causes of variation.

Choosing Relevant Variables

The most important factor in choosing a relevant variable is that it be meaningful. The following discussion of accident rates and accident counts illustrates the meaning of "meaningful" for statistics. Accident rates, and accident counts are presented in Chapter 6. Accident data can be analyzed in either form, but rates, and counts are not equivalent. At a site where the number of hours worked does not vary by more than 10 percent from month to month, either accident rates or counts are *meaningful variables* for analysis. However, when the number of hours worked varies by more than 10 percent from month to month, accident counts could be very misleading since the count makes no reference to variation in exposure hours of the workforce. In that case the accident rate is the more effective variable, helping to assure that significant changes in the data are due to changes in the site's accident producing system, and not due merely to changes in the number of hours worked.

Having properly selected a variable for analysis, the next steps involve determining whether the data are suitable for traditional control chart analysis. It is important to establish suitability for charting because standard control chart analysis makes two assumptions (called normality, and independence) that often go untested. When these assumptions are violated, standard control chart analysis can lead to false conclusions. The following Red Flags list several situations where normality, and independence are likely to be violated.

Red Flag 1—Situations where Independence May Be Violated

- reporting bias—managing the numbers to make them look either good or bad
- presence of individuals who have multiple incidents.
- more than one person involved in the same accident.
- systematic changes in reporting methods
- systematic changes in exposure, in hours worked, in weather conditions, and so on

Red Flag 2—Situations where Normality May Be Violated

- very low accident rates or counts
- small number of exposures hours
- small employee population
- combining workgroups that have remarkably different accident rates

Where any one of these Red Flags is present, safety managers should look for faulty assumptions in their data. A technical discussion of normality, and independence is beyond the scope of this section, but the interested reader is referred to the section on Advanced Statistical Techniques in this chapter.

After determining conditions of independence, and normality, the next step is to select the proper control chart for graphing the data. In companies where behavioral data is available, it should be analyzed along with incident data. To say that accident frequency is a random variable is not to say that safety is a matter of luck. In everyday usage random means something like luck. Things that happen at random, unplanned, and unlooked for, are spoken of as lucky or unlucky. In statistics, however, random means something different, Table 7.2. This difference of terminology is especially important in the field of safety because managing safety performance has nothing to do with luck, and everything to do with minimizing exposure to hazards to create a safe workplace. Man-

TABLE 7.2 Standard Definitions

	Definitions
Accident frequency rate	(number of accidents × 200,000)/ hours worked
Statistical process control	The use of statistical analysis methods to improve performance
Control chart	Graph showing observed values of a variable over time
Mean	Average
Variable	Quantity of characteristic that varies
Variation	Observed differences in values of a variable
Random variation	Difference in value of a variable due to chance or unknown causes
Standard deviation	Standard measure of amount of variation that occurs
Upper control limit	Three standard deviations above the mean
Lower control limit	Three standard deviations below the mean
Common cause	Variation associated with no identifiable cause
Special cause	Variation associated with an identifiable cause

aging safety has to do with hard work, statistical literacy and other good management practices, cooperation and involvement of employees, proper design and equipment, and so on. To use SPC for behavioral data or incident frequency data (Table 7.3), the steps are

1. Construct control charts for safety data.
2. Analyze the plotted chart for special causes.
3. If special causes are a factor, establish statistical control in the system by correcting identified special causes. If special causes are not a factor, and the system is already in control, go directly to step 4.
4. Continuously improve the system's performance by using behavioral data to develop action plans that correct common causes of incidents.

TABLE 7.3 Constructing and Using a Standard Control Chart To Address Accident Rates

Question: Is your facility's rate "in control" or "out of control?"
1. Calculate the mean of the periodic accident totals (monthly, quarterly, etc.).
2. Calculate the standard deviation of the periodic accident totals
3. Plot the accident frequency rate on the chart by period.
4. Plot the mean on the chart.
5. Plot the upper and lower control limits as defined in Table 7.2.
6. Identify special causes and develop action plans to address them.
7. Identify common causes and develop action plans to improve the system.

These are the basic steps for using statistical methods to improve safety perform-ance. Without control charts an organization does not know the meaning of its safety data. Statistical illiteracy of this kind continues to cripple the safety efforts at even Fortune 500 companies to this day—a situation that this book is written to address, at least in part. However, the equally bad news is that many organiza-tions who *do* chart their incident data, immediately misuse them in ways outlined in Chapter 6 on the uses and abuses of measurement. This chapter addresses the issue of how to collect, and analyze behavioral data, upstream data; but before leaving the subject of basic charting, first a word about determining whether acci-dent frequency is in control or out of control.

Even the most effective management focus cannot do away with random vari-ation. Accident occurrence remains in part a random variable—*that is a given.* When the accident-producing system is improved what improves is the overall accident frequency rate. Basic statistical analysis answers the question, "Is our accident frequency rate in control? "This can be taken to mean inside or outside of our control limits, and it can refer to patterns of variation that occur within control limits. For most practical purposes this question translates to the ques-tion, "Is the periodic variation in our accident rate due to common cause or spe-cial cause?" The first, and most basic thing that managers do is distinguish com-mon cause variation from special cause variation using statistical analysis.

BASIC STATISTICAL ANALYSIS OF ACCIDENT DATA

Here is typical accident frequency rate data for a period of just over three years. In this form it is fairly difficult to determine anything useful from this informa-tion, Table 7.4. However, when the same data is displayed graphically on an X-Chart, it is much easier to visually see a pattern (Fig. 7.2). However, rendering the data as a charted pattern is only the beginning; the point is to discover whether the variation in the pattern is from common causes (in control) or special causes (out of control). The basic question to answer is: Is the performance charted here in control or out of control? Before management overreacts, either positively or negatively on the basis of this data, they need to know whether the data reveals anything significant. To proceed on the basis of statistical illiteracy is to risk creating safety superstitions in the entire organization. Consider Table 7.5 for a data set showing four years of recordable accident rates. Once again, it is plotted on a control chart (Fig. 7.3) with the upper control limit (UCL), and lower control limit (LCL). In addition, the chart plots the first two standard deviations on either side of the mean, labelling them as LCL 1 and 2, and UCL 1 and 2 respectively. Note that none of the data points lies beyond the outer control limits of this system of performance. This means that the outlying variation shown here

TABLE 7.4 Tabular Data—Difficult To Read and Interpret

	Jan	Feb	Mar	Apr	May	Jun	Jul	Aug	Sep	Oct	Nov	Dec
Hours worked	61,455	61,109	68.585	60,699	69,588	60,467	61.999	67.994	65,699	65,449	63.708	63,004
Recordables	1	1	6	6	2	0	3	5	5	6	2	4
Rates	3.25	3.27	17.5	19.77	5.75	0.00	9.68	14.71	15.22	18.33	6.28	12.70
Hours worked	61,114	63,936	70,013	64,147	69,203	67,397	67,574	72,587	65,281	66,047	64,582	60,366
Recordables	3	4	1	2	9	5	8	3	4	3	0	2
Rates	9.82	12.51	2.86	6.24	26.01	14.84	23.68	8.27	12.25	9.08	0.00	6.63
Hours worked	69,461	58,792	62,488	58,402	63,958	64,244	66,220	67,492	56,296	65,932	57,704	58,241
Recordables	1	1	1	1	3	4	6	3	0	2	4	6
Rates	2.88	3.4	3.2	3.42	9.38	12.45	18.12	8.89	0.00	6.07	13.86	20.6

		Mean	Std. Dev.	Sum
Hours worked	63,238	64,174.89	3903.63	2,374,471
Recordables	1	3.19	2.27	118
Rates	3.16	9.84	6.88	

TABLE 7.5 Tabular Data—Difficult To Read and Interpret

	Jan	Feb	Mar	Apr	May	Jun	Jul	Aug	Sep	Oct	Nov	Dec
Hours worked	48,711	62,742	63,599	61,788	63,637	47,496	64,350	60,141	59,753	63,566	60,884	53,779
Recordables	14	16	12	17	21	12	21	23	13	17	20	9
Rates	57.48	51.00	37.74	55.03	66.00	50.53	65.27	76.49	43.51	53.49	65.70	33.47
Hours worked	63,062	52,968	61,138	66,604	68,491	78,995	65,833	72,534	74,497	74,270	59,332	61,446
Recordables	8	11	11	10	17	13	14	16	12	21	11	23
Rates	25.37	41.53	35.98	30.03	49.64	32.91	42.53	44.12	32.22	56.55	37.08	74.86
Hours worked	42,589	47,208	49,350	57,839	57,839	54,175	57,260	54,466	53,386	48,015	39,433	40,497
Recordables	16	17	10	18	18	20	18	10	21	13	9	11
Rates	75.14	72.02	40.53	62.24	62.24	73.83	62.87	36.72	78.67	54.15	45.65	54.33
Hours worked	54,907	50,575	49,401	49,401	44,105	46,601	53,767	52,260	50,762	51,630	46,401	
Recordables	10	5	12	17	16	11	19	12	14	14	10	
Rates	36.43	19.77	43.58	68.82	72.55	47.21	70.68	45.92	55.16	54.23	43.10	

	Mean	Std. Dev.	Sum
Hours worked	56,627.30	9165.67	2,661,483
Recordables	14.53	4.34	683
Rates	51.90	15.06	

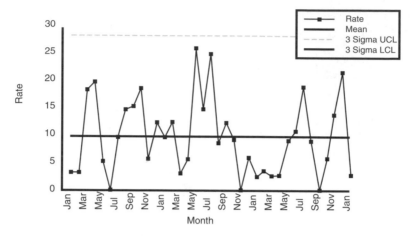

FIGURE 7.2 X chart: recordable accident rate for three years.

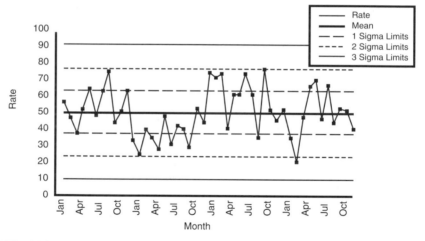

FIGURE 7.3 X chart: recordable accident rate for four years.

is normal random variation in the system. The outlying variation in this chart provides no grounds for either positive or negative feedback to employees.

Nonetheless, there are some seeming patterns in the chart, described in Table 7.1. For a discussion of a statistical approach to identifying these patterns, see the section subheaded Advanced Statistical Techniques. However, most individuals will be tempted to search for anomalies with the naked eye (see Table 7.6). It is very important not to over-manage cycles and clusters. It is very easy to see them where they do not exist. For instance, consider the four graphs in Fig. 7.4. Each graph represents accident frequency across a two-year period. On

TABLE 7.6   Interpretive Rules

---

1. Trends are indicated by gradual change either upward or downward.

2. Clusters indicate unusual changes in the system.

3. Cycles indicate repetitive variation that may very well have a special cause.

4. Bias ("creative reporting and classification") is often indicated by lack of variation from the center line. In terms of behavior-based safety, this bias could be observer or sampler bias. (For more on this, see Chapter 9 on behavioral observation as a continuous improvement procedure.)

---

numerous occasions the author has used this figure to administer a knowledge survey about safety statistics. In a majority of cases respondents say that they detect important trend and cycle information in these four graphs, information about which they feel a high level of confidence. This figure of four graphs is another case of trick data. Each of these graphs was randomly generated by a computer. Not one of these graphs represents anything more than random variability. The variability in each graph is just "noise in the system." One important lesson to draw here is that to be interesting, and helpful to management, safety data has to show *more* variation than this. Safety data that looks like this is no different from random data, a fact which is easier to see when the four graphs are converted as in Fig. 7.5 to data in the form of 12-month moving averages. In this form it is obvious that this data has no trends or cycles or clusters, and that no inferences can be drawn from the data.

Note—it is very easy to misread data that is actually random as though it showed the influence of special causes. The very strong temptation is to see special causes everywhere.

The first error to avoid is treating a common cause as though it were a special cause. To achieve this basic level of clarity, chart accident frequency data to answer the fundamental question, "Is our safety performance in control or out of control?" Steps 1 through 5 below lay out the construction of a chart showing accident frequency rate by month. Steps 6 and 7 indicate how to analyze the charted data for the presence of special causes, and step 8 does the same for common causes.

1. Gather accident frequency rates for a set period of time.
2. Plot the accident frequency rates by month on a chart: months along the X-axis, accident rate along the Y-axis.
3. Compute the mean accident frequency rate, and add it to the chart, plotting it across all months.

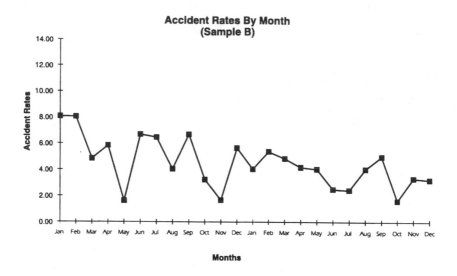

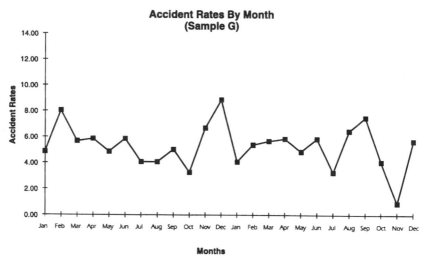

FIGURE 7.4 Four samples (B, F, G, and I) of accident rates by month. (continues)

4. Compute the standard deviation for the accident frequency rates. Various methods for doing this are described in introductory, and advanced books on statistics (ref. IBM, Ott).

5. Multiply the standard deviation by three, then add this to the mean. This is the Upper Control Limit to be plotted on the chart. Next subtract three standard deviations from the mean. This is the Lower Control Limit to be plotted on the chart.

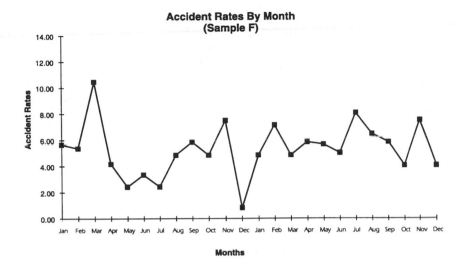

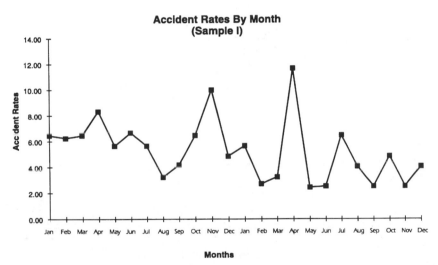

FIGURE 7.4 (continued)

6. Identify any points beyond the Upper or Lower Control Limits. These are usually part of special cause variation. Variability within the Upper, and Lower Control Limits is generally part of common cause variation.

7. If the special causes are present, investigate them, and develop action plans for each of them.

8. Where common cause variation is unacceptable, improve the system itself by (a) developing upstream measures of common causes, (b) discovering

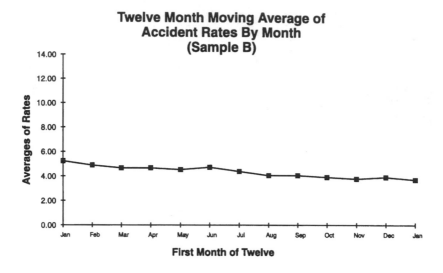

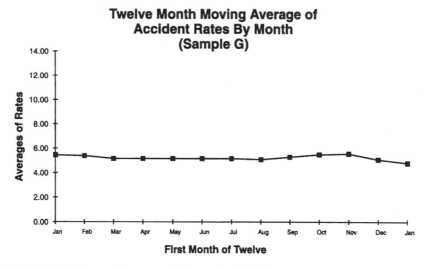

FIGURE 7.5 Twelve-month averages of the samples in Fig. 7.4. (continues)

improvement opportunities, (c) analyzing data, and (d) developing action plans to correct systems issues.

Using the Basic Injury Data to Manage Safety

To highlight the importance of the distinction between common cause, and special cause variation, the control chart shown here in Fig. 7.6 is heavily shaded

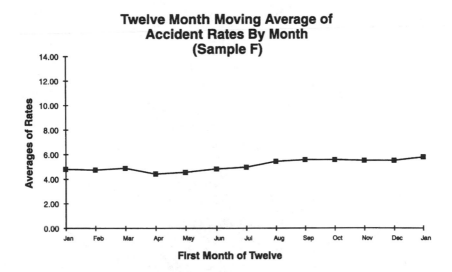

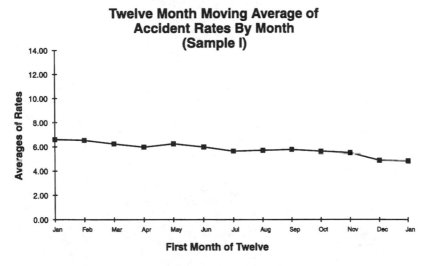

FIGURE 7.5 (continued)

within the "bandwidth" of the first two standard deviations. The reason is to discourage inaccurate interpretation of variation that falls well within the control limits of the system. Other types of variation within control limits are considered below.

The chart presented here is a modified control chart with shaded areas to highlight the areas most important to analysis. So as not to be distracted by the first two standard deviations on the chart, that area is heavily shaded, and the points

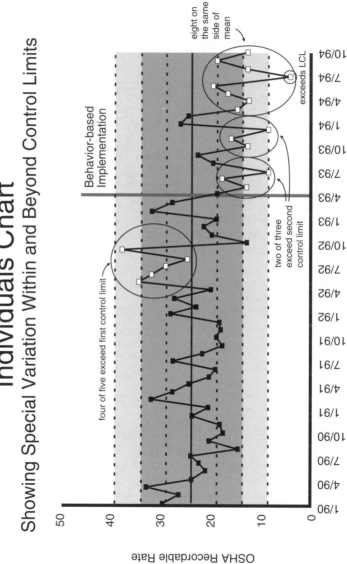

FIGURE 7.6 Individuals chart showing special variation both within and beyond control limits.

that fall within that range do not show up very well. The third standard deviation is lightly shaded, and above that, no shading at all. This graphing represents the fact that for basic analysis the place where the dot falls within the shaded area is less important than whether or not it is out of the shaded area.

Analysis within Control Limits—Normal or Abnormal Sequence?

The procedure for analysis is

- Identify data points beyond the control limits, and patterns within limits, and treat them as special causes
- Identify other data points within control limits, and treat them as common causes.

To see the possibilities for further analysis *within control limits*, look again at Fig. 7.6, showing some suspicious sequences of data points. This same observation was mentioned earlier in connection with abnormally long runs of similar numbers. Identifiable patterns of data within control limits also indicate special causes.

Sequence Patterns Indicating the Effect of Special Cause

Same side, exceed second level control limit
- Two out of three consecutive data points on the same side of the mean exceed a second level control limit.

Same side, exceed first level control limit
- Four out of five consecutive data points on the same side of the mean exceed a first level control limit.

Same side, any level within control limits
- Seven or eight consecutive data points on the same side of the mean.
- Ten out of 12 (or 12 out of 14) consecutive data points on the same side of the mean.

The following is a list of Sources of Variation in Accident Frequency. The reader is invited to decide which are common causes, and which are special causes.

1. changes in exposure
2. quantity of work being done
3. type of work being done
4. new employees
5. changes in equipment or process
6. new equipment or process
7. atmosphere or quality of worklife
8. changes in leadership
9. changes in labor relations

10. changes in production pressure
11. conflict, and stress
12. weather

Now it's a bit tricky to determine which of these are special and which are common causes. The primary distinction between common and special cause as used in relation to these sources of variation has to do with whether the source of variation is a normal, natural, common part of the existing system or something from outside the system. For example, Source 10, Weather, would generally be a common cause, but it could be a special cause. In the case of heat of the kind that occurs every summer, weather would be a common cause. But a tornado that tore down half the factory would be considered a special cause. In the case of changes in exposure or quantity of work being done—if it's within the normal limits of variation of quantity, it would be a common cause. If the amount of work being done changed in such a way that overtime increased by 500 percent, that would be a special cause. The same principle applies in the case of the type of work being done. Change in the type of work would be a special cause if the entire process were changed or if all of the equipment were changed at the same time. New employees would be a common cause ordinarily but if for some reason the workforce doubled in size, that could be a special cause. Similarly with changes in equipment and process, similarly with atmosphere and quality of worklife—those things tend to vary naturally within any system. On the other hand if, for example, a downsizing occurred in which three-fourths of the plant were laid off, and other huge changes occurred of a similar kind, that could be considered a special cause. The same holds for leadership changes and also with labor relations issues, production pressures, conflict, stress, and weather.

In daily practice, what is at issue in distinguishing common cause from special cause is how the source of the variation is viewed. The temptation is to see special causes everywhere, and to blame ourselves for having four injuries in a month when the average expected is two. By now we know that four incidents is within control limits for a mean of two. The month with four incidents does not reflect any change in the system, and therefore does not require that we redesign, re-engineer, replan, change everything, and generally over-react. On the other hand, the parallel temptation is to pat ourselves on the back when a month or two goes by and we have zero or one injury. By now we also realize that we should not be misled into thinking that something about the system has actually changed.

ADVANCED STATISTICAL TECHNIQUES

Standard control charts are valid only when the charted data are independent, that is, when the individual data points are not correlated with each other in any way.

Correlations of this kind can be caused by reporting bias, systematic changes in reporting methods and seasonal effects, among other things. Obvious trends and cycles are also indications of non-independence, but sometimes the correlations are not easily detected. Two errors are more likely to occur when data are not independent, and both of these errors fail to distinguish variation due to common causes from that due to special causes. First, the control limits may be miscalculated too close together, increasing the risk that certain system values that actually arise from common causes will be mislabelled as having special causes. Second, there may be substantial runs above or below the mean that will appear as isolated special causes when the cause actually pervades the entire process, and is therefore a common cause.

Such non-independence does not mean that data cannot be analyzed, but it does mean that a more comprehensive type of control chart analysis is needed: Time Series Analysis. Time series control charts adjust for non-independence of data while permitting a comprehensive study of the nature of the non-random variation. Illustrating this point is actual data from a paper company (Figs. 7.7 and 7.8). Figure 7.7 is a standard X-chart, showing a few points beyond the control limits. If these data were independent, those extreme points would be cause for concern. But as it happens, this data violates the independence assumption because previous observations were strongly related to later ones. This linkage makes the data points appear to be out of control when they really are not, an error that is corrected in the time series control chart in Fig. 7.8. The control limits set by this kind of charting take into account the fact that the data are correlated. On this adjusted chart none of the data points is out of control. Although

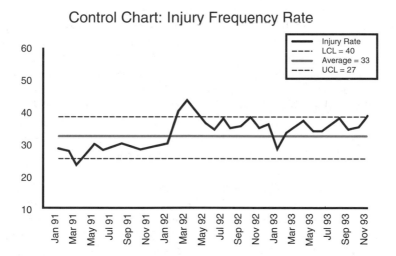

FIGURE 7.7   Control chart: injury frequency rate.

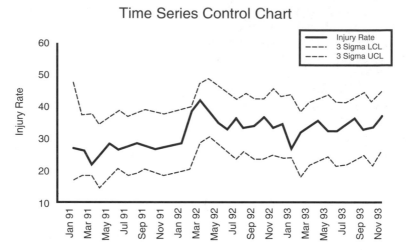

FIGURE 7.8 A time series control chart.

non-independent data do not permit traditional control chart analysis, a great deal of information can be gained from time series analysis of the correlations in the data.

Normality of the Distribution

Normality refers to the distribution of data. The normal distribution is a symmetrical, bell-shaped distribution of data about their mean value. Incident data tend to approach a normal distribution at rates of ten or more incidents per measurement period. All companies should scrutinize their data to make sure that their distribution is normal. For instance, larger companies usually have no worry about the normality of the distribution of their incident data because they typically satisfy the minimum threshold of ten+ per month. Smaller companies, however, may have to chart their incident data by multiple months before it achieves normality. One of the numerous advantages that behavioral data offer over incident data is that behavioral data accumulates rapidly even for small work units within a company. This means that such a workgroup can use the power of statistics to measure, and manage their performance—something they could not do using incident data alone.

Tests for normality are incorporated in many statistics software packages, but a histogram illustrates the idea. The histogram in Fig. 7.9 developed from Table 7.4, demonstrates that these data meet the normality assumption. Notice how the histogram follows the normal curve, which is also shown on the chart. In the case of this data, statistical tests for normality showed that the fit was close enough. Figure 7.10 shows the same histogram positioned on the control chart,

Histogram of Data in Table 7-4
Recordable Accident Rate for Three Years

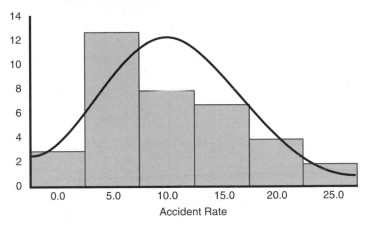

FIGURE 7.9   A histogram of the data in Table 7.4.

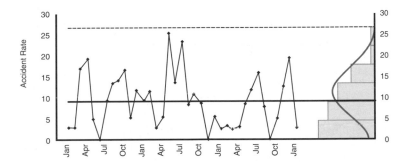

FIGURE 7.10   A control chart and histogram of the data in Table 7.4.

indicating how the two are related. On the other hand, when very skewed data are placed on a control chart, there is an increased risk of registering some data points as significant (out of control) when in reality they are not. Figure 7.11 shows a control chart in which the data are skewed toward the higher numbers. In this case, the user of the chart cannot be certain that the extremely high value logged in August of 1991 is significant because the skew creates an increased chance of logging extremely high values. In the same way, the user of the chart cannot be sure that the run of 12 below the mean logged between January, and December of 1993 was significant because of the disproportionate amount of data that falls below the mean. Fig. 7.12 also has a skewed distribution, but this time the non-normal tail is on the low end. Under this circumstance the user of

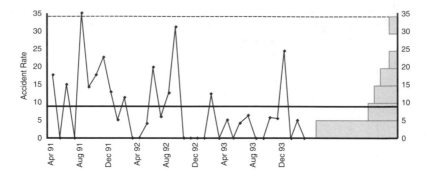

FIGURE 7.11   A control chart for data skewed toward the high end.

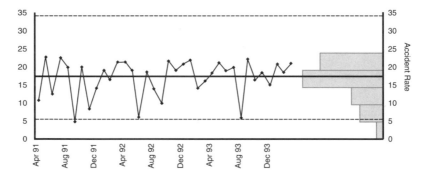

FIGURE 7.12   A control chart for data skewed toward the low end.

the chart cannot be sure that the low point logged in September 1991 was significant because the skew increases the likelihood of logging extremely low values.

Attribute Control Charts

The control charts used for counts are called attribute charts, and to be valid they must satisfy the normality assumption. This may seem counterintuitive at first since some attribute charts (C and U charts) are designed for data having the Poisson distribution. However, to be valid even the Poisson distribution must meet the normality assumption.

The Poisson distribution is defined by any attribute whose mean equals its variance. Figure 7.13 shows a Poisson distribution for an attribute whose mean equals 1. It is moderately skewed. Figure 7.14 shows a Poisson distribution for an attribute whose mean equals 3. Notice that it is less skewed. Figure 7.15 shows the Poisson distribution for an attribute whose mean is 10. Notice that this is a

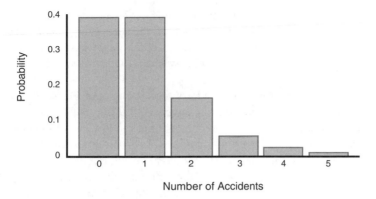

FIGURE 7.13 Poisson probability distribution with a mean equal to 1.

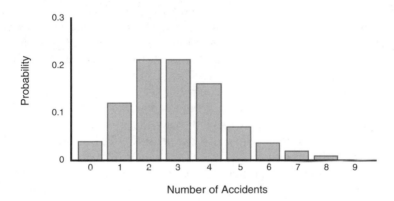

FIGURE 7.14 Poisson probability distribution with a mean equal to 3.

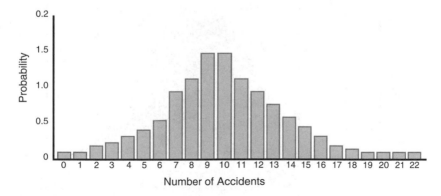

FIGURE 7.15 Poisson probability distribution with a mean equal to 10.

close approximation to the normal distribution (Fig. 7.16), but it also follows a Poisson distribution because the mean equals the variance. Plotted on a C or a U chart, this type of attribute permits the usual techniques of interpretation. One finds this type of attribute when the probability of an accident is very low, and the sample size is very large.

There is some risk of error with standard control charts of Poisson variables with a mean less than 10. With Poisson means of 1.9 the usual techniques of interpretation are liable to set the upper control limit too low and/or to detect too many runs below the mean. The first error would cause the unsuspecting interpreter to see too many significant events above the mean. For example, when the mean of a Poisson distribution is 1, the standard normality assumption sets the upper control limit at 3 because normally distributed data are said to have less than a 0.1 percent chance of exceeding this limit. But by definition, for Poisson data the chance of an observation of 3 or more is not 0.1 percent but 6 percent, or 60 times more likely. Therefore, to build into Poisson distributions the same protection against false positives as is found in normal distributions, the upper control limit for a mean of 1 needs to be raised from 3 to 5. Table 7.7 gives the correct Upper, and Lower control limits for Poisson distributions of data with means of 1 through 9. Once the Poisson mean reaches 10 or higher, it becomes approximately normally distributed, and the control limits are set at the standard three deviations above, and below the mean. With Poisson means smaller than 10, the control limits need to be corrected to avoid errors of interpretation.

Uncorrected Poisson distributions also run the risk of erroneously registering too many runs below the mean. The usual techniques of interpretation say, for instance, that a run of seven or more data points below the mean is significant. With Poisson distributions, this rule is only approximately true. Table 7.8 gives the correct rules for interpreting runs for Poisson distributions with means of 1

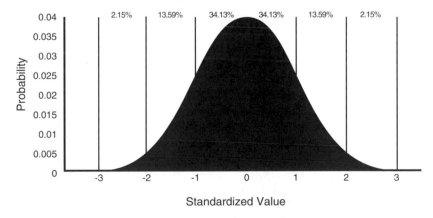

FIGURE 7.16 The normal probability distribution.

TABLE 7.7   Correct upper and lower control limits for Poisson distributions of data with means of 1 through 9.

P< .001   P< .001

Mean	LCL	UCL
1	0	6
2	0	7
3	0	9
4	0	11
5	0	13
6	0	14
7	0	16
8	0	18
9	1	19

TABLE 7.8   Rules for interpreting runs for Poisson distributions with means of 1 through 9.

Mean	A significant low run is seven in a row equal to or below:	A significant high run is seven in a row equal to or above:
1	0	1
2	0	2
3	0	3
4	0	4
5	0	5
6	0	6
7	0	7
8	0	8
9	1	9

through 9. Standard techniques for detecting runs are discussed earlier in this chapter under the heading Analysis Within Control Limits.

Selecting a Control Chart

The flow charts in Figs. 7.17 and 7.18 present guides for selecting control charts. Figure 7.17 is for accident rates while Fig. 7.18 is for accident counts. In those cases where the data satisfy conditions of independence, and normality, the decision tree is very simple (indicated in the figures by darkened arrows). There are control charts for data that do not satisfy conditions of normality or independence, and the decision tree for those cases can be rather involved. These guides illustrate the many alternatives available in cases where data *do not* satisfy conditions of independence or normality.

When the number of hours worked changes from one month to the next, accident rates are recommended over accident counts for control charts

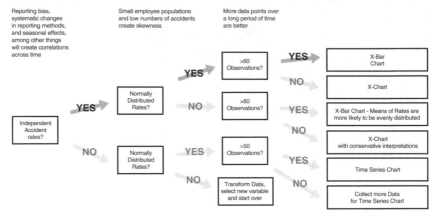

FIGURE 7.17   Decision pathways for selecting accident rates versus accident counts.

When the number of hours worked is the same from one month to the next, accident counts will make meaningful control charts

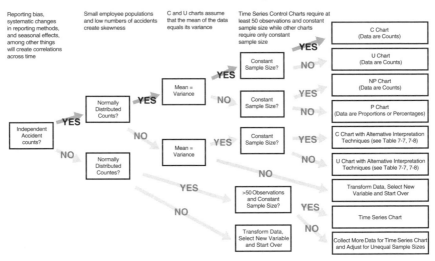

FIGURE 7.18   Decision pathways for selecting accident counts.

8

The Behavioral Inventory as a Continuous Improvement Instrument

Continuous improvement requires continuous measurement of the correct system variables. Although the theory is simple, putting it into practice is often challenging. Even in seemingly straightforward applications such as basic production or quality control, difficult questions come up almost immediately. Just which inputs need to be measured—how often and with what degree of precision? Although these issues are analogous for all areas of performance management, including safety, quality, and productivity, an example from production may be clearer at first. Consider the impact of statistical process control (SPC) techniques in the metal stamping industry.

In a 1994 issue of *MetalForming* magazine, an SPC observer reported that the metal stamping industry faces a number of challenges trying to implement statistical process control. Each of the main points of the report has a safety equivalent.

FIVE QUALITY POINTS

1. Incentive

Although the incentive to implement SPC is clear, companies are overwhelmed by the sheer range of SPC parameters that can be extracted from modern manufacturing technology, and monitoring is necessary even in the case of machines with sophisticated built-in microprocessor closed-loop controls. The effects of environmental changes, power fluctuations, and material changes are still significant.

2. Measurement

Although manufacturers are installing accurate sensors in their die-presses and other hydraulic and load sensors, the frequency of measurement using those sensors remains unsatisfactory. With infrequent measurement there can be long delays between the time when substandard parts are made and the time when someone realizes that they are unsaleable. The result can be an entire shift of scrap production, all of which has to be charged against the cost of producing good parts.

3. Implementation

Large manufacturers are in the forefront of the effort to implement SPC, particularly those who now require their suppliers to provide proof of continually increasing levels of quality. These days such proof includes documentation not only that parts are free from defects, but that the manufacturing process itself was in control. This is interesting confirmation of the inherent validity of system measurement versus the more primitive defect measurement, and a good argument for system measurement in safety.

4. Cost

The cost of materials has become another important factor favoring SPC. As materials themselves become more varied, sophisticated, and expensive, it is not practical to stock large quantities of them. "Do it right the first time" takes on new meaning under these conditions.

5. New Technology

Even if the new sophisticated production technology did not require SPC (and they do), most facilities are not equipped exclusively with new machines. The typical site has a few profitable machines, and several not-so-profitable machines. Some companies have retrofitted their older machines with third-party monitoring systems. To get an overview of the whole plant floor, this solution requires management or supervisors to access several systems. One result is that problems can be missed.

FIVE ANALOGOUS SAFETY POINTS

Each of these fairly standard quality issues comes up in relation to safety efforts.

1. What to Measure

The incentive is there to implement SPC for accident prevention, but companies are overwhelmed by the sheer range of parameters. A workforce of 100 people at a modern paper plant, for instance, can be exposed to risk in what seems like literally thousands of ways. The same is true at any modern petroleum refinery, chemical plant, utility, or pharmaceutical or food manufacturing plant. Faced with the typical complexity of the modern workplace what can management do? Moreover, safety comes down to performance, and performance is a human factor. What is the proper way to measure the human factor?

2. Inadequate Frequency of Measures

Although organizations have put in place many new safety programs, the frequency and quality of the "measurement" in those programs remains unsatisfactory. With infrequent or inappropriate measurement there can be long delays between the time when substandard safety performance is happening, and the time when someone recognizes it as such. The result can be an entire quarter (or year) of "scrap" procedures, directives, and incentive programs. (See Chapter 6 for more on the limitations of traditional safety statistics such as the recordable injury rate.)

3. Demonstrated Progress

Companies that are safety leaders are in the forefront of the effort to use SPC for safety. But asked for evidence that the safety system is in control, many safety leaders would be hard-pressed to supply it. Even if they have the correct control chart in use, they usually employ it to chart incidence frequency, a measure that offers no obvious system improvement method when it is found to be in control.

4. The Cost of Status Quo

Analogous to the cost of modern materials is the cost of modern medicine and treatment for work-related injuries. According to the National Safety Council's 1993 edition of *Accident Facts,* in 1992 American industry suffered 8,500 work-related fatalities, at an average cost of $780,000 per death. In the same year lost work time came to 105 million days, and there were 3.3 million disabling injuries, at an average direct cost of $27,000 each. A recent *BusinessWeek* article suggested $3,400 as the average combined direct and indirect cost of each medical treatment injury, whether disabling or not. The cited indirect costs include lost productivity, time spent in investigations, and time spent filling out and submitting paperwork. In *Accident Facts,* the National Safety Council estimates the total cost at $115.95 billion dollars—an astounding sum that equals 78 cents of every dollar of 1992 corporate dividends to stockholders, or 31 cents of every dollar of 1992 pre-tax corporate profits. In safety, the quality imperative of "Do it right the first time" becomes "Perform the safe behavior every time."

5. *Discredited Programs*

Analogous to the shop floor with some new and some old machines is the mix of old and new safety practices. Side by side with the latest in personal protective equipment, many sites have a fairly mixed bag of tired, off-the-shelf safety programs, video tapes, and incentive schemes. The result is an overall safety effort that is doomed to be "catch as catch can." A related problem is that some companies have departments or areas that are retrofitting or re-engineering their safety systems in the direction of SPC measures. However, as long as the progressive units remain pilot areas surrounded by traditional safety programs, management is required to use a variety of accountability systems. One result is that problems can be missed. Each identified problem is an opportunity for improvement.

Safety management needs what quality management needs—a unified, systematic approach. The unified safety system answer presented by this book is the employee-driven approach. Under the headings of parameters, sensors, and data analysis respectively, Chapters 7 through 9 present the behavior-based equivalents to the quality systems in place at many companies. Chapter 7 is concerned with the parameters of behavior-based safety. These parameters are embodied in two characteristic instruments, an inventory of site-specific safety-related behaviors, and a data-sheet for measuring the incidence of those behaviors. The "sensors" of employee-driven safety (Chapter 8) are trained observers. The observers, usually wage-roll personnel, apply the parameters of the behavioral inventory to their coworkers. Through ongoing observation, these human sensors register and record levels of safe and at-risk behavior as specified by their site's inventory. They also deliver verbal feedback on the spot to the coworkers they observe. As in any other case of quality grading, the quality and consistency of the group of graders or observers determines the quality of the data they produce. Chapter 9 presents the data analysis that grows out of the data-collection activities of the observers.

THE BEHAVIORAL INVENTORY AS A MEASUREMENT INSTRUMENT

Safety-related behavior is *what* to measure. The behavioral inventory is *how to* measure it. Many important benefits follow from the use of this instrument for continuous safety improvement:

- Problem solving that is driven by this accumulating data is accurate instead of being superstitious. This answers safety point 2, about inadequate measures.
- Performance feedback based on a behavioral data base is true feedback, not false feedback that impairs people's judgment about the causes of accidents (safety point 3, charted progress).

- Safety training based on an inventory of a site's critical safety behaviors is training that enhances the adaptive readiness of the workforce, maximizing safe performance for rookies, and veterans alike (safety point 5.) Chapter 12 addresses the important topic of safety training transfer, and adaptive readiness to safety. This kind of safety training answers Deming's call for a workforce that is always learning.

DEVELOPING THE INVENTORY OF CRITICAL BEHAVIORS

In most accidents at-risk behavior is the final common pathway. Each facility, characterized by particular production processes, products, and workforce, has a characteristic cluster of these final common pathways that are responsible for a highly significant percentage of its safety incidents.

The task is to

- identify this cluster of safety-related behaviors,
- write operational definitions of them to form the inventory, and then
- prepare a data sheet for observers to use.

The operational definitions are framed completely in terms of how something is done. This set of definitions provides the facility observers with a resource that tells them exactly what behaviors to look for when they are taking samples of workplace safety performance. The definitions are clear enough for the observer to recognize safe, and at-risk behavior without interpreting a situation or guessing at someone's attitudes, alertness, and other internal states.

Behavioral analysis of accident reports lays the foundation of the facility's inventory of critical behaviors. It identifies the behavioral categories, and items that are most often associated with the facility's accidents, and injuries. A combined group of managers, and veteran wage-roll employees are typically the best source of knowledge about these behaviors. Once this group understands the concept in practice, they appreciate the strict safety-related focus of the behavioral approach. Wage-roll employees often serve with distinction on the steering team that conducts a behavioral review of facility accident reports to produce an inventory of critical behaviors. Their contribution to this important safety resource for their facility is one of the more important instances of employee involvement in the employee-driven safety process. The groups of people who do this work need to be representative of each major area at the site. These people need to be carefully selected for the correct attributes. They need to be very familiar with the work in their departments and have some knowledge of the accidents that have occurred there.

Focusing on Accident Reports

To construct a behavioral inventory it is necessary to know what kinds of at-risk behaviors are occurring. Most companies collect various kinds of summary information on injuries, including information on injury type. Usually these injury types are named after the categories used for government reporting purposes, categories such as *struck by, struck against,* and so forth, as well as a number of other classifications. However useful these categories are for government record keeping, they are not very helpful for behavioral inventory development.

Consider the case of a worker who suffers contusions by striking her hand against something when her wrench slipped as she was tightening a bolt. If the contusions were severe enough she might have had difficulty holding hand tools for a while, restricting the kind of work she could do until her hand healed. In this case, the accident report would probably classify this injury as an instance of *struck against.* However, what happened that caused the wrench to slip so that the worker struck and injured her hand? The possibilities are various. Here are three possibilities.

1. The bolt might have been rusted in place, or the head of the bolt might have been rounded off—either case calling for the worker to burn the bolt off with a cutting torch instead of trying to use a wrench on it.
2. Or the worker might not have seated the wrench properly on the bolt. Or perhaps she seated the wrench properly but then jerked on the wrench or applied too much force.
3. The worker might have been able to position the wrench differently so that in the event that it did slip, she would not have struck her hand against anything.

As a safety performance parameter, it is far more useful to know the operational definition related to tool use than it is to know how many injuries were caused when workers *struck against* something. Supervisors who tried to use this *struck against* information proactively would find themselves using very vague terms and warning their workers to be careful not to strike against things. The warning is not specific enough to be useful to the workers. It is like saying, "Pay attention." Furthermore, the supervisors would find it difficult to know whether the workforce was being careful not to strike against things. So the *struck against* category is not specific enough to be a useful parameter for the supervisors or to the workers.

The operational definition, on the other hand, addresses all three of these points. Operational definitions are something that both the worker and the supervisor can be aware of before an injury takes place, and the damage is done. They can be spelled out in sufficient detail that both the worker and the supervisor know what counts as safe behavior, and what counts as at-risk behavior. The aim of behavioral analysis of accident reports is to arrive at the set of behavioral parameters that account for a significant portion of a facility's accidents. In most cases, even long-time employees at a facility are surprised to discover just which parameters of behavior lie at the core of their recurring safety problem-areas. They are also usually surprised to discover how great a proportion of their total accident frequency is associated with this core of behaviors.

Information concerning the behavioral components of injuries is often lacking in standard accident investigation reports, (a defect that is corrected as the behavior-based safety process achieves maturity in integrated accident investigations, and safety meetings). When such information is present in standard investigation reports, it is rarely summarized. However, behavioral information can be extracted from accident reports fairly reliably by carefully answering two questions for each injury.

1. In behavioral terms, what was the worker doing when he/she was injured?
2. What might the worker have done differently in order to avoid the injury?

The combined answers constitute a set of statements that specify what workers need to do to avoid injury. These statements are of the form, "When workers are performing such-and-such a task, here is what they need to do." For instance, "When uncoupling hoses, first check that valves are closed and that product has been cleared from the hose." Even at this preliminary stage of developing the facility's inventory of critical behaviors, the emphasis is on producing clear operational definitions of safe and of at-risk behavior. At the outset this sets the stage for accurate performance feedback that simultaneously minimizes superstitions about safety and maximizes safety training transfer. Readers interested in a detailed presentation of the behavioral inventory are referred to chapters 6, 12, 18, and 19 in *The Behavior-Based Safety Process.*

Generic and Job-Specific

The items in a facility's inventory of critical behaviors divide into two kinds: generic and job-specific. Generic categories name the broad underlying patterns discovered in pattern search. Job-specific inventory items are tied to a particular job that has been identified as a target. The procedure for developing job-specific behaviors is so similar to JSAs that it is not reviewed here. However, it is important to note that JSAs are not usually written as *operational definitions of behavior.* This means that when JSAs are used as a source for inventory development they need to be reviewed and usually upgraded to behavioral standards.

Operational Definitions of Critical Behaviors

An effective operational definition for the inventory is perhaps best understood in contrast with a poor or non-operational definition. Remember that an observer must know whether a behavior he is watching is safe or at-risk by referring to the operational definition of his data sheet items.

First the good definition:

> *Body Placement.* The walking surface and working surface must be stable. Body position should not be cramped or over-extended. The worker should be balanced and have stable footing. The worker should not be in the line of fire, or in the fall pattern of objects.

Now the unclear, non-operational definition:

> Body should be kept out of way of hazards, and worker must be aware of body placement at all times.

This is a poor definition for observation purposes because it does not spell out what the workers must do to keep their bodies out of the way of hazards. By watching the workers how is the observer to know whether they are aware of their bodies placement at all times?

Observation Data Sheet

The end product of inventory development is two documents, the data sheet and the set of operational definitions. The definitions provide a standard of safe performance; they state what to look for, and they increase the consistency and reliability of the observations. The data-sheet provides a place to record observation data.

Cautions

A number of pitfalls await the overzealous behavioral inventory developer.

Copying. Why not use the inventory of a sister site? Copying is tempting but always a mistake for three reasons:

1. A significant part of the gain associated with inventory development is the effect on the personnel who do the development. Wage-roll employees have heard for years that safety behaviors are critically important; they will believe it when they work on behavioral inventory development.
2. Without the buy-in resulting from point 1 above, it is unlikely that a site can achieve the quality of training necessary for excellent observation.

3. Operational definitions are highly specific by nature. To generalize is to miss the point.

Getting Stuck in the Mud. Behavioral inventory development is a vigorous procedure, requiring hard work and careful attention under the trained and experienced eye. In the absence of proper guidance, a committee can spend months in never-never land and still not end up with a useful inventory.

Biting off Too Much. It is not hard to take on more than can be processed. The untrained person may want several hundred behaviors in an inventory when only twenty-five are needed. The idea is not to write procedures for every job in the factory, but rather to identify those behaviors that cut across jobs.

SUMMARY

The facility inventory of critical behaviors sets the parameters of excellent safety performance. Used in conjunction with ongoing observation, and problem solving it is an instrument of continuous improvement.

9

Behavior Observation as an Instrument of Continuous Improvement

In Chapter 8 a site's trained behavioral observers are referred to as *safety sensors*. Admittedly, to speak this way is to stretch the point a bit, but perhaps not as far as it may seem at first. Every continuous improvement process implies measurement, and measurement requires the registering or sensing of critical data points. In a metal stamping mill such as the ones referred to in Chapter 8, it is common to install quality control sensors in the die-presses where the metal is formed. In addition, the production machinery is usually monitored with load sensors and others for hydraulic pressure and vacuum pressure. Each of those sensors contributes its data to the overall data stream monitoring the quality of the stamped metal fittings and goods. In that way, if output quality drifts or slips, the crew can check for correlations with slippage in the upstream production inputs.

When it comes to safety performance, workforce behavior is the critical system to monitor. The constant stream of ongoing workplace behavior is like the constant performance of the hydraulic and vacuum systems, or the electrical and gas utilities. By fine-tuning this behavioral system, a site's workforce *produces* excellent safety performance. The result is fewer and fewer injuries of less and less severity. In a matter of years, sites that were concerned to bring down their recordable injury rates find themselves in the enviable position of having too few such incidents to measure. They move on in turn to managing a decline in their first-aid cases and near-misses.

The *installed* sensors that make this possible are the site's observers. By steadily taking readings of the site's performance of critical behaviors, the observers collect the data that alert managers to safety trends and allow for acci-

Kim Sloat, Ph.D., contributed to the development of this chapter.

dent prevention. A very interesting side development is that some managers have begun to see correlations between their behavioral safety data and their quality data. The manager of a chemical plant has told the author that he is able to use his safety data as a leading indicator for quality because he has regularly seen that when behavioral safety begins to slip, quality frequently slips also.

Such data is only as good as the parameters (the behavioral inventory), and the sensors (the behavioral observers). Observer training is critical. Observers are trained to interrupt behaviors that put people at immediate risk. Not all critical safety-related behaviors happen fast, but many of them do. Seasoned behavioral observers are also responding to very high stakes. They know that by their efforts they actually prevent injuries from happening. Within their respective companies, and communities that is a very important service to deliver. In addition to the human suffering they save, there are substantial dollar savings too. In the established industrial countries of the world, accident prevention offers an important return on investment. One wonders whether the stockholders of the world know about the National Safety Council (NSC) estimates cited in Chapter 8. If 78 cents of every dollar of 1992 corporate dividends to stockholders were spent or lost on poor safety performance, then surely there are big gains to be realized, and when safety savings are thought of as safety *revenues*, then the NSC's estimated $115.95 billion ranks up there with a number of entire industries.

It is now widely recognized that in a plant with a strong and healthy safety culture, workers also watch out for each other, and they feel comfortable talking over their thoughts about safety. Some hazardous industries have formalized this approach by assigning people to be spotters. Spotters are detailed to watch others who are doing an especially hazardous task, warning them whenever they see their fellow workers put themselves at risk. For instance, as a safeguard against danger, power company crews working around hot wires often rely on a spotter for an additional pair of eyes. A trained behavioral observer also functions as another pair of eyes. In addition to keeping their fellow workers from getting hurt, the trained observer is a pair of eyes who gathers data on an array of critical behaviors.

When the observations are performed and recorded with consistently high quality across observers, the result is completed data sheets that represent the %safe performance level for a specific area during a known period of time. By itself, one observation may not be a good indicator of safety performance. During one observation there will be behaviors that the observer misses. However, with an effective inventory of critical behaviors, one observation is a good sample of workplace safety, and the accumulated samples provide a very reliable indicator of workplace safety performance. In the same way that upstream production sampling helps to increase the quality of what is produced, so behavioral sampling helps increase the safety of how the product is produced. Behavioral observation data is crucial to workplace safety. When the level of critical, at-risk behavior is on the rise, people need to know it before the related accidents happen. To produce data that is of high-quality, effective observers standardize their methods and procedures. One of the more important standard practices of observers is that they sample behavior—not individuals. They are interested in the overall critical mass of workgroup at-risk behaviors.

ESTABLISHING A SITE'S BEHAVIORAL BASELINE

The usual sequence is that after a site's inventory and data sheet have been drafted, reviewed, and fine-tuned, trained observers measure the site's level of %safe and %at-risk behavior. The purpose of this measurement is to give the site a behavioral reading of its safety system. Suppose, for instance, that the site has freed itself of the accident cycle only to see its performance level off and plateau with a 5.0 incident frequency rate. For the sake of presentation, also suppose that the site's managers have used statistical analysis on their accident data and have come to a sobering conclusion. Although their 5.0 incident frequency rate is as unacceptable to them as ever, they nonetheless realize that it is *in control*. The common causes at work in the system of the site are *producing* this incident frequency rate year in, and year out. By random variation some quarters are better, and some are worse, but on average their improvement has stalled. Short-lived programs are not having any effect on baseline performance. Therefore, the resources spent on such programs show no return on investment. Many companies come to the behavioral safety process at this juncture because they are looking for a way to shift their performance baseline, and they are hoping to make the step-change to continuous improvement. Behavioral observation is one of the critical instruments that helps them to make this step-change.

Trained observers use the inventory and its data sheet to sample the sheer mass of behaviors at the site. In some cases it is useful to start with a baseline measurement stage during which observers withhold verbal and charted feedback. For the first four to six weeks the observers just gather data. Established in this way, the performance baseline is valuable as a reference point. However, it is not always worth the effort required. Sometimes it can make the safety communication process more difficult since, in the absence of feedback, workers may begin to be suspicious of what is going on. In cases where it is crucial to give the workforce feedback from the outset, the first four to six weeks of data can be treated as a moving baseline. Performance improvements are not usually difficult to detect, so the moving baseline usually does not present a problem.

As sites complete this measurement stage it is common for them to discover that their baseline performance includes literally thousands of critical at-risk behaviors per week. For instance, a baseline performance of 65 to 75 percent safe is common. Stated in terms of at-risk behaviors, those numbers correspond to a performance baseline of 25 to 35 percent at-risk. Even using a weighted scoring procedure (for an example, see Chapter 14 of *The Behavior-Based Safety Process*), the 25 to 35 percent at-risk ratio can mean very large numbers of at-risk behaviors daily. This is a sobering thought when one remembers that with a well developed inventory the observers are counting only critical behaviors, behaviors that have provided the final common pathway to the bulk of the site's incidents. In other words, these levels of at-risk behaviors are accidents and injuries poised to happen.

The challenge is to manage a continuous decrease in the level of at-risk behaviors. Consider the following thoughtful statement by a maintenance superintendent at a Fortune 500 paper plant—a company and industry leader before implementing the behavioral process. Since 1989 the maintenance department, and the site as a whole, achieved impressive gains in safety performance. In 1992 the maintenance department %safe level stood at 89 percent, reflecting a marked improvement in the department baseline. In other words, they were continuously removing the common causes of accidents from their system. However, this superintendent was in no way resting on his laurels. In commenting to the author on the 89 percent safe level, the maintenance superintendent said, "Although the maintenance department averages 89 percent safe, the 11 percent at-risk continues to be of concern. From the observation data we have estimated that this 11 percent at-risk figure translates into 1,106 critical at-risk behaviors *per day*" (emphasis added). Chapter 2 presents the interpretive and problem solving techniques that such managers use to zero in on new opportunities for performance improvement.

OBSERVER SELECTION

Ongoing behavioral observation is essential to continuous improvement in safety performance. Very different from the traditional supervisor audit programs, behavioral observation is not disciplinary but positive, and it involves peer-to-peer observation, and feedback. Far from being a punitive approach in which supervisors are expected to fill the role of *safety cops* who lie in wait catching offenders and writing *safety tickets*, behavioral observation is usually best carried out by wage-roll personnel who have been trained in their site's inventory of critical behaviors. The observer or sampler is a key player in employee-driven accident prevention. In addition the observer is the champion for the accident prevention process itself. This second function is very important. Credibility in the organization is essential in an effective observer, especially at the beginning of the behavioral process. At companies that emphasize employee involvement, a high proportion of observers—sometimes 100 percent—are wage-roll employees. Managers and supervisors can also be effective when they have had observer training. It gives them hands-on experience with the process and puts them in a position to understand fully what the inventory and data sheet are like to work with. Whether or not managers and supervisors should be observers depends on the site's barriers to improvement, and on its safety and organizational culture. Ideally, all employees from all levels would do regular observations. At the beginning of the behavioral process, however, this arrangement is not practical in many organizations because of varying degrees of trust, and communication.

Characteristics of good observers include

- high credibility with peers
- demonstrated commitment to safety
- knowledge about the work to be observed
- good verbal and interpersonal skills

The effect of these traits is that people will listen to the observers. This is a very important factor. The most effective way to change a behavior is to change its consequences, see Chapters 3 and 4. One of the most powerful consequences is information or feedback about performance.

PURPOSES OF PEER-TO-PEER OBSERVATION

The three main products of observation are regular sampling of the safety process for measurement, feedback to individuals and small groups of workers, and data gathering for employee problem-solving.

Sampling for Measurement

The at-risk behavior may be the kind that directly exposes a worker to injury—using the wrong tool. Or it may be behavior that indirectly exposes other workers to injury—the mechanic who fails to reinstall a safety guard he removed while he was fixing a machine. In the first case, the %safe rate can be measured for tool use by observing numbers of workers who are using tools. In the second case, the mechanic might be directly observed to walk away from the machine without replacing the safety guard, or the observer might later note the *footprints* of the mechanic's behavior by observing that the repaired machine was missing a safety guard. Systematic observation of safe and at-risk behaviors is a way of monitoring whether a facility's safety system needs adjustment, and ultimately whether the causes of at-risk behavior are common or special causes (see Chapter 7 for more on this SPC connection).

Feedback

The second main reason for doing systematic observations is to provide feedback to small groups individuals. Injuries often occur when people are doing jobs that they do routinely and in a way that puts them at risk. Workers are often unaware that they are doing a job in a way that puts them at risk. Workers new to a task may be anxious about safety but ignorant of the task-related behaviors critical to safety. In their ignorance they are not in a position of adaptive readiness for safety. On the other hand, workers very familiar with a task often become complacent about the at-risk behaviors they routinely perform. They also lack adaptive readiness for safety. (For more on the subject of maximizing adaptive safety readiness, see Chapter 12.) Correcting for this dual situation of ignorance or habituation, a systematic observation procedure ensures that workers regularly receive information from an observer about their safety-related behaviors. Since this information emphasizes the positive aspects of safety performance by consistently noting areas of improvement, observer feedback becomes a soon-certain-positive consequence for safe behavior.

Problem Solving

In addition to individual feedback, the workgroup as a whole receives performance feedback in charted reports posted in their work area, and discussed in their safety meetings. A natural motive exists for workgroups to want to know why their charted performance is either down or up. Engaging the workgroup in a discussion of their behavioral data is a natural way to create employee involvement. An observer questioned by a workgroup is able to discuss factors related to the overall performance rating. Analysis of this data yields insight into the system (common) causes of incidents. From this analysis it is a short step to action planning to reduce the levels of at-risk behaviors reflected in the data. In this way the behavioral process provides workgroups with a structured mechanism to engage them in data-driven, solution-oriented problem solving (see Chapter 2).

Supervisors

It might seem that a peer observation system is not necessary, and that a supervisor could give feedback to workers in the normal course of events. Supervisor feedback is helpful when properly given, however its value is limited. In most cultures observations made by supervisors have a different effect on workers than does peer observation. On the more traditional model of supervisor as boss, supervisor observation of workers is loaded with nuances—evaluative, authoritative, possibly disciplinary. Given this fact, it is much more difficult for the supervisor-worker interaction to have the behavioral effect of positive feedback. Further, the ideal atmosphere for safety interaction is one in which both parties have no other motive than worker protection. Peer feedback creates this atmosphere best. The old model is changing fast in contemporary industry, and the role of the supervisor is shifting from boss to coordinator or facilitator. However, even on the new model it is inappropriate for supervisors to be the sole observers since responsibilities of this kind are shifting to the work team as a whole.

OBSTACLES TO HIGH-QUALITY OBSERVATION

Behavior-based observation takes time to learn. A good training course is at least two full days in length, and it covers the following elements:

- operational definitions of the site's identified critical behaviors
- interaction skills
- feedback techniques
- models of observation strategy
- %safe calculation

There are a number of obstacles to performing behavioral observation well, and three of the obstacles make their appearance as resistance from wage-roll employees, from unions, and from supervisors.

- *Resistance from wage-roll employees*
- *Resistance from unions*
- *Resistance from supervisors*
- *Over-familiarity with the work:* Observers who know the work may take for granted the way things are done, and thereby overlook some hazards. People tend to accept what they are used to. They can lose their adaptive safety readiness. They lose respect for the hazards. Many at-risk behaviors and practices that were taken for granted in the 1890s would shock us today. On the one hand, we should be grateful that safety standards have improved over the years. However, the safety standards that we currently take for granted regularly produce accidents. Current standards still need continuous improvement. Behavioral observation provides the data for this continuous improvement.
- *Unfamiliarity with the work:* Observers who are not familiar with the work have a different problem to overcome. They do not understand where the hazards lie. They must first grasp the situation before recognizing the hazards.
- *Unfamiliarity with the facility's data sheet:* This is a typical problem for new observers. Thorough familiarity with the data sheet, and with the list of definitions of critical behaviors cures this difficulty.
- *Behavior that happens quickly:* It doesn't take very long for a worker to assume an at-risk wrist position when using a tool. For new observers this

behavior can happen so quickly that they are not sure whether it was done properly. Or they may not even notice the behavior at first. With training, however, observers become behavior-focused. During an observation they are undistracted by non-behavioral aspects of the scene before them. They learn to take a very professional approach to observation because the know that *little things* can mean the difference between safety, and injury.

- *Small but important things:* Little things, or the absence of them, may be hard to observe. For example, while observing a bus driver, does the observer notice whether the driver's eyes scanned continuously between the mirrors, the sides of the vehicle, and the road ahead? The importance of little things is compounded by the fact that when things go wrong they can go from safe to at-risk in a moment. The importance of little things is magnified in a crisis. A door that is half open may not appear to be a hazard, but if the lights suddenly go out, that door can become a serious danger. People have been injured walking headlong into the edge of such doors during an emergency. A wheelbarrow in an aisle may not amount to much of a hazard, until there is a fire and that escape route is obstructed. Not cleaning up a spill right away can seem like a little thing that does no harm; but the law of averages is at work here too, and that harmless little spill of water or oil on the floor can suddenly become a critical contributing factor in an accident.

Other Contributions of the Peer Observer

Safety meeting resource. Observers play an important role at safety meetings when the behavioral data is analyzed by the group for the purpose of problem-solving. By amplifying the information contained in the summary data sheet reports, providing general impressions, the observers give the benefit of their unique perspective based on experience with the observations in question.

Accumulating Data for Action Planning

The result of professional quality behavioral observation is an accumulating data base that allows a facility to target the common causes of its accident *producing* system. After three to six to nine months of active observation, the workforce as a whole begins to see the results. This is the time when the charted data can be collated and compiled into reports that a workgroup can use to identify new targets for improvement. For streamlining this task computer software is essential. This closure of the facility feedback loop represents the threshold of the safety improvement process itself, the third behavior-based instrument of continuous improvement in safety performance.

SUMMARY

In practice, after behavioral observation the next step in the sequence is data analysis and problem solving, which was presented in Chapter 2. As a workgroup learns to manage its more initial behavioral problems areas, they move on to a new round of inventory development (Chapter 7), further observation (Chapter 8), and new efforts at problem-solving and action planning (Chapter 2). This is the crux of the employee-driven safety process as a mechanism for continuous improvement. At the same time that this round of activity is ongoing, a number of special issues typically come up for consideration. The chapters of Part III present some of the most important of those current issues in employee-driven safety.

Part III

Current Issues in
Employee-Driven Safety

10

Behavior-Based Safety: The Paradigm Shift beyond the Failures of Attitude-Based Programs

Although the 1980s have seen the arrival and development of the behavior-based paradigm of safety management, some managers remain confused about behavior-based safety. Contributing to this confusion is the fact that some safety consultants are using the name *behavior-based safety* to relabel old attitude-based models and practices that are not behavior-based at all. Calling something behavior-based doesn't make it so. Nonetheless, well-meaning people who are unfamiliar with the new paradigm can be misled by names, and even people who are familiar with the new paradigm can easily lapse into the old ways of thinking. See the Paradigm Checklist (Fig. 10.1), and the profile of A Misguided Pep Talk (Fig. 10.2).

IN THE OLD PARADIGM, SAFETY IS PERSONAL

Counterproductive strategies of the past 20 years are still alive and well. Management confusion about behavior can be increased by people who try to talk about behavior using the old attitude-based paradigm. Not surprisingly, the attitude-based paradigm sees everything in terms of attitudes, including behavior. When people talk about behavior using the old paradigm of safety management, they do not really mean behavior but things that go on within the individual.

An example of this mistake is the reference to so-called *psychological behavior,* Error no. 7 in the Misguided Pep Talk. This emphasis on the personal or individual is a fatal confusion that has no place in a continuous improvement model. In quality this mistake shows up as the tendency of management to see every defect as a special cause event. In safety the result of this misconception is an

---

This chapter was written by John Hidley, M.D.

Paradigm Checklist

The Old Paradigm is Attitude-Based

The New Paradigm is Behavior-Based

☐ **Safety Concept:**
The Personal fallacy — erroneous conclusion that because persons suffer accidents, safety efforts need to focus on the internal states of persons.

☐ **Safety Concept:**
The Systems Approach — sees safety as a systems issue (not a personal issue), requiring a systems answer.

☐ **Underlying Assumptions:**
The Accident Cycle is inevitable and therefore repeated efforts are required.
If outside consultants or management can change what goes on inside of individual employees, then they can get employee behavior to change.

☐ **Underlying Assumptions:**
Continuous Improvement in safety is possible and desirable.
Since individuals have direct control of their actions but not of their attitudes & beliefs, effective management of behavior is the place to begin — then both individual and cultural change will follow.

☐ **Indirect Focus:**
Efforts center on changing the personal beliefs and attitudes of individuals in the hope of thereby changing their behavior.

☐ **Direct Focus:**
Efforts are focused directly on behavior, actions, and performance. What goes on inside the individual is respected as private.

☐ **Wage-roll Accountability:**
At wage-roll levels this old paradigm leads to campaigns to get people to feel responsible for safety, and to get them to give up whatever beliefs they have that supposedly stop them from behaving safely.

☐ **Wage-roll Accountability:**
Individuals can act in accordance with the inventory of crital behaviors and therefore protect themselves. They do behavioral observation and feedback, thus protecting their co-workers while building a data base for continuous improvement.

☐ **Management Accountability:**
At the management level this old paradigm results in campaigns to get managers to lead the effort, to inspire and motivate so as to create the changes inside of individuals.
And all of this because managers are held accountable for bottom-line injury frequency results.

☐ **Management Accountability:**
Management can act to create the organizational consequences that reinforce safe behavior, i.e., compliance with the facility's inventory of critical behaviors.
Managers are accountable for the quality of the safety culture and atmosphere, and for the expanded sphere of wage-roll activity levels that they involve in safety.

☐ **Top-Down Model:**
Management bosses, motivates, entices, supplies incentives, coaxes.
Wage-roll personnel attend meetings, win prizes, lose prizes, suffer disciplinary action.
Safety problems are prioritized and solved by management, sometimes with wage-roll input.

☐ **Collaborative Model:**
Managers are not seen as bosses but as people who empower the whole team.
Wage-roll personnel serve with distinction as steering committee members and as behavioral observers, helping to develop their facility's inventory of critical behaviors and giving their peers ongoing verbal and charted feedback on safety performance.

☐ **Low Effectiveness:**
Continuing accident cycle or performance plateau.

☐ **High Effectiveness:**
The step-change to continuous improvement in safety performance.

FIGURE 10.1   Checklist for behavior-based versus attitude-based safety paradigms.

A Misguided Pep Talk

Consider the following pep talk given by a manager who mistakenly thinks he is encouraging his supervisors to use the new behavior-based paradigm. The way this well-meaning manager lapses into outmoded attitude-based errors provides a textbook case of confusion about behavior-based safety. The errors are numbered for further discussion in this chapter.

Operations Manager to his Supervisors:

We have good employees here, and

Error 1   if we can just get them to be more aware of safety, then they will behave more safely.

Error 2   We need to get at the attitudes that underlie the behavior of our employees. Only then will we begin to see our injury rate come down.

No one comes to work wanting to get hurt, but

Error 3   sometimes some of our employees take safety for granted; they go to sleep psychologically, and then an injury happens.

We want them to have a

Error 4   more "proactive attitude".
Error 5   We want a "behavioral" approach to safety where each employee assumes total responsibility for his or her own safety, and for the safety of their co-workers

To make this happen

Error 6   you supervisors must be leaders and commit yourselves to this goal.
Error 7   People's psychological "behavior" is the key, so
Error 8   wake them up, get them paying attention,
Error 9   get them responsible and committed, and then they will behave safely.

If this pep talk rings true for you, read on.

Not only is this manager off-track; he's dead wrong. Each numbered statement here repeats at least one piece of counterproductive, outmoded thinking. Even though he is using some of the language of behavior-based safety, he is really relying on the Old Paradigm of attitude-based safety. Some of his wording may be new, but his approach is no different from that of his predecessors of twenty years ago.

FIGURE 10.2   A common but misguided pep talk.

old, misguided paradigm that wastes time and resources on initiatives that are supposed to raise something called "individual safety consciousness."

This state of heightened awareness is supposed to be brought about by

- the right training, and
- reflection on experience which, in turn, is supposed to result in
- positive safety attitudes, and commitment (Pep Talk Errors 2, 4, 6, and 9)
- attention to the job and awareness (Pep Talk Errors 1, 3, and 8)
- a heightened sense of personal responsibility (Pep Talk Errors 5 and 9).

To achieve these things management often thinks that it is supposed to

- actively provide leadership (Pep Talk Error 6), to
- motivate (Pep Talk Error 8), and to
- sustain these attitudes in the employees.

What is Wrong with This Picture?

There is a great deal that is counterproductive in the person-based approach. Awareness, learning, experience, commitment, attention, personal responsibility, and management initiative—this is the same old mix that people have tried to use for safety for the past several decades at least. There is nothing wrong with many of these things but not one of these is a behavior-based strategy. Each of them appeals to personal things that go on inside of individuals.

Just What is Safety-Related Behavior?

When people using the old paradigm of safety management talk about behavior, they are referring to actions that are socially acceptable, and to ideals about how they wished people felt and acted. (Pep Talk Errors 1, 5, 8, and 9) That is why they go on to spend so much time on motivation and attitudes (Pep Talk Errors 2, 4, and 9)—they are really focused on the social setting. This is the proper setting for annual fund drives and other types of cheer-leading activity, but it has shown itself to be wholly inadequate as an approach to managing continuous improvement projects of any kind, including safety.

Contrary to that older, vague, socially oriented meaning of behavior, in the new paradigm, *behavior* is a technical scientific term. The behavior-based approach to safety is focused strictly on those observable, measurable actions that are critical to safety at a particular facility. As presented in Chapters 2, 3, and 7, this is a very task-oriented view of behavior, and it treats safety-related behaviors as critical work-related skills to be identified and inventoried. The inventory typically contains a cluster of 15 to 25 behaviors that are implicated as the final common pathway in most of the accidents at the site. The behaviors that emerge from many analyses are such things as

- three-point contact on all ladders, stairs, and catwalks
- body position in relation to task
- wearing personal protective equipment (PPE)

These behaviors are critical no matter what people's attitudes may be.

To see how irrelevant attitudes are to results, consider the following scenario. A plant manager is getting a progress report on safety initiatives in two different departments of the plant. One department is using the old person-based approach, and the other, the new behavior-based approach.

Plant manager:

"What kind of results are we getting from the person-based safety initiative?"

Typical person-based report from operations manager:

"Well, our supervisors have all been talking up safety in their crew meetings, and now if you ask our people they will tell you that safety is their responsibility. I think we're beginning to make believers out of them."

In response to a report like this a plant manager might well repeat his request for results data. By way of contrast, consider the typical report on a behavior-based safety effort.

Plant manager:

"What kind of results are we getting from the behavior-based safety initiative?"

Typical behavior-based report from operations manager:

"Well, the employees have developed their inventory of critical behaviors, and they have trained behavioral observers for each workgroup. The observers have established the department's baseline %safe ratings. Furthermore, over the past three months all crews are up to at least 85 %safe from their original baseline rating of 55 %safe on performance of 3-Point Contact. Improvement is also good—up to 75 %safe—on Wearing Personal Protective Equipment. However, %safe ratings for Body Position in Relation to Task remain a concern, showing almost no improvement over the baseline rating of 60 %safe. The crews are developing action plans to get at this area of their performance."

When plant managers are provided with data of this kind, they do not go on to say, "Well, all that workgroup safety data sounds good, but how is their attitude?" or, "Are they safety-aware?" The reason is that when plant performance of critical safety-related behaviors is up, managers don't even think to be concerned about safety *attitude*. This is because when it comes to safety, behavioral performance is the true bottom line. The other important reason that behavior-based managers don't have to worry about attitude is that attitude *follows* performance. When a workgroup makes demonstrable progress as measured by peer observation on the basis of a behavioral inventory developed from hard data, and endorsed by the workgroup itself, their safety attitude also makes progress.

BEHAVIOR-BASED DOES NOT MEAN PERSONAL

It may seem reasonable to focus a safety effort on persons. After all, when there is an injury, some person gets hurt, and it is a person who benefits from accident prevention. The trouble is that focusing on the person is *not* the way to achieve continuous improvement. The mistake of the old paradigm is that because our safety efforts are *for* persons, it was assumed that the effective approach must necessarily be *personal*. We could call this the "personal fallacy." This fallacy is comparable to concluding that because it is persons who suffer in highway accidents, the way to improve highway safety is to have people change their attitudes or feelings or consciousness. But in fact, when we are on the freeway, we don't think about the attitudes of the drivers around us. Our concern is for whether they signal their lane changes and observe the other important principles of safe driving behavior.

The personal fallacy thinks that because persons suffer or benefit from safety practices, the responsibility for those sufferings and benefits must "lie within" individual persons. This confuses cause and effect. Responsible feelings are not the cause of improved safety (Pep Talk Errors 5 and 9).

- The proof of this is that people can be made to feel responsible for safety, and yet not improve their safety performance and, conversely,
- Employees sometimes have very cynical feelings and attitudes about safety, and yet they perform their jobs with admirable levels of safe behavior.
- Furthermore, programs that focus on attitude don't work in the long term. At best they succeed in heightening this sense of responsibility for a short time, and therefore they have to be redone continually.

Not surprisingly, advisers who recommend approaches based on this fallacy recommend hiring external consultants to do extensive training to get people to develop their insight into the importance of safety—and then more training to get them to maintain this insight. In fact, in a well-functioning safety process (not a program) individuals do increasingly feel responsible for safety—but their feelings are the result, *not* the cause, of an effective behavior-based safety initiative. We talk about this more in a moment.

Focusing on the person has had its day. It is what people have been trying to do for years. Its uses are limited, and its drawbacks are numerous. We know about them under headings like punishment, disciplinary action, investigation, incentives, and the many motivational schemes that companies large and small, prestigious and marginal, have tried in every conceivable mix over the years. Those who advocate the personal approach to safety continue to believe, in spite of decades of evidence to the contrary, that the problem is inside the individual. He or she doesn't have a sufficient sense of responsibility, the right safety beliefs, the proper respect for safety, and so on. The surest sign that this approach is mistaken is that when it is practiced it misfires. Just think about the problems associated with the personal fallacy as embodied in top-down initiatives, incentive schemes, punitive accident investigations, and motivational programs:

- At best, these measures provide only a temporary fix.
- Focusing on the person often creates resistance—either in the person who receives negative attention, or in the person who is passed over for positive citation.
- The personal approach in injury investigation creates adversarial them-versus-us conflicts in the culture.
- Focusing on the person invariably creates a cycle of increased energy (fear or excitement), and then letdown and withdrawal.
- Focusing on the person eventually creates indifference or cynicism about management's real commitment to safety because it diverts attention and resources away from the real issues. In management it inclines well-meaning individuals toward the view that the wage-roll people who get hurt are defective human beings who just don't take their own safety seriously, and who would rather blame the company or work the system.

THE NEW PARADIGM—BEHAVIOR MEANS ACTION

Contrary to all of this the new paradigm advocates focusing instead on the one thing that people who are properly fit for their jobs can directly control—namely their task-related actions. The new paradigm says since effectiveness lies in the realm of task-related action or behavior, expanding the individual's sphere of action is the key to improving safety. Consequently the recommendation is that a facility install a systematic methodology to identify, measure, and alter antecedents and consequences in favor of maximizing safe behaviors and minimizing at-risk behaviors. In this way people expand their control over those critical behaviors. Employee committees use the methodology to drive continuous improvement in safety performance and cultural safety standards, thereby increasing their actual effectiveness and their sense of empowerment and responsibility for safety.

Note which comes first (cause), and which is the result (effect). Beginning by controlling what is in their power, their behavior, people act responsibly. As a result of this consistency of performance (behavior) they then develop a sense (attitude) of increased responsibility and empowerment. Responsibility follows from action. In the new paradigm, behavior is the focus, not persons. Since under the new paradigm's analysis of the safety situation, behavior is the key variable, this paradigm focuses directly on behavior—first, middle, last, making an end run around the old, counterproductive appeals to awareness, attitudes, beliefs, feelings, and motivation.

The personal fallacy really is a very indirect way of trying to help people improve their performance. In fact, the indirect approach of the personal fallacy is itself directly responsible for much that is frustrating and ineffective in the old paradigm of safety. The old paradigm fails by failing to specify behaviors.

- *No scientific inventory of critical behaviors.* The identification of behaviors that are critical to safety is left up to opinion and controversy.
- *No valid measurement.* There is no effective technology in place for systematically sampling and measuring behavior.
- *No proactive data collection.* There is no system for collecting and analyzing safety data before people are injured. In a classic reactive pattern, accidents are relied on to steer the safety effort.
- *No answer for barriers.* Invariably there are cultural barriers to safety (unidentified antecedents and consequences) pressuring people to routinely perform at-risk behaviors. The old, person-based paradigm has no systematic way to identify and remedy cultural barriers to safety. Instead it seeks to simply *inspire* a safer culture.
- *Subjective and unfair.* Typically, the *behavioral* focus of the old paradigm has been inconsistent, unjust, half-hearted, and negative or even punitive.

People who try to get results with the old, person-based paradigm find themselves in a difficult, and frustrating struggle against its inherent limitations. It is no wonder that supervisors and managers alike have suffered burn-out under such a system. In the old paradigm, management's role is a fantastic and impossible mix of drill sergeant, traffic cop, and cheer leader. In the new paradigm, management's role is not to boss but to empower.

WHERE IS THE PERSON IN THE NEW PARADIGM?

The person is there in the new paradigm as a *professional*. The new paradigm respects the individual more than does the person-based approach. In fact, it is because the new paradigm respects the power of attitude that it does not try any clumsy or ham-handed attempt at attitude modification. Attitudes, beliefs, feelings, motivation, awareness—these are closely related to things like hope, anticipation, and enjoyment. Just because those things are very personal and very private, it does not follow that private individuals can control their own, let alone someone else's. In fact, the sources of these things in us are not accessible to us (personal fallacy). We can order ourselves or others to be punctual, but we cannot order anyone (ourselves included) to value punctuality. We can order ourselves or others to meet the train, plane, or bus, but we cannot order anyone to eagerly look forward to the meeting. We can promise that we will attend an event, but we cannot promise that we will enjoy it. People who talk as though we or they could command, order, or promise in those ways are guilty of committing the personal fallacy. "Now hear this—after our next safety workshop, you *will* be aware of safety."

The behavior-based safety of the new paradigm does not get confused about any of those issues. Instead it treats persons well by not expecting unrealistic things of them. It doesn't tell people to try to manipulate their feelings, beliefs, and awareness. Neither does it abuse the limits of people's powers of attention, alertness, focus, commitment, and so on. Hypervigilance is no virtue, even if it is hyper-vigilance to safety. (For more on this subject, see Chapter 15 on behavior-based safety training for adaptive readiness.) Sustained hypervigilance is an illness. Far from being some kind of desirable, responsible, sustainable state, people who are really and truly hypervigilant are ill, and doctors treat them as such.

All the calls for *constant safety awareness* and *permanently heightened attention to safety* are just so much loose talk. (Pep Talk Errors 1, 3, and 8.) No productive person really lives and works in that way. Secret service agents guarding the President of the United States can only do what they do for short periods. The same is true for all professional watchers, sentries, and guards. By falling into the personal fallacy, the old paradigm has proven itself very inadequate to meeting the complex challenge of managing continuous improvement in safety. A good safety attitude and a high level of individual safety responsibility are a wonderful side benefit of an effective safety process. They are not its cause.

11

Employee Selection for Safety: Reducing Variation in Human Performance

Focusing as it does on levels of at-risk behavior, the behavioral safety process is concerned essentially with human performance. Human activity is one of the important inputs of the manufacturing process. Other inputs are raw materials, utilities, equipment, and facilities. The outputs are product, and in the middle zone there is the transformation of inputs into outputs. Even in plants that make extensive use of robotic devices, human performance remains one of the most important of the inputs, since people install and service the robots. Since the pioneering work of Deming, many people have contributed solutions to questions of how to limit variation in raw materials, equipment, and facilities. What about variation in human performance? For the most part, effective strategies for managing human variation have been few. Deming has worked with service industries to help them develop TQM measures for the delivery of their services. This quality approach perhaps comes closest to addressing this area, but it remains an indirect approach in most cases, focusing as it does on the output of the particular service industry.

It is in the field of safety, not quality, that human performance has been addressed directly. That direct approach is the one presented in this book—the behavior-based approach. To the question, "How can managers limit variation in human performance?" behavior-based safety answers, "By measuring and managing safety-related behaviors."

There are two kinds of variation managers are concerned with here—between-variation and within-variation—and the behavior-based approach works to limit both. Between-variation is the variation in performance between individual workers, as in the following contrast.

This chapter was written primarily by Kim Sloat, Ph.D.; Ron Finley also contributed.

Most of the time worker A avoids at-risk behaviors while worker B has an individual %safe rating of only 50 percent, performing as many at-risk behaviors as safe ones. Within-variation is the variation in performance within an individual worker. For example, although worker A avoids at-risk behaviors most of the time, on some days he, too, scores only 50 percent safe.

As a workforce becomes fluent in the operational definitions of safe and at-risk behaviors that compose their site's inventory of critical behaviors, the large majority of employees, from 90 to 95 percent, consistently perform with higher and higher standards of excellence. Ongoing observation and feedback strengthens their adaptive readiness for safety challenges and, on the whole, workforce performance makes the step-change to continuous improvement. For that 90 to 95 percent of the workforce, this step-change means a decrease in both the between-variation and the within-variation of their performance.

LIMITING VARIATION DURING THE HIRING PROCESS

Applicant screening has been a common practice in manufacturing and industry for decades now. It is designed to limit between-variation. For instance, because of the extensive use of color coding in the electrical trades, applicants for those positions are routinely screened for standard color vision. In such a case, screening for color blindness is something the employer owes to everyone concerned— to the existing workforce, to the company stockholders, and to the applicants themselves. In addition to screening instruments for assessing physical aptitude and intelligence, recent years have seen the development of instruments designed to predict levels of safe and at-risk performance.

The incentive for developing and using such screening instruments is that variation between workers in safety performance can be quite high, and it can cost everyone concerned a great deal. It is not unusual to find that 6 to 10 percent of a workforce accounts for 30 to 65 percent of a company's injury frequency. The author has found this to be true for dozens of companies he has worked with. Readers are encouraged to review their own data to see what portion of their workforce is involved in a disproportionate number of incidents (Fig. 11.1). This group of workers with repeat incidents is clearly an important factor for any continuous improvement initiative. When workers who are liable to have repeat incidents are already part of the workforce, the most effective approach is to work with them individually to develop their personal inventory of critical behaviors. For an outline of this method, readers are referred to Chapter 19, "Managing Employees Who Have Had Multiple Accidents," in the author's book, *The Behavior-Based Safety Process.*

Another good management solution is to screen for predictors of at-risk behavior during the selection process. The long-term benefits of such screening can be

1. In alphabetical order by employee name, print out all incidents over a three-year period. Calculate the total incidents.
2. Subtotal the counts for all individuals with two or more incidents.
3. To determine the percentage of all incidents attributable to the group of employees with multiple incidents, divide the number arrived at in Step 2 by the total found in Step 1.
4. To calculate the proportion of the workforce that has had multiple incidents, count the individuals who have been involved in more than one incident and divide their number by the total number of employees.
5. These two data points yield the percentage of the workforce that has had multiple incidents, and the percentage of the total incidents represented by those multiple incidents.

FIGURE 11.1   Steps for determining the proportion of accident frequency attributable to employees with multiple incidents.

very substantial. For all practical purposes, a facility with a 10 percent annual turnover rate in personnel will have a new workforce every ten years. And it is not unusual to see newer employees over-represented in a facility's incident frequency. The potential for hiring *poor safety performance* is quite high, therefore, and very serious gains in overall safety performance could be compromised or cancelled outright by the steady arrival of new personnel with a tendency to have repeat incidents. The most effective way to minimize the effect of poor selection on company performance is to screen for safety during the hiring procedure. This chapter reviews two methods for selection, employee testing and situational interviews or inventories. Both are presented following a review of the Human Resources perspective.

HUMAN RESOURCE DEVELOPMENT

When it comes to employee screening, most HRD officers and personnel are justifiably wary of quick-fixes. Over the years, most HRD personnel have seen fads come and go. The abiding fact is that the soon-certain-positive that HRD wants is new-hires who fit in well, catch on quickly, and more than earn their paychecks in short order. Having been disappointed in that happy outcome many times, HRD officers are concerned and cautious.

This is not to say that they are resistant to change. In fact, HRD people are more open to change than most people in the normal business setting. However, by definition, HRD is people-business. And there are no simple answers for people-business. HRD people may question just how valid any of the various screening instruments can be. HR managers may need to be educated about the similarity between techniques used to validate selection instruments and the techniques of statistical process control (SPC). Through their interface with the line organization, HRD professionals know about batch sampling, tolerances, and ranges of quality specifications. Using these same methods, employee selection procedures allow a quantifiable approach to performance prediction. An SPC-based instrument lets HRD know what they are doing. This helps them make their hiring calls with a judgment that is informed by scientific principles.

CANDIDATE SCREENING

A variety of instruments for screening applicants is available. Used as part of a comprehensive personnel screening procedure, these instruments help managers to select safe, dependable, productive employees by measuring applicant characteristics that are predictive of actual on-the-job performance. The types of factors measured by pre-employment screening tests are such things as:

- *Dependability:* likelihood of following company rules, policies, and work schedules, and of avoiding on-the-job misconduct
- *Working safety:* likelihood of avoiding on-the-job injuries
- *Driving safety:* likelihood of avoiding on-the-job driving accidents
- *People relations:* likelihood of working well with customers and fellow employees

On one pre-employment screening instrument, these scales were developed and validated using a concurrent validation strategy. Employee test scores and job performance information were gathered from companies in diverse fields—supermarket, department store, manufacturing, long-haul trucking, heating and plumbing services, and soft drink bottling.

Figure 11.2 shows some of the data for low and high scorers on the Working Safety Scale. Across companies, people who score low on this scale of the instrument cited here average five times more on-the-job injuries than the high-scorers. The data bear out this correlation for the other three scales, too. Compared to employees who score high, people who have low scores on the test also tend to have two times higher absenteeism rates, three times as many on-the-job driving accidents, and five times more customer and co-worker arguments.

Pre-employment screening instruments such as these may be either computer-based or paper-and-pencil tests. Working through the questions the prospective applicants indicate to what degree the items are descriptive of themselves. The resulting profile is designed so that applicants are asked several questions that relate to each of the scales, e.g., Dependability, Working Safety, Driving Safety, and People Relations. Administrative functions are handled usually on-site with the software, allowing employers timely use of applicant scores for hiring decisions. These instruments need to be fully validated, showing that they predict actual on-the-job performance in each Scale area. Furthermore, they need to be designed so that they do not discriminate unfairly on the basis of race, gender, or age, meeting all EEOC legal requirements.

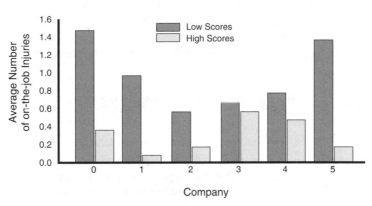

FIGURE 11.2   Data for high and low scorers on the Working Safety Scale.

VALIDITY

Validity has a technical meaning in employee selection instruments. It means the degree to which the instrument can be demonstrated to predict on-the-job performance (behavior). An instrument that demonstrates statistically significant correlation coefficients between test scores and predetermined outcome criteria is valid—that is, it is predictive of job-related behavior.

Validity studies usually follow either a *concurrent* or a *predictive* methodology. Concurrent studies examine the validity of the instrument with current employees, while predictive studies examine the same relationship with applicants. Concurrent strategies are easier to conduct since the results are available immediately. Predictive strategies are more scientifically rigorous but less practical since they require testing the applicants, hiring them all, and then measuring outcome criteria over a period of years. Concurrent validation methods are considered acceptable and they are most commonly used to validate screening instruments.

A well validated screening instrument will have been validated in multiple settings over an employee population of several thousand people. Its use will be limited to the types of employees (wage-roll, for instance) included in the validation strategy. In some cases it is appropriate for a company to conduct additional validity studies within its own ranks. The basic method for a concurrent validity study is as follows:

1. Select employee groups to study. Usually this group should include at least 200 people.
2. Administer and score the screening instrument.

3. Determine outcome criteria and gather data. Typical outcome criteria would include the accident frequency rate over several years, supervisor ratings, absenteeism, and self-reported alcohol and drug use.
4. Do statistical analysis, determining the degree of correlation between score on the selection instrument and outcome criteria.
5. The instrument is valid to the degree that the questions predict the outcome measures.

APPLICANT SCREENING—TWO CASE HISTORIES

Case History 1

This Midwestern printing company (company A) employs approximately 600 people. Company management creates a corporate climate that supports positive attitudes toward safety improvement. This company uses a pre-employment screening instrument to screen all new wage-roll workers. Production-related positions account for 90 percent of new hires, while the remaining 10 percent are office personnel. To begin the hiring procedure, the prospect fills out an application. A phone screen follows. Prior to a supervisor interview, the safety screening instrument is administered. For jobs that are classified as high-risk, there is also a physical examination and a drug screen.

Results

Since including the instrument in hiring procedures in mid-1990, management reports that the turnover rate has fallen from 40 to 20 percent. In addition, as Fig. 11.3 indicates, worker's compensation claims decreased dramatically from 12.1 per 100 employees in 1989 to 3.9 per 100 employees in 1990.

Case History 2

This southeastern manufacturer of military training simulators (company B) employs approximately 825 people. At this site there is a low level of commitment to safety—the pre-employment screening instrument is virtually the only safety-related instrument implemented by this company. All new wage-roll applicants are screened. As in Company A, production-related positions account for 90 percent of new hires, the remaining 10 percent being office positions. In making hiring decisions, managers review supervisor interviews, and job knowledge and screening test scores.

Results

This company began using the a candidate profile in 1990. The data in Fig. 11.4 show that worker's compensation claims fell from 37.3 per 100 employees in

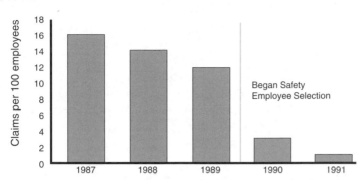

FIGURE 11.3   Company A workers' compensation claim frequency before and after using a candidate profile.

FIGURE 11.4   Company B workers' compensation claim frequency before and after using a candidate profile.

1989 to 20.6 per 100 employees in 1990. This decrease occurred despite the company's overall low commitment to safety.

Legal Issues in the Use of Screening Methods

This chapter is not intended to replace the legal advice necessary to determine the suitability of these methods for a particular company, but to paint a broad picture of some of the legal considerations involved in the use of screening techniques.

The primary concerns are that the selection procedure be job-related and not discriminate against protected groups. This concern exists for all selection methods, including the interview, screening tests, telephone screens or review of applications.

Job-Relatedness

The method used to select employees should be related to on-the-job behavior, to the requirements of the job. Screening devices offer an advantage in this area if they are properly validated because they have demonstrable predictive ability. Applicants who score high on the screening instrument are more likely to perform in accordance with job-related behaviors.

Nondiscriminatory

The test manual that accompanies any properly validated selection instrument should show evidence of non-discrimination against protected groups. The EEOC publishes Guidelines to assist with this determination.

CANDIDATE SCREENING—SITUATIONAL INTERVIEWING

The basic aim of any selection procedure is to help an employer predict what the candidates will do in particular job situations. Will the candidates perform effectively or ineffectively in those job situations? The selection approach presented in this section is founded on a simple, direct idea—to predict better what people will do, ask them what they would do in a given job situation. Other selection methods use less direct approaches. For instance, one fairly well supported approach does not ask about specific job situations but rather identifies what a candidate has done in similar situations in the past, and then infers that his or her behavior will be similar in the future. Another, more involved, inferential approach identifies characteristics or traits of the candidate, and infers his or her future situational behavior based on what others with the same traits have done in situations of interest.

The rationale behind the direct situational approach is that, as a predictor, it has high validity and it is very straightforward and aboveboard. The validity of the direct situational approach has been established in studies that compare how people respond to situational questions and how they subsequently perform the tasks covered in the situational questionnaire. The predictions made on the basis of this approach are better than traditional approaches. Furthermore, the straightforwardness of the questions adds another dimension to the selection process. It is reasonable to ask people what they would do, and it turns out that it is reasonable to credit the accuracy of their answers.

In using the situational approach, the challenge for a company is to formulate the right questionnaire. It does not work to use a set of random questions. An effective situational questionnaire taps various dimensions of the desired job performance at the site. Questions that select for safety-related behaviors, for instance, elicit answers that bear on risk-taking and similar factors. Another requirement of the question set is that it be consistent across candidates, and non-discriminatory for factors that are not job-relevant.

Well considered selection procedures that satisfy these strict criteria are not produced by informal brainstorming sessions about situations that might be important to safety performance. To meet these criteria an effective situational questionnaire needs to emerge from a fairly careful development scheme. The development scheme presented here is known as the critical incident methodology. The critical incident methodology can help site personnel meet the twofold challenge,

1. Identify the incidents (situations) in which employees perform very well or poorly.
2. Extract from those situations the underlying dimensions of safe performance.

USING THE CRITICAL INCIDENT METHODOLOGY

One application of the critical incident methodology is to do behavioral analysis of a site's injury or incident reports.

Incident Reports

This analysis produces a brief description of the situation and of the behaviors performed by the employee in the situation. At most sites the best team for this work is a combined group of supervisors, safety professionals, and wage-roll personnel who know are very familiar with the situations covered in the incident reports. These are people who are very knowledgeable about the site's procedures and production processes.

Internal Interviews

Internal interviewing is the second application of the critical incident methodology. The interviews are conducted with the same site personnel who are helpful during behavior-based analysis of incidents—supervisors, safety professionals, and veteran wage-roll personnel. The interviews need not focus on incidents in which the interviewees themselves were involved. The questions can be about any situations that the interviewees know about. Supervisors are typically the group that is interviewed here, and that is relevant if they are adequately familiar with what has gone on. The basic internal interview request is twofold,

1. Please describe a situation in which an employee did a particularly good job with respect to safety. What was the employee's behavior, and why was it particularly apt for safety?
2. Describe a situation in which an employee performed behavior that was particularly at-risk. What was the employee's behavior, and how did it put him or her at risk?

To be sufficiently exhaustive for use, the initial database requires descriptions of this kind for upwards of several hundred critical incidents. Once a wide range of these incidents is in the database, they are organized into performance and selection dimensions.

Performance and Selection Dimensions

To avoid individual biases in the categories of the organized database, a small team of knowledgeable people performs this sorting procedure. To avoid the biases of the group, it is helpful to have a second team sort the same database independently of the other team. Usually each team works with stacks of index cards, each card bearing the description of one critical incident identified in the preceding step. This team sorts the cards into groups. Each group contains incidents that, in the opinion of the people doing the sorting, describe an underlying dimension such as risk taking, poor job planning, and insufficient personal protective equipment. Each team goes through the card set of critical incidents, sorting them into what they take to be categories of underlying dimensions of the incidents. Using two groups allows comparison to see whether they have sorted consistently with each other. Inconsistency of sorting appears when one team puts a particular incident in one dimension (personal protective equipment) and another puts it in a different dimension (poor job planning). Comparison brings out this discrepancy. If on reconsideration the incident remains ambiguous to the combined teams, it may not be a good exemplar of either dimension. They then discard it, continuing their search for examples on which they agree. Comparing the two sets of sorted cards, the combined team retains only those incidents that have been categorized consistently by the two teams.

Labeling the Dimensions

After sorting comes labeling. Whoever is doing the development work generates names that capture the underlying dimension and then writes the definition for that dimension. To validate the dimension labels and the loading of the incidents onto the dimensions, a third team is used. Along with the proposed dimension labels, this team receives the incident cards that passed the preceding test of clarity and specificity. This third team then sorts the incident cards back onto the dimensions. This is another test for the consistency of the dimensions. If there are discrepancies between this sorting and the combined sort then, once again, the incidents are probably not good exemplars of the dimensions because different groups of people put them into different categories.

Only those incidents that are sorted consistently through the whole process are retained as a source for the situational questionnaire for selection candidates. The validation steps leave the team with a much reduced set of dimensions. This is the reason to begin this procedure with a large number of incidents. In cases where the validation steps drastically reduce the critical incident pool, the teams may have to go back to incident reports and interviews to generate more incident descriptions. The teams then recapitulate the steps of the method. For this reason it is better to err on the side of collecting too many incidents than too few, reviewing as many as several hundred incidents to begin with. The result of the method is a set of dimensions and incidents that exemplify either good or poor performance on a particular dimension.

Composing the Situational Questions

To select incidents for our situational questions, the team orders the incidents for a particular dimension in a continuum or range. However, since it would be too tedious to ask questions about each incident in the range of incidents, the team selects two or three incidents that are representative for each dimension. These incidents form the basis of the selection questions for their respective dimensions. It is a good idea to have more than one question for each dimension. For the sake of accurate prediction, it is better to have a candidate's answers to multiple procedures, rather than just one incident. Since each incident will differ at least slightly from others, an array of them is selected for each dimension. In fact, the actual incidents may be too specific. In that case, the incidents are slightly rewritten to modify some of the details but retain their essential character. A candidate's answers about what he or she would do across this mini-range of incidents presents a number of behaviors that are predictable.

Scoring Standards

Scoring standards are developed in advance. Suppose that a team has four dimensions relevant to safety, for each of which they have selected two representative incidents. Typically a five-point rating system is used to score the responses the candidates give when questioned on these incidents. A response that indicates no element of safety performance is assigned 1, the lowest score. An answer that embodies absolutely ideal safety performance is assigned 5, the highest score. A rating of 3 is for an answer indicating acceptable, but not ideal, performance. On such a five-point scale, ratings of 1 and 2 are for unacceptable answers, and ratings of 3 through 5 are for answers that are acceptable in varying degrees.

1. most unacceptable
2. unacceptable
3. least acceptable
4. acceptable
5. most acceptable

In addition to the scoring system itself, the selection team also develops scoring criteria in advance to assure consistency of scoring across candidates, applying the same standards for each candidate. To avoid arguing after the fact about scoring standards, the team develops the scoring standard beforehand. Following the validation pattern of "involving another set of eyes," another group of people develop the scoring criteria. Supervisors or managers can be used effectively for this. In most cases, some wage-roll employees are also involved in the standard-writing group. This group can actually meet as a group to consider the incident set, or they can work in smaller numbers or by themselves. The important thing is that as they consider each incident, they draft an entire range of responses to the situation described. That is, each of them drafts an exemplary response, one they think merits the highest score of 5. Each drafts an adequate response (3-rating), and an unacceptable response (1-rating). In effect, this group writes behavioral *anchors* for each of the range of incidents in each category. The rating scales serve as guides because the actual candidate's response may be somewhat different from any of the five answers drafted by the standard-writing group. Nonetheless, it is usually fairly easy to match a candidate's response to one of the five answers.

At this stage of developing the selection procedure, there are

- dimensions that are labeled
- dimensions or categories with representative incidents
- rating points
- scoring criteria

The Trial Interview

The trial interview can be done with candidates or with current employees. At this early stage, if candidates are used in the trial interviews, their responses are not used for selection purposes. If current employees participate in the trial interviews, it is important to maintain confidentiality so that preliminary interview results do not reflect negatively on the employee. Disciplinary action or reprimand has no place in the trial phase. The point is to test the questions and see what kind of responses they actually get from people. The test is to see whether the scoring anchors cover the situations and whether several raters can form a scoring consensus on the responses. Several raters listen as candidates or current employees answer questions about what they would do in the representative situations in each category. The raters record the answers and then discuss them to arrive at agreement on ratings. If need be, these scoring anchors can be modified so that they are better guides for consistency.

Administering the Situational Questionnaire

Once the interview questions have been tested and revised where necessary, the questions are ready for use. Whoever administers this battery of situational questions needs to have some training in the general methodology of the interview, and they need some experience with the interview questions and with the scoring procedure. During the general administration of the test, the candidate is interviewed by a panel. More than one person should do the rating. For example, there is a panel of three people, the questions are asked orally, and the test is explained to the candidate. The panel gives descriptions of situations that could occur on the job, and the candidate is to respond by telling what he or she would do in the situation. The question may be repeated but not explained. An explanation might give one candidate more information than another. The question is read to the candidate by one of the panel members. Then all panel members write down the response and go on to the next question. There might be eight questions—for, say, four dimensions, two questions per dimension. It only takes a few minutes to go through each question so that the entire procedure may last only 15 minutes. The raters need to go through some trial runs where a response is given them. Ideally they do this live, compare their ratings, and then discuss them. They are given guidance on how to reach consensus and how to apply the scoring criteria. All raters go through the same training, and if raters shift around over time, new ones coming in are given the necessary training.

In practice, a panel of trained assessors/raters gets together and administers the questions. The responses are written down as nearly verbatim as possible. There is no probing of the responses. The panel does not ask any follow-up questions of the candidate, unless a term is unclear or the candidate could not hear what the person said. The raters do not probe at all; they just take down the response as given. Probing may give information differentially to candidates, or may give them clues as to how to modify their response. The question is read;

the person responds. The raters write down the response as completely as possible, and then go on to the next question. It does not matter whether only one rater reads the questions or the raters take turns. After the candidate is finished, the panel goes through the answers independently. This should be done fairly soon after the session, preferably immediately. Each rater independently rates the response to each question by applying the scoring criteria. Raters use the rating anchors to rank each response on a scale of 1 to 5. Then there is discussion among the group, question by question. People share their ratings, and if there is disagreement on them, they discuss the response in light of the scoring criteria to arrive at a scoring consensus for each question. The responses to each question are combined into a rating for the dimension. If there are two questions, for instance, on a dimension, an overall rating is developed for that dimension for that response. That information is the consensual rating by dimension, which then feeds into the overall assessment process and is one additional consideration in the selection.

Developing a Situational Inventory

Very similar to the situational interview, the situational inventory is a paper-and-pencil instrument that is well suited for mass screening of applicants. In development, the inventory is also based on the critical incident method presented above for the situational interview. Situations are identified that exemplify the performance dimensions in terms of which the candidates are to be screened. The two instruments diverge at this point, however. Since the candidates completing the paper-and-pencil inventory do not give oral answers, there is no need here for scoring anchors and rating guidelines for a panel of questioners. Instead, for each situation in the inventory the applicant is required to select one response from a multiple choice array of alternatives. The team that develops such an inventory generates a set of rated response alternatives for each situation.

The sets of response alternatives are best produced by job incumbents or supervisors. After carefully reading the situation statement, they describe a range of responses. For each situation, four or more of those descriptions are evaluated by senior supervisory personnel. They identify the best and worst of the range of alternatives for each situation. To produce an adequate range of possible scores, a situational inventory needs more questions than does the situational interview. An inventory needs to cover 35 or more situations, compared to the eight to twelve situations asked about in an interview. To complete the inventory, for each situation description the applicant indicates which alternative response it is most likely that he/she would, make and which is least likely. The applicants answers are scored by comparison with the range of scores established by the senior supervisory personnel.

A Case Example

A petrochemical company developed a situational inventory as one assessment procedure for screening applicants for mechanic positions. The inventory presented 39 situations that reflected the underlying performance (behavioral) dimensions of: Initiative, Responsibility, Teamwork, Communication, Judgment, Dedication, and Safety. Before using the inventory to screen applicants for the position, it was validated on forty job incumbents roughly half of whom were high performers and half, low performers. The 18 high performers were drawn from a list of employees who served as temporary supervisors, and who were therefore in line to be promoted to supervisory positions. In the year preceding, supervisors at the site had ranked their supervisees on overall performance. Twenty-two of the lowest ranked personnel were given the new situational inventory. On completion the average score of the high performers was one-third higher than the average score of the low performers—a statistically significant difference between the two groups (p < 0.0001) (Fig. 11.5).

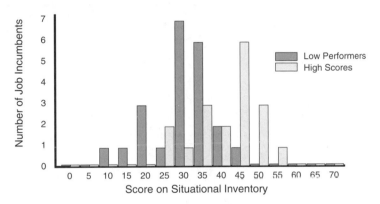

FIGURE 11.5   On the situational inventory, response distributions show that high performers scored significantly higher than low performers.

SUMMARY

Such results demonstrate the power of this approach to candidate assessment. Answers to situational questions reflect job performance, and behavior-based assessment methods can differentiate between potential high and low performers.

12

The Behavior-Based
Approach to Ergonomics

Since 1980 the number of occupational injuries and illnesses reported has increased dramatically. The U.S. Bureau of Labor Statistics reports that more than half of workplace illnesses reported are cumulative trauma disorders (CTDs). The cost of these ergonomics injuries is alarming. The reported cost per individual case has ranged from $800 to $80,000. Average costs are estimated to be $2,400 per case. By the year 2000, CTDs are expected to account for approximately half of every dollar spent on medical care. In 1984, the American Academy of Orthopedic Surgeons estimated that CTDs cost $27 billion a year in lost earnings and in medical expenses. (See Fig. 12.1 for a survey of ergonomics problems.)

A cumulative trauma disorder (CTD) is any of a wide variety of injuries and illnesses that appear in an individual worker who is exposed to a physical stressor (ergonomic risk factor) for a period of weeks, months, or years.

- Examples of upper extremity injuries include tendinitis, bursitis, epicondylitis (tennis elbow), carpal tunnel syndrome, trigger finger, white finger, and DeQuervain's disease.
- Back injuries that cannot be associated with one specific episode of lifting or twisting are often the result of cumulative trauma.
- Eye strain from working without adequate lighting or from cumulative work with video display terminals (VDTs) has also been considered in this category of occupational injury and illness.
- Often, other general muscle strains and sprains that can't be directly related to a single exposure are identified as simulative trauma or ergonomics issues.

FIGURE 12.1 Survey of ergonomic problems.

Portions of this chapter were written by Garnett Langston, Ph.D.

Too Many Remedies? Thus far the typical strategies have been hit or miss. One reason is that the ergonomics bandwagon has gotten very crowded. Industrial engineers, industrial hygienists, physical therapists, occupational therapists, physicians, academicians, and inventors have all joined the chorus offering remedies to companies plagued by ergonomics problems. This flurry of activity has brought many "ergonomic" products to market. In terms of work stations and equipment alone, a short list would include chairs, rests and supports, lean stands, and hand tools—all engineering solutions designed to minimize the physical discomfort of workers performing at-risk jobs. Another reason for the hit-or-miss approach is that ergonomics issues do not fit the old model of workplace injury. See Fig. 12.2 for an overview of ergonomics risk factors.

CTDs: Difficult to Diagnose. Ergonomic issues represent a special challenge to traditional safety efforts. As the name of this disorder indicates, rather than being the result of an exposure to a specific event, the onset of a cumulative trauma disorder is something that accumulates gradually. And although related facility issues are often easily identified, management typically remains unsure of the

Although research on CTDs is still somewhat limited, and some of the findings are controversial, there seems to be agreement on the risk factors listed below. Jobs that involve repetitive exposure to these factors are likely to result in injury even if the exposure is of low intensity.

- *Posture* becomes a problem when the worker maintains a position that creates excessive force on the muscle and connective tissue at the joints of the body. For example, awkward postures of the wrist joint may be required in manipulative tasks such as typing on a keyboard, scanning groceries, or packing objects into a container. A more comfortable and less stressful position for the wrist is a neutral posture (see Fig. 12.3).
- *Force* refers to the amount of work or effort required to manipulate an object or tool. The type of gloves that workers use, or their grip on their tools, are factors that contribute significantly to the amount of force they must exert to perform the task. Although these may seem like small exertions, over time soft-tissue injury can result from even slightly excessive stress on the small muscles of the hands and forearms.
- *Mechanical stress* is the injury risk factor that is operative when a worker's body repetitively makes contact with an object or surface. In some cases, the pressure exerted on the soft tissue of the body results in nerve damage.
- *Vibration* of the tools or equipment that an individual works with or leans against can also result in cumulative trauma problems, including a serious injury called Raynaud's disease, or white finger. This is characterized by a loss of sensation to the finger. Repetitive exposure to vibration has also been linked to back injuries—in the case of long-haul truck drivers, for example.
- *Extreme temperatures* can also place physical stress on workers. Heat may be a factor in some environments or in jobs that require the worker to wear extensive protective gear. Work environments that are both hot and humid place even more stress on the body. Cold can also be an issue, as in food manufacturing and processing operations where workers perform their tasks in very cool environments or in cold climates where work is performed outdoors.

FIGURE 12.2   Ergonomic risk factors.

real causes of the injuries. Part of the confusion regarding the causes and serious-ness of these injuries clearly has to do with their internal nature. CTDs such as hearing loss, carpal tunnel syndrome, or disc damage cannot be seen like a lacer-ation, bruise, or burn.

Symptoms for carpal tunnel syndrome, for instance, include numbness, tin-gling, burning, and aching. These symptoms are not always accompanied by vis-ible signs such as swelling or a contusion, bruise, abrasion or other cut to the skin. Without any visible sign of an injury, a supervisor, or even safety manager, typically may not know how to react. Unless supervisors and managers are edu-cated about these injuries, they may feel that these vague symptoms are just *men-tal* or even *fake*. Managers may even be reluctant to talk about carpal tunnel syn-drome for fear of *touching off an epidemic*.

Since there is no time-specific event that *happens to* the worker reporting cumulative trauma symptoms, it can be difficult to know just which at-risk behaviors and conditions contributed to the problem. Consequently the accident report often includes vague statements such as, "Employee used improper lifting technique." Not surprisingly, employees can feel as though they are being blamed for their own discomfort.

Hit-or-Miss Approaches. There remains a great deal of confusion regarding the best strategy for minimizing the occurrence of cumulative trauma disorders in the workplace. Some safety audits may include a *behavioral* component that looks at worker performance in addition to facility issues. To truly address ergonomic problems, however, any behavioral audit worthy of the name needs to be steered by a skillfully prepared inventory of operational definitions directed to the spe-cific observable behaviors that underlie ergonomics hazards.

Lacking such an inventory of behaviors critical to safe ergonomic perform-ance, the audit won't draw attention to manageable factors. Assessments will remain vague, and recommendations will remain unfocused, "Encourage employees to be careful and to lift properly." What is needed is a mechanism that produces action plans using operational definitions to address and correct critical upstream factors of safe ergonomics performance.

AN INTEGRATED APPROACH

The behavior-based approach offers an integrated way to address to this array of CTD-related issues. Grounded in scientific methodology, the upstream focus of the behavior-based approach is particularly well suited to managing ergonomics issues. In fact, the safety management approach that CTDs seem especially to call for—careful monitoring of the critical mass of accumulating indicators of exposure—is standard operating procedure for behavior-based safety. It treats *every* safety situation this way. Nor is the behavioral approach stymied by the *invisibility* of the problems. By the time any problem is visible, the most that is possible is reaction. From the behavioral perspective, ergonomics issues represent just one area among many where it pays to prevent injuries before they happen—while they are still *invisible*. The behavior-based approach establishes a mechanism for identifying and correcting the upstream factors of safe work—namely the behaviors that ultimately lead to a cumulative trauma injury.

Observing Ergonomics Behaviors. Behavior-based ergonomics observation uses the same two instruments presented in Chapters 8 and 9:

- an inventory of operational definitions
- its related data sheet

The data sheet may list generic behaviors such as Wrist Posture (Fig. 12.3), PPE, and Pushing/Pulling, or it may be more job-specific in its focus. A job-specific

---

When performing a repetitive task, is the worker's wrist in a neutral position (avoiding extreme flexion or extension)? Is the worker minimizing excessive gripping of tools or objects (not forcing, pushing, or straining)? Is the worker minimizing pressure on hands when making contact with a tool or object?

Examples include the following:

- a "T-stacker" slipping (not forcing) Ts through a coil
- a press operator keeping wrist straight when lifting units out of the press
- a press operator wearing gloves and/or using limited force when using a pick to clear a jam

Operational definitions for ergonomic risk factors often include pictures of safe behavior as guidelines for observers (e.g., diagram of neutral wrist position, below).

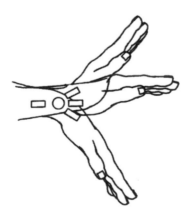

FIGURE 12.3 General operational definition of repetitive wrist movement.

data sheet lists the numerous behaviors essential to the safe performance of a specific task such as packing product, loading cases, or trim and pare. The facility's inventory of critical behaviors is the foundation of the behavioral observation and feedback process. This inventory is a customized document that lists the behaviors that are critical to safe performance at the site.

The Behavioral Inventory. Generic behavioral items on the facility's inventory might include

- body position
- lifting
- pushing / pulling
- wrist posture
- pre-job planning
- tool use and selection

For each of these behaviors there is an accompanying definition that describes safe behavior in operational terms so that it is obvious to an observer what represents safe versus at-risk behavior. The Job-Specific data sheet lists the numerous critical behaviors involved in completing a specific task or aspect of a job in a safe manner. There are five steps involved in writing job-specific ergonomics operational definitions such as those in Table 12.1 for Trim and Pare.

1. Select the Job

Good candidates for job-specific definitions are jobs that are by nature repetitive and that have typically been associated with a higher incidence of cumulative trauma injuries. These jobs likely require a person to stand or sit in one area and/or to repeat the same cycle of physical movements frequently.

2. Select Worker or Workers

As initial models for the job, identify one or more employees who are successful at the job and who do not have a history of work-related injuries. Watch them work and make gross observations of their behavior. If they appear to be working in a safe manner (i.e. using good body mechanics, proper tools, body position, speed of work), then plan to return to the work scene to videotape their performance.

3. Videotape the Job Being Performed

Videotape more than one employee performing the job. Move about the work area while videotaping to insure that you record static postures and movements

TABLE 12.1   Job-Specific Operational Definition: Trim and Pare (from Food Manufacturing)

Safe	At-Risk	
____	____	Waits for product to advance on conveyor
____	____	One foot is on foot rail
____	____	Wears proper gloves for task—good selection and fit
____	____	Employs proper tool selection and condition—knife sharp, handle size and design appropriate for worker
____	____	Hips are clear of workstation
____	____	Elbows are 20° or less away from sides of body while performing task
____	____	Forward bending from hips is limited to less than 5° when reaching for product
____	____	Product is grasped with whole-hand grip
____	____	Product is lifted to cutting area with whole-hand grip
____	____	Minimal wrist rotation or deviation is used when picking up moving product
____	____	Takes rest breaks—simple stretch/relief exercises every 20 minutes for hands, arms, and shoulders
____	____	Worker sets knife down during idle times
____	____	Non-cutting hand is kept out of line of fire
____	____	Eyes are on task
____	____	Discards product with minimal force, sliding with one hand to outgoing conveyor
____	____	Takes scheduled breaks

of all parts of the body. Consider the cycle time of the job. Behavior happens fast—before moving to another location or focus it may be necessary to focus the camera on one aspect of the job while several cycles pass.

4. Identify Observable Behaviors

Review the videotapes and identify the observable behaviors that you want to include in the definition. When determining behaviors, consider the following aspects that are involved in most repetitive jobs.

- *Seated/standing posture:* position of the neck, hip joint, legs, arms
- *PPE:* appropriateness for job condition, fit
- *Tools/equipment:* condition of tool, grip on tool, force used to operate tool.
- *Body mechanics:* movements of joints while work is being performed, lifting/reaching/fine hand movements (avoidance of extreme posture, extreme force)

- *Body position:* out of line-of-fire, pinch points
- *Breaks/relief period between cycles:* changes in posture, tool use during breaks
- *Housekeeping:* environmental conditions in immediate area that impact job
- *View of work:* focus of attention and vision on work

5. Write Operational Definitions for Each Observable Behavior

Operational definitions are then written for each identified behavior. These definitions need to be concise and descriptive of each step, and they should be listed in a logical manner on the job-specific data sheet to aid the observer. Table 12.1 is a sample job-specific data sheet for an assembly line food manufacturing job known as Trim and Pare.

Inventory as Resource. The facility's inventory of critical ergonomics behaviors is primarily used as a guide for observers in the behavioral process but can also be used by others in the organization. The ergonomics inventory becomes a valuable training tool for new employees because it goes beyond the description of hazards in a job, to accurately describe what visible steps individual workers should take to reduce their exposure to a cumulative trauma injury. The facility inventory can also be used by engineers to help them better understand the nature of the work being done and to design out problems in advance of construction.

BEHAVIORAL ERGONOMICS DATABASE

When inventory design, and behavioral observation and feedback are implemented effectively, ergonomics issues in the workplace are uncovered before they result in epidemic or serious injuries and illnesses. The behavior-based approach helps to identify these problems through behavioral analysis of accident reports and computer analysis of

- accident data
- observation data
- observer comment reports

After being exposed to the problem solving tools developed to address the issues uncovered through behavioral observation and feedback, the steering committee determines a strategy for training a core group of problem solvers in the facility.

This core group should consist of wage-roll representatives from the departments with the most exposure for injury, trained observers, engineering and/or maintenance technicians, and management. This problem-solving group is then trained in the following strategies that result in clearer definitions of the issues and solutions to problems:

- investigative interviewing of co-workers through the observation process
- cause tree analysis
- behavior analysis
- data analysis of observation software reports
- idea generation through probing questions and brainstorming
- action planning

Once the problems are identified, the problem solvers are trained to select a focus area to work on. This is done by identifying the issues that are resulting in the most injuries and/or are showing up most frequently as at-risk behaviors on the data-base reports. Once a focus area is identified the problem solving team can work on determining solutions to these ergonomic issues. After determining possible solutions, the problem-solving team is trained in how to evaluate and select the best ideas and to initiate action and follow through on their plans. It is important that none of these steps are ignored. As problems are solved, new ones can be addressed.

Certain types of exposure to ergonomics risk is due primarily to equipment design. In some cases these exposures can be reduced behaviorally, but the best solution—and sometimes the only solution—involves re-design of equipment and facilities. In these cases the at-risk behavior should still be included on the behavioral inventory. This allows for data gathering about the frequency, nature, and extent of exposure, and provides managers with exposure data on which to base their decisions about priorities for re-design action.

CONCLUSION

Cumulative trauma injuries are a serious industrial issue. Risk factors for these injuries have been identified and many engineering and administrative solutions have been suggested. Companies are faced with the challenge of identifying the specific risks in their environments and determining cost-efficient manageable strategies. The behavior-based approach is a comprehensive approach to injury prevention that provides a framework for identifying ergonomic issues and solutions. Through the identification of at-risk behaviors, the development of operational definitions, behavioral observation and feedback, and team problem-solving, exposure to cumulative trauma injuries is reduced and a mechanism for continuous improvement in safety is installed.

13

Behavior-Based Incident Investigation

Fact-finding accident investigation is a crucial part of establishing continuous improvement in safety performance. The behavior-based approach to accident investigation is well suited to this end. The emphasis in this approach is on investigation as a scientific procedure rather than as a disciplinary action. The person or persons involved in the accident are included in the investigating team to help the site identify which at-risk behaviors provided the final common pathway for the incident. Rather than *make an example* of the injured workers, this approach makes them partners in further development of the site's inventory of critical behaviors.

Accident investigations sometimes have a bad reputation. From a behavioral point of view this is not surprising. Most people have experienced soon-certain-negative consequences in connection with accident investigations—and as behavior analysis shows (Chapter 3), consequences of that kind discourage interest and participation. Without the benefit of good behavioral science principles an accident investigation can seem like a thankless task that produces a reactive solution at best. However, safety facilitators using a behavior-based process approach have found that accident investigations are one of the best sources of insight into safety at their facilities. The key to their approach is that they integrate their accident investigation data with other relevant data to develop strategic action plans that take into account the big picture. This integration of accident investigations into an ongoing safety process is keyed to four important actions:

1. discovering the common cause in single events
2. redefining accidents

Portions of this chapter were written by Larry Russell, CSP.

3. making accurate reporting the norm
4. establishing collaborative investigation teams and accident review committees

The result of these efforts is no-fault accident investigation. This is investigation as a primary source of data gathering, not police work or a jury process.

DISCOVERING THE COMMON CAUSE IN SINGLE EVENTS

In the terms of statistical process control (SPC), by virtue of focusing on single events most accident investigation methods implicitly assume that an accident results wholly from a special cause. This assumption is always inappropriate. When an accident reflects a special cause, that aspect of the incident should indeed be investigated and addressed. For example, if an employee is injured by the failure of a piece of equipment, investigation of the cause of failure is appropriate. However, accidents usually result from known factors in the workplace and therefore result from common causes in the system itself. Further, single events have little meaning. It is the pattern of events that describes the underlying system. Continuing this book's extended comparison with total quality management (TQM), the old approach to accident investigation amounts to *defect management*. This old focus is primed to blame the incident on some special cause, perhaps characterized as *lack of attention*. The usual effect of this approach is to add insult to injury—the faulted worker can get the message that management thinks he or she *wanted to get hurt*. The main point here is that even though in most cases employee behavior is the final common pathway of an incident, the workers know that for some time those at-risk behaviors have been part of the way work is conducted at their site. In other words, the at-risk behaviors that are the common pathway of incidents at a facility are part of the plant culture, the work system at the site. This is the same thing as saying that such at-risk behaviors are among the common causes of production at work at the site.

Example
A chemical operator is breaking into a line and is sprayed in the face by a substance.

Related Facts
Operator was not wearing required PPE or was not following prescribed procedure for body position.

Reactive Response
The typical reactive response to the above example sees individual operator negligence (special cause) as the cause of the injury. The usual options for investiga-

tion follow-up involve disciplining the injured operator, re-writing the safety rules, and making an example of this case in subsequent safety communications.

This scenario plays itself out with numerous negative consequences for accident prevention. Committees end up recommending all manner of facility and equipment upgrades, rule and regulation changes, and various "enforcement" activities. The workforce may see this as hypocritical, self-defeating, and even ridiculous. For example, in one facility when an employee bumped his head on a valve it was moved high enough that it then required a ladder to reach it. But when an employee fell off a ladder getting to the valve, the valve was moved back down to within reach. Later, however, the valve was moved back up when another employee bumped into it again. In another facility, an opening to the roof of a building was welded shut when an employee cut his hand opening it. Investigation committees operating in this mode are often divided over which options to take. Some members will favor discipline, others not. Often the parties polarize and extended discussions occur. No one is happy with the final result in either case.

The flaw here is in the very premise of reactive accident investigation. From the beginning, this approach to an accident expects to find and deal with special causes. In a manner of speaking, that is the unwritten charter of reactive accident investigation—identify, discipline, and publicize the special cause of the accident. This entire enterprise is off on the wrong foot from step-one. It is no wonder that polarization, frustration, and repetition are typical results. Even professional, well meaning investigators are handicapped once they are boxed in by this mistaken premise.

Common Cause, Not Special Cause

When a behavior-related injury occurs, the probability is extremely high that the behavior involved has occurred previously without the resulting injury. Fig. 13.1 illustrates this by showing some at-risk behaviors whose results happen to fall outside the accident triangle. The behavior at issue most frequently is one that occurs regularly at the facility. This means that the at-risk behavior is part of the system (common cause). It has been seen, observed, condoned, and probably encouraged (indirectly) by management systems, and usually for an extended period of time. In other words, the at-risk behavior in question is part of *how we do things around here*.

This is the premise of behavior-based accident investigation. The charter of investigation of this kind is to identify and address the root cause or causes (common cause/s) of the accident in question. Consequently a behavior-based investigation considers such questions as:

• Has the at-risk behavior at issue has been previously identified and operationally defined?

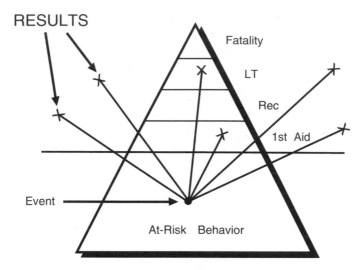

FIGURE 13.1   The results of some at-risk behaviors fall "within" the accident triangle, but others do not.

- Has the at-risk behavior been observed and, if so, with what frequency?
- Has the workforce been trained about this critical behavior?
- Are action plans in place to address these behaviors?
- If not, why not?
- Where is the accident-prevention system breaking down?

Answers to these questions do not usually identify special causes; they identify common causes. These findings don't require reactions—discipline, new regulations, and so on. They require system improvements, and when management addresses these requirements the response from the workforce is very positive. Across regions and industries the result of this approach is that employees get involved in accident investigations, rather than feeling resentful and resistant to them. The most significant safety payoff is that future injuries are prevented. In the course of this work, the worn-out distinction between incidents and accidents is redefined for the entire workforce in a new way.

REDEFINING ACCIDENTS

Traditionally an accident is defined as an unplanned act or event that results in property damage, injury, or fatality. However, this definition misses the very important fact that most acts that result in accidents are planned. They are even calculated—they are calculated risks. To reflect this important point, the behavior-based definition says,

An accident = the unplanned *result* of a behavior that is very likely a part of the culture of the facility.

The conventional definition hides this fact. According to conventional wisdom, when behaviors result in injury, damage, or loss, we have an accident on our hands, and we had better investigate it. If we are *lucky*, however, and experience *only* a near-miss, then that is *just an incident*.

Incident or Accident: The Behaviors Are the Same

Because it is framed in terms of the result, the conventional definition of an incident/accident is reactive. Proactive safety facilitators know better. They know that—incident or accident—the behaviors were the same.

The proactive definition of an incident might run as follows:

An incident = the unplanned result of a behavior that *happens not to cause* injury or damage.

The key point is that although accidents and incidents look different downstream—upstream they look the same.

Consider the familiar accident triangle of Fig. 13.1. At the bottom of the triangle are at-risk behaviors that occur everyday. The figure shows these at-risk behaviors as launching points for various outcomes. An at-risk behavior whose outcome lies off of the triangle is an incident. An identical behavior whose result lies on the triangle is an accident. Behavior-based safety investigators are not confused by the difference in chance outcomes. They investigate back to the upstream behaviors that were the final common pathways of the incidents or accidents. This tracking procedure lies at the heart of no-fault accident investigation. And the identified behaviors are prime candidates for subsequent inclusion by the Accident Review Committee into the facility's inventory of critical behaviors.

PREVENTION REQUIRES ACCURATE REPORTING

The goal of no-fault investigations is accident prevention. Accident prevention is upstream work that improves the common causes of safety performance. To achieve this it is necessary to identify all contributing behavioral causes and address them through action plans involving behavioral observation and feedback.

Preventive work of this kind requires accurate accident and incident reporting. Even a quick consideration indicates the importance of accurate reporting. Used properly, accident and incident data has the potential to help:

- Plan immediate activities to improve systems.
- Determine which areas/systems/conditions need improvement.
- Decide where to allocate resources to make cultural changes for safety.

Many safety efforts are seriously flawed by the under-reporting of accidents and incidents. By making accident investigation dependent on single events, the traditional approach is misleading and unproductive. An investigation that focuses on a single event fails to take into account the system that produces the event. This is like investigating why a single tree fell in a storm. The factors that contribute to one tree falling need to be determined by investigating the pattern found across multiple data points, not single events.

A forester who asks questions about a single tree is going to get answers that apply only to that tree—its trunk was weak or rotten, the wind was high, the roots were uncared for. However, any forester who was satisfied with those answers would be a forester who had lost sight of the forest. Forest management requires a systems approach, one that inquires into the system causes of tree loss. Why haven't we previously checked root strength, soil characteristics, mineral content, water composition, and so on, for this forest? In the future what ongoing procedures could we take to improve these conditions in the entire forest system under our care? One very important ongoing procedure that effective foresters use is investigation across sufficient data points to show the pattern of forest as a whole. Then the system effects can be addressed.

Under-Reporting is the Norm

Most organizations have a policy that *all* injuries must be reported, no matter how minor they are. As we all know, policy is one thing—practice is another. What percentage of first-aid injuries are reported in your organization? What percentage of OSHA recordables? Since 1980 the author and his colleagues have asked these questions of all levels of numerous organizations. Typically the reporting rate for OSHA recordables is 70 to 85 percent, but for first aid injuries a reporting rate of 10 percent or lower is very common. Since recordables and first-aids are often preceded by the same at-risk behaviors, this low rate leaves a big gap in valuable decision-making data.

- *Question:* How many of the upstream events do you need to know about for accurate decision-making?
- *Answer:* All of them.

High-performing organizations such as the Eastman Chemical Company understand the need for improved reporting levels.

Using the behavioral safety process along with other measures, many units at the Texas Eastman Division of Eastman Chemical Company have significantly reduced their OSHA recordable rate while at the same time encouraging accurate reporting of total injuries including first aids. The Shops and Maintenance (S&M) area is a good example. The Shops and Maintenance safety effort had successfully freed itself of the accident cycle only to see its performance plateau in 1987-1989 (Fig. 13.2). In 1989 the S&M division implemented the behavioral safety process and has achieved continuous improvement since. Committed to genuine data gathering, workers were encouraged to scrupulously report first aids and near misses. At Texas Eastman, a first aid or non-recordable injury is one that does not require prescription drugs, sutures, work restrictions, or follow-up treatment. The campaign to increase reporting levels has been successful—since 1989 the ratio of total injuries to recordables has improved to healthy levels (Fig. 13.3). For more on context of this story, see Chapter 16.

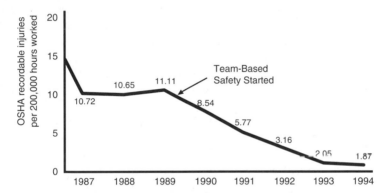

FIGURE 13.2   Texas Eastman's Shops and Maintenance Division incidence rate.

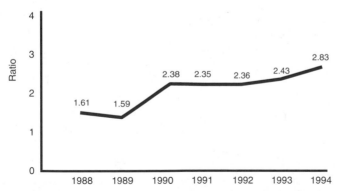

FIGURE 13.3   Texas Eastman's Shops and Maintenance Division ratio of total injury rate (including first aids) to OSHA injury rate.

Addressing Under-Reporting

Behavior analysis shows some important reasons that facilities do not get complete accident/incident reporting data (Fig. 13.4). For more on this subject, see Chapter 3.

Behavior: failure to report accidents/incidents

Antecedents: things that elicit the stated behavior from an employee

Consequences: outcomes that the employee experiences as a result of the stated behavior

Antecedents 1 through 6 are some of the things that trigger employees not to report accidents/incidents. The next step is to list the consequences of the stated behavior and note their values.

Consequences with the most power to influence behavior are the ones that are soon-certain-positive (SC+). In our example the SC+ consequences favor the behavior of NOT reporting incidents. Note: these are consequences delivered by the organization. In fact, disciplinary and reward systems account for all of these counterproductive consequences. The only naturally occurring consequence shown here that favors reporting is no. 6: Injury gets worse. But notice that this consequence is of the weakest kind, late-uncertain-negative (LU–). When the misuse of the disciplinary and rewards systems is combined—as here—with a misunderstanding of why it is important to report all incidents and accidents, the systemic result is under-reporting.

Integrated Accident Investigations

The behavioral approach to safety emphasizes the information-gathering function of accident investigations. Furthermore, the information is integrated into

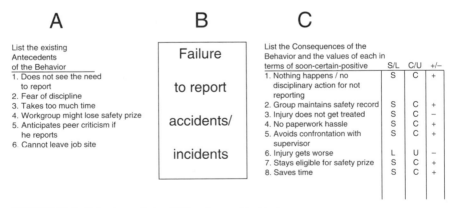

FIGURE 13.4   Behavior analysis of failure to report incidents.

the facility's inventory of critical safety-related behaviors. Taken together these two points go a long way toward removing disciplinary action from the investigative process. For instance, a primary behavioral recommendation is that the injured person be included on the investigating team as a source of important information.

Guided by principles of scientific analysis, behavior-based investigating and interviewing procedures focus on fact-finding aimed at preventing future incidents rather than on discipline and faultfinding. Since ongoing training is a key element of continuous safety improvement, there are many opportunities to address and change workforce Antecedents (Fig. 13.4) such as (1) does not see the need to report, and (5) anticipates peer criticism for reporting.

Management and Supervisor safety process training addresses Antecedents such as (2) fear of discipline and (4) workgroup might lose safety prize.

In addition, Safety Meeting problem-solving and action plans can address such matters as Antecedents (3) reporting takes too much time and (6) worker cannot leave job site to report.

The combined impact of training, problem solving, ongoing behavioral observations, and no-fault accident investigations is that the workforce consistently receives a very different set of consequences for reporting accidents/incidents. By systematically addressing both the Antecedents and the Consequences of the existing behavioral norm of Under-Reporting, the behavior-based approach resets the norm in favor of accurate, complete reporting

INVESTIGATION TEAMS AND ACCIDENT REVIEW COMMITTEES

In the behavior-based framework, the accident investigation team discovers and reports important factors of safety to the accident review committee, which considers strategic issues and formulates appropriate action plans. These include such things as

- adding identified behaviors to the facility's inventory of critical safety-related behaviors.
- developing additional training
- recommending changes to policies and procedures
- recommending changes to equipment and facilities

In this climate, the information-gathering function is healthy—leadership gets accurate, complete data. The groundwork is laid for a safety mechanism that is both responsive to emerging safety challenges and productive of well focused action plans to address them.

The Three Interlocking Activities

Although they are related, the three activities shown in Fig. 13.5 are best understood as distinct functions. First there is the ongoing behavioral observation process of problem identification and problem-solving based on observation data (see Chapters 8 and 9). This is a workgroup function.

When an investigation is called for, the accident investigation team draws upon facility behavioral inventory data and uses the tools of observation and behavior identification. In turn they report their findings to the accident review committee. The accident review committee is an oversight group that integrates the Investigation findings along with other data to develop appropriate action plans.

The Accident Investigation Team

As its name indicates, this function is a team-based activity. Comprising a leader with wage-roll employees, including trained behavioral observers, the accident investigation team

- meets on each accident
- investigates single events
- does observations to identify behaviors related to the accident
- reports to the accident review committee

The Accident Review Committee

Paralleling the activities of the accident investigation team, the accident review committee

FIGURE 13.5   Three interlocking activities.

- meets quarterly
- reviews data of numerous events looking for patterns and trends
- analyzes connections with the facility's behavioral inventory
- recommends appropriate interventions in action plans

The accident review committee is also team-based, including Safety Steering Committee members, Safety Department representatives, Management representatives, and wage-roll employees.

Using the Behavioral Inventory in Investigations

The accident investigation team uses the facility behavioral inventory to guide a re-enactment of the accident. Always taking precautions to avoid any repeat of the injury, they walk through the event in slow motion and with no power or energy applied to any equipment. The Team is looking for things that witnesses may have overlooked or failed to report during interviews.

Trained behavioral observers score the walk-through on the facility's inventory data sheet, seeking answers to the following questions:

- What items would observers have scored "at-risk" if they had been present at the scene immediately before the injury?
- Would an observer have been able to prevent the accident?
- Does the facility's behavioral inventory contain all of the critical behaviors that apply to this accident?

The answers to these and related questions are reported to the accident review committee for their quarterly consideration. On the basis of their analysis of ongoing behavioral observation data and reports from accident investigation teams, the review committee might add new item/s to the facility's observation data sheet. The Committee would add relevant behaviors to the observation data sheet and monitor safety performance to check for improvement.

CONCLUSION

Taken together, these three initiatives establish accident investigations as a part of a self-correcting safety mechanism with an emphasis on information-gathering rather than fault-finding.

By redefining accidents as unplanned results of behaviors that are otherwise rewarded or condoned by the culture of the facility, attention is focused on the upstream similarity between accidents and incidents. The effect is a safety effort committed to managing an injury-free culture.

By correcting the root-causes of under-reporting at a facility, the organization begins to have the benefit of information that is crucial to its accident prevention efforts.

And by establishing accident investigation and review on scientific principles of information gathering, analysis, and problem-solving, the behavior-based approach lays the groundwork for procedures that are both rigorous and no-fault—two signature traits a sustainable safety process. Rigor brings accountability and demonstrated performance improvement. No-fault drives out fear and fosters genuine involvement—two key actions for promoting continuous improvement.

14

Behavior-Based Safety in a Union Environment: A Natural Fit

In the question-and-answer periods during countless conference, seminar, and workshop settings since the early 1980s, one of the common questions addressed to the author and his colleagues has been, "The behavior-based approach to safety sounds great, but how well does it work at unionized facilities?"

When asked, most of the people who raise this matter acknowledge that their question is based on two generalizations:

1. A unionized workforce is harder to work with.
2. Unions are not interested in the behavior-based approach to performance issues.

Drawing on a decade of experience with fully-developed implementation efforts across industries and regions, the authors have found that the answer runs counter to both of these generalizations. Although it is true that implementation efforts at unionized facilities have their own dynamic, given the focus of the behavior-based process on adaptation versus adoption, each successful implementation effort is bound to have its own dynamic. And contrary to the expectations of many—the unions included, sometimes—it turns out that there is a very natural fit between behavior-based safety and the charter of labor unions.

USING COMMON SENSE TO MANAGE COMMON GROUND

Most unions have long agreed with one of the most central points of behavioral safety management, namely that safety is too important to be treated in an adver-

John Hidley, M.D., contributed to the development of this chapter.

sarial way. Once the membership understands it, another point of agreement is the strict reliance on the objectively observed performance of operationally defined behaviors—a hallmark of the behavior-based approach. This moves safety beyond the short-lived realm of personalities, fads, and programs. An equally important point of agreement is the focus on the upstream factors of incidents and injuries. In fact, this last point is represented by a cluster of desirable results that most unions identified long ago—results such as no-fault accident investigations, careful ongoing attention to work conditions, a safety culture in which the only acceptable injury rate is zero, employee input and representation at all phases of the process, and so on.

There are so many common-sense aspects to the foregoing list that it is really another way of saying that the concerns of unionized labor are the concerns of labor everywhere. Having said that, however, it is important to acknowledge that where labor-management relations have a history of struggle, behavior-based implementation includes a special emphasis on communication about the process and ownership opportunities for the workforce. If the trust level is low, better communication is required more frequently, and it is more important to have good, demonstrable results early in the implementation effort.

NOT BLAME, BUT THE FINAL COMMON PATHWAY

Blame is perhaps the single issue that best characterizes the adversarial side of workplace safety. In facilities, unionized or not, where there is the perception that workers get blamed for *their* accidents, very clear communication is needed during the presentation of the central reasons for tracking behavior. When they first hear that work behavior is going to be under ongoing scrutiny, most people think—and many people fear—that this is just another way of blaming workers for accidents and injuries. This worry arises from a common misunderstanding. It is true that one of the primary reasons to focus on behavior is that in a majority of cases unsafe worker behavior provides the final common pathway of the incident. However, this statement emphatically does not mean that the injury or accident is simply the fault of the employee. This is because the unsafe behavior is itself a part of the management system, implicitly encouraged or condoned by management. Therefore, to blame employees is counter-productive. The effective approach is the behavior-based process approach that identifies critical safety-related behaviors, measures the sheer mass of them, and manages their levels so that the system stops precipitating accidents (see Part 1 of this book for an overview of these issues.)

However, unions are often sensitive to the observation and feedback system. *Potential* exists in this part of the process for punitive action toward employees. Unions may have a natural resistance to what may be perceived as *ratting on my brother*. Workers may fear that their activity is being documented and filed for use against them. To address these concerns it is essential to present the non-punitive nature of the behavioral safety approach. Appropriate settings for open discussion with everyone must be built into the process. As is indicated by the company profiles presented here, communication about one set of concerns often leads to improved communication in other areas. In many cases, seeming obstacles bring opportunities with them. Sites that take advantage of these opportunities can increase the overall morale and level of trust within the organization.

Other key factors in the successful implementation of a behavior-based safety process include the ability to be responsive and to address problems as they arise; defining appropriate roles and responsibilities for everyone in the organization; major involvement of hourly employees in driving and implementing the process; and keeping safety out of the political arena (Fig. 14.1).

Since 1980, the author and his colleagues have implemented the behavioral approach to safety in diverse industrial settings in the United States, Canada and abroad. To preserve the anonymity of the companies described in this chapter, identifying information in each case history has been altered. Drawn from a large pool of implementation efforts, the following six case summaries illustrate four lessons of implementation at unionized facilities:

- Communication is the key.
- Roles and responsibilities must be defined.
- Solve problems immediately.
- Safety is nonpolitical.

Communication is the Key

Case 1. Starting in July 1990, a large paper manufacturing plant in Georgia involved over 200 union workers in two departments in the behavioral safety process. One of the facilitators of the process is an active member of the United Paperworkers International Union, and he confided that initially there were concerns that this new approach would be, "just another short-lived program"—or worse yet, that it would be used for disciplinary purposes.

- Involvement of union and management from the beginning
- Wage-roll workforce given major responsibility for steering and implementing the process
- Observations never the cause for disciplinary action
- Good fix-it program in place
- Communication on the spot when misunderstandings arise
- Willingness to make changes in the process when necessary
- Appropriate roles and responsibility for everyone
- Keeping safety out of the political arena

FIGURE 14.1 Key factors in successful implementation of a behavior-based safety process in unionized organizations.

A long history of labor-management tensions at this facility showed itself at the very beginning. A group of union members arrived at a meeting to be introduced to the process only to discover that without their knowledge they had been chosen to be on the steering committee. Their reaction to this bit of poor communication?—they were ready to leave the meeting then and there. The Consultant persuaded them to stay, however, and learn about the process.

At the close of that first session, management arrived with apologies for the mistake, and the union people agreed to continue on the steering committee. They decided, however, that they wanted to include one manager on the committee to act as a liaison and a resource person for management. By the time this plant was ready for kickoff, conflict between management and union had been laid aside by both parties in the area of safety. Of particular interest in this regard is the story of one union officer who had been selected to be facilitator of the process. He felt he had been chosen because, "The union membership knew if anyone would rock the boat, it would be me, and they wanted me to be on their side." Just before the kickoff, he heard from several union people that he was "too radical" and that his usually adversarial stance was endangering the success of the process.

As a result, he decided he would change his approach and he began to discuss safety with people he normally was unwilling to talk to. He and the site manager made a promise to each other that they would not let the process fail. This facilitator also decided to select some of the more antagonistic individuals to participate in observer training. Many of these people then volunteered to be behavioral observers. The 2.5-hour kickoff meetings were conducted in groups of no more than 20 people to foster participation by everyone. The atmosphere of openness resulted in candid discussion, and people were able to air their concerns thoroughly. Union leadership powerfully demonstrated its endorsement of the process by placing its logo alongside the company's on the list of critical behaviors and on the charts used to provide graphic feedback on observed behaviors. Both the company and union leadership are very proud of their mutual effort and success with the safety process.

An issue later brought to the attention of the steering committee at this facility highlights a common fear unions have concerning the observation process. An employee was terminated for "failure to follow established lock-out procedures." Even though the termination was in no way associated with the behavioral process, word spread quickly that it was related to an observation of the facility's inventory of critical behaviors. The situation was resolved by holding informational meetings for all workers. During these discussions the company stressed that the firing was a result of a supervisor's repeated warnings over several months and not the result of a behavior-based observation. The process was thus put back on track. Overall communications have improved to the point that in the words of one participant, "the union and the company have grown closer in all areas." "It's a great process all around." Currently this company is forming departmental steering committees plant-wide.

After implementation of the behavior-based safety process in this facility, seat belt use increased 28 percent in three months. As an interesting side note, one facilitator mentioned that, "Safety is now being carried home." Safety has become a personal priority, and many employees are now wearing safety shoes, hearing protection, safety glasses and other personal protective equipment at home while performing household chores.

Case 2. Another plant enjoying a successful behavior-based safety process is major producer of ketones belonging to an international chemical corporation. The plant currently has 40 observers, all members of various unions. According to a senior engineer and steering committee member, "Neither the company nor the union has experienced any problems implementing the process since informational meetings were held for union committees and company staff."

These meetings were held early in the implementation phase of the process, well before kickoff. The meetings were conducted by the steering committee, which presented the steps of the process in small groups composed of management and hourly workers together. Because everyone shared information and concerns early in the process, the rumor mill was effectively short-circuited and people felt included in the process. The most stubborn barrier encountered by the steering committee at this facility was the motivation of observers to make their scheduled number of observations. Workers did not believe that facility and equipment problems discovered during behavioral observation would be followed up by management. To address this concern, the company has recently begun sending personal thank-you notes for each observation made. This note also includes comments on how areas of concern tagged by the observer will be addressed and/or corrected. The steering committee reasons that this effort will "demonstrate results, and so increase the level of trust and commitment."

The engineer's advice to other unionized facilities considering the behavioral approach to safety is to, "make sure that they gain union buy-in before ever beginning." He added that this was a simple process in his company, because "Safety sells itself." But for the process to succeed, "It must be driven and controlled by the workforce because this builds ownership."

Define Roles and Responsibilities

A key part of implementation is determining what the appropriate role is for everyone. The particular dynamics of each organization will require somewhat different solutions. Much of this should be uncovered during the assessment stage of the process. In the assessment process, it is necessary to meet with the union officials who will be concerned with implementation to make sure they are in tune with what the process will require in terms of their support and leadership.

Case 3. In 1988, in approaching implementation of the behavior-based safety process at a major pharmaceutical company, the union had two very basic concerns: that the process would be used as a disciplinary tool, and that the data gathered would be used to eliminate jobs. Management, union leadership, and the Consultants sat down together and explored what the union required from the process so as to feel good about it. As a result, the company asked the union to select eight of the twelve members of the steering committee. They selected union officers, including the union vice-president. The other four seats were filled by first-line supervisors.

To address the union concern that the process not be used for disciplinary purposes, the company and the union drew up the following contract, "No data gathered through the behavioral process will be used for disciplinary purposes in any way or fashion." Both the union president and the company personnel director signed the contract and distributed copies to everyone, union workers and supervisors alike, at the kickoff meetings. In addition, the company asked the union to select all observers. The steering committee developed the criteria list by which the union officers made the selections. And in a completely separate process, the union put together a corps of Trainers chosen from hourly ranks. These Trainers conducted all of the observer training, including organizing and scheduling the classes, as well as follow-up sessions with the observers.

After the first group of observers was trained and the process was up and running, the original steering committee disbanded and individual steering committees were formed in the four departments. Most of the original steering committee members now sit on these department committees. Each department team now runs its own behavior-based safety process completely autonomously, with its own list of critical behaviors, observer training schedule, and so forth.

Previously, the relationship between management and the union at this facility had been extremely adversarial. In the early 1980s the company became interested in developing a more self-regulatory style of operation, with hourly workers taking responsibility for their own activity. The safety process offered a good opportunity to continue in that direction. The result was improvement not only in the area of safety but in union relations altogether.

Supervisor Involvement

Interestingly, it was the first-line supervisors who required some attention as the process developed. At the outset the only involvement of this group was with the four seats on the original steering committee. There had been virtually no communication about the process with the 45 other supervisors. First-line supervisors can be a pivot point for the operation of the safety process, and their involvement and support are essential. It was necessary to backtrack in this case, to give the supervisors clearly defined roles in the process, particularly in the safety-related maintenance program. They were also asked to lead the departmental safety meetings, collect observer concerns, and see that departments came up with action plans for safety based on observation data. The company installed measures of performance for supervisors that included the safety process as a part of their ongoing responsibility, making it clear that a real commitment to the process is expected from them. Because they now have a clear role in the process, these supervisors are synchronized with management and the union, and the process is proceeding effectively. The key is establishing appropriate roles and responsibilities for everyone.

Solve Problems Immediately

Case 4. This Gulf-state oil refinery has implemented the behavior-based safety process at six facilities throughout the U.S., four of which are unionized. Five hundred of the 600 employees currently involved in the process work in union shops. The division's Health and Safety Manager, who acts as their national coordinator for the process, made sure that implementation was carried out in the same manner at all locations, union or not. He stressed that, "This organization felt that it was imperative that all workers understand the process completely before beginning."

The major concern of the unionized employees was a fear that the process would be used to conduct time studies that would lead to workforce reductions. In fact, a previous time study had eliminated jobs, so their fears were based on recent experience. During the initial informational meetings, the company was able to demonstrate that there would be "no strings attached to this process", and it invited the employees to participate fully. Because the company was genuinely interested in safety and did not have anything "up its sleeve", management was able to reassure people and allay their fears. Later in the process a union member in one of the facilities refused to be observed. Management met with the employee and his union steward, carefully explaining the process completely and discussing the worker's reservations. They invited the employee to participate in any way he would like. He is now an active observer himself.

In situations where there is friction or resistance timely communication can eliminate mistrust. And a direct invitation to a reluctant person is often extremely effective.

Safety is Nonpolitical

Case 5. One issue touched on here deserves further discussion. Sometimes management's perception is that the union views the safety process as a bargaining tool to achieve other aims. In another major chemical plant, located in Texas, management decided to switch several jobs from one department to another. In the first department, these jobs included significant overtime possibilities, with the resulting increase in pay to those employees. In the new department, the jobs would be straight-time, and would result in rehiring people.

A union individual from the first department opposed the management move, and made safety the hostage in his fight. He persuaded his fellow workers in the department to withdraw from the behavior-based safety process unless the jobs were returned. They attempted to draw in the other departments but were unsuccessful in this. This troublesome conflict brought up emotions on both sides, but it was obvious to most participants that the safety process itself had nothing to do with the conflict and should not be sacrificed. Eventually the person who began the struggle backed off, the company moved the jobs to the new department, and the safety process remains in place.

Case 6. A Louisiana paper mill in the early stages of implementation recently decided to slow the process before launching the observer training phase. Union elections were coming up and the complex politics of the union at this facility had resulted in a tradition of almost complete turnover in union offices in every election. The steering committee didn't want to make safety a political issue for the election, so they slowed the pace of the Implementation effort. They hoped that introducing the behavioral safety approach to the newly elected leaders at the beginning of their three-year term would provide the opportunity for them to make a genuine journey with the process. With ample time for the process to take root, it may not be as vulnerable to the political ups and downs of the next election.

CONCLUSION

In most cases the success of a comprehensive accident prevention process is directly related to strong employee involvement and direction from the very beginning. When everyone feels involved, they can build a foundation that supports cultural change and continuous improvements in safety performance. Every organization has its unique concerns and characteristics. Ongoing communication, together with the tools provided by the behavior-based safety process, make it possible to exchange ideas and concerns, address fears on the part of management and the union as they arise, and build a company culture based on the shared commitment to safety. This often results in increased morale and improved communication over other issues in the company as well.

It is important to structure the process in each organization so that appropriate roles are assigned to management and union alike. In some facilities, the union president sits on the steering committee. This generally works very well. In some facilities, the observers are drawn entirely from union rosters. In others, there is supervisory participation as well. When the people responsible for the implementation of the process have a real interest in safety, the process is enhanced. It is essential to involve representation of all groups from the outset, beginning with the first introductory meeting with the Consultants. This provides the opportunity to deal with mistrust right from the beginning. When people make the decision jointly to adopt the process and then work together to build it, they share in the responsibility and in the commitment to make it work. This results in the improvements in the workplace that are effective in achieving an injury-free environment, as well as quality performance on all levels. It also establishes a working basis to solve problems as they arise.

There are many advantages to exempting safety from the political arena. Safety is not a legitimate area for management and unions to fight about, but one in which the common good is easily shared. This kind of cooperation is a positive tool that unions can offer to their membership and that management can offer to the union, to everyone's benefit.

15

Using Behavior-Based Methods to Sharpen and Sustain Adaptive Readiness for Safety

Adaptive readiness, the manifest ability to respond appropriately to a safety challenge, is a crucial but often unrecognized aspect of any effective, total approach to safety. Sharpening and sustaining workgroup adaptive safety readiness requires several things. First, it means that the employees understand the hazards that are critical to safety at their facility. They need to be able to identify the hazards associated with performing their jobs. Second, they need to know exactly which behaviors put them at risk and which behaviors are critical to their continued well-being throughout their working lives. Finally, to sustain adaptive readiness, the workgroup needs supporting systems that encourage and allow them to make continuous improvement in their safety performance—as time goes by identifying new and emerging behaviors that are critical to safety at their facility, and removing barriers to safe behavior.

SUSTAINING ADAPTIVE READINESS IN SAFETY CAN BE DIFFICULT

The reason it can be difficult to sustain an optimal level of adaptive readiness is that in some important ways our lives reward us for routine or automatic behavior. We are biologically predisposed toward automatic behavior since under many circumstances that kind of behavior is quite appropriate. In the course of a normal day everyone receives many soon-certain-positive consequences for doing many things on *automatic pilot*—reading and writing, typing, doing errands. These automatic behaviors can be valuable because they save time and energy. To remember what it was like to learn those routines in the first place, we can

Portions of this chapter were written by John Hidley, M.D., and Don Groover, CIH, CSP.

move them back into our adaptive, problem-solving mode by significantly altering how we do them. For instance, people who can type fluently (automatically) on a standard keyboard can become rank beginners again just by crossing their hands and trying to type. With the new alignment between fingers and keys our problem-solving capacity has to take over the task in an overload of hunt-and-peck typing.

PERFORMANCE PLATEAUS AND OLD HABITS

Of course, this is just an exercise—people don't take up cross-handed typing in an effort to improve their performance. However, there are cases where people do willingly take up something like cross-handed typing to improve their performance. These are cases where their habitual performance is no longer acceptable to them because it somehow puts them at risk of failure in an area where they very much want to improve. In sports, for instance, many people take tennis or golf or swimming lessons in order to help them unlearn old, automatic habits that put them at-risk of poor performance. Many self-taught athletes find that no matter what they do, the old way they picked up the skills of their favorite sport limits their performance.

In search of a remedy they buy new clubs or a new racket—no improvement. They play harder and longer—no improvement. They fine-tune their shoes and other gear—no improvement. They are stuck on a performance plateau. Given their current habits, their performance is as good as it will ever get. Either they have to settle for their performance plateau or else find a way to move their performance back into their adaptive readiness mode for a new period of learning and improvement.

PARALLELS WITH SAFETY

Safety performance has many important parallels with this situation. Even facilities that are company or industry safety leaders can see their performance level off and stall on a plateau. Needless to say, they find this performance plateau discouraging. These are companies that have already learned how to get beyond faultfinding and other adversarial reactions to incidents. They have also usually learned how to avoid the swings of the Accident Cycle by keeping their safety focus constant. This means that even when their incident rates happen to be low, they continue to maintain a high priority on safety. Nonetheless, their continuing efforts do not lead to continuous improvement.

The Old, Ineffective Model

We often hear frustrated managers and supervisors say, "We want our people to be safety conscious." This seemingly common-sense reliance on *safety con-*

sciousness can cover a multitude of confusions. Just what is this *safety consciousness* and what is it actually supposed to achieve in the way of safety performance? In practice, this statement about safety consciousness ranges all the way from vague descriptions like

1. *Safety is no. 1 at our facility.*

to the equally vague recommendation,

2. *If the workforce were as constantly aware of safety before an accident as they are after a major injury, this facility would not have any injuries.*

Statement no. 1 is counterproductive because it gives no objective guidance for workgroup performance. For instance, at the site in question exactly which behaviors represent safe work, and which critical behaviors put workers at-risk? In the absence of objective specification of *working safely* workers and managers alike can only fall back on subjective definitions. Continuous improvement has never been achieved in any field on the basis of a welter of subjective definitions of excellent performance. Organizations that lack objective standards for their statements about safety experience frustrating reruns of the Accident Cycle.

Statement no. 2 is also counterproductive. There is no such thing as healthy *constant awareness.* People who work at tasks requiring continuous vigilance usually work in short stints, and that is all they are doing—their *product* is alertness. Secret Service agents guarding the President, for instance, are not producing some other product and at the same time being alert.

Distracted by the Extraordinary

In fact, it is unnatural and unhealthy for people to work a 40-hour week producing goods and services and at the same time to live in a state of hypervigilance. Hypervigilance or constant alertness is actually a symptom of illness. In cities facing severe flooding, people may exert themselves and achieve extraordinary levels of group alertness and performance—raising levees, evacuating entire towns, taking measurements around the clock. However, these admirable achievements carried out under the extraordinary conditions of natural disaster are not a good model for how to sharpen and sustain adaptive readiness for safety. In a normal environment this level of alertness is called post-traumatic stress disorder. (For more on this, see Chapter 10.)

In business and industry the point is to make continuous improvement as *ordinary* as possible, not extraordinary. Managers distracted by the supposed object lessons of war and emergency rescue operations completely miss this point, only to find themselves caught in the spiralling need for bigger and bigger pep rallies, incentive programs, and, on the negative side, disciplinary measures.

Performance Is the Point—Consciousness Is Beside the Point

In business and industry the whole point is continuous improvement in safety performance, not in safety beliefs, attitudes, or a vague safety *consciousness*. The best way to get results in safety performance is to start with safety performance. An appeal to *safety consciousness* is as beside the point as an appeal to *quality consciousness*. Deming and other pioneers of quality settled this debate years ago. A workforce that is hyped up into a state of anxious watchfulness about quality produces the same defects as before. The only difference is that now they are more anxious about them. The same pattern shows up in safety.

Effective safety initiatives don't harangue people about safety, trying to raise their *safety consciousness*. Instead, the workgroup as a whole undertakes to measure and track behavior-based, upstream factors predictive of safety performance. Then through ongoing problem-solving, the workgroup practices the kind of adaptive performance-correction that brings continuous improvement (see Chapters 2 and 9).

The challenge therefore is both to sharpen and to sustain adaptive safety readiness both for the workgroup and the individual.

- To achieve improvement, this readiness is first sharpened and focused by behavior-based analysis of available data, including accident reports.
- To achieve continuous improvement, readiness is sustained through management support of peer-to-peer behavioral observation and feedback, and workgroup-centered problem solving based on accumulated behavioral data.

THE STEP-CHANGE TO CONTINUOUS IMPROVEMENT

Without pep rallies, incentive programs, and unpopular disciplinary measures, behavior-based safety sharpens and sustains the adaptive readiness of the individual and of the workgroup as a whole. Behavior-based safety helps employees who are new to their tasks by sharpening their responsiveness to the critical at-risk behaviors associated with their jobs. At the same time, the behavior-based approach helps veteran employees to sustain higher levels of adaptive readiness for safety by interrupting their habitual work routines periodically to reassess critical issues.

Many companies have adapted this behavior-based approach to achieve the step-change to continuous improvement in safety performance. Those safety leaders have gotten their results by focusing on behavior (performance) rather than wasting time on appeals to employee attitude, beliefs, and so-called *safety consciousness*, and by gearing the entire initiative to the relevant workgroup as a whole rather than worrying about *motivating* the individual to *take more responsibility for safety*. In addition, those successful companies have revisited and revised their old training assumptions about *rookies and veterans*.

Revisiting the Rookie and Veteran Concept

An informative example of these issues can be seen in what could be called the rookie and veteran concept. Some facilities mistakenly believe that they only have to worry about whether new employees (the rookies) know the hazards of a given task. The implication of this model is that because of inexperience *new hands* are most likely to perform at-risk behaviors, while veterans will know and recognize job hazards and therefore perform their tasks with a minimum of at-risk behaviors. Both of these assumptions are wrong. A common observation in industry is that both new employees and old hands are over-represented in the injury statistics.

It is true of course that employees require training on new jobs, but experience has shown that actual safety training needs are more complex than this. As Figs. 15.1 and 15.2 show, there are three important Stages of Task Familiarization—not merely the two assumed by the rookie and veteran concept.

- Stage 1—Anxiety (rookies)
- Stage 2—Maximum adaptive readiness
- Stage 3—Habituation (veterans)

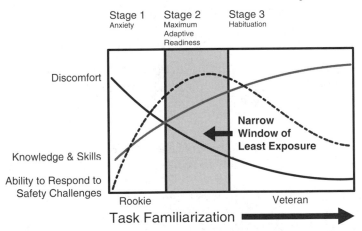

FIGURE 15.1 Task familiarization without behavior-based safety.

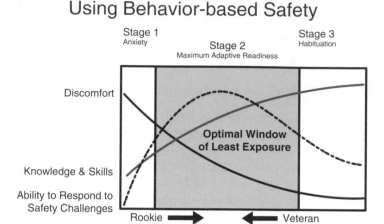

FIGURE 15.2 Task familiarization using behavior-based safety.

Furthermore, Fig. 15.1 illustrates the relations of these three Stages before the implementation of the behavior-based approach. Fig. 15.2 shows how the behavior-based approach widens Stage 2 to optimize the window of least exposure for both rookies and veterans. Using the old, ineffective model, both rookies and veterans suffer from low adaptive readiness to safety challenges. During Fig. 15.1, Stage 1, the Anxiety stage of task familiarization, when employees begin a job they are at risk of injury because

- their knowledge and skills level is low, and although
- their subjective discomfort about hazards is high, owing to their inexperience
- their adaptive readiness is low because it is *not sharply focused.*

On the other hand, veteran workers pass through Stage 2 and occupy the other extreme of the task familiarization time line. They are in Fig. 15.1, Stage 3, the Habituation stage of task familiarization, and they are also at risk of injury because

- their knowledge and skill level plateaus, and as
- their subjective discomfort and concern decreases they may become complacent, and
- their adaptive readiness *is not sustained* and it decreases with time.

Thus, like the rookies, the veterans are unable to respond appropriately to safety challenges. The complacency of Fig. 15.1, Stage 3 arises because, by this stage of acquaintance with their jobs, individual employees may have years of experience in which they happen not to have been harmed by the hazards and at-risk behaviors characteristic of their workplace. Under the old model of attitude-based safety, facilities have no ongoing way to interrupt this complacency and refocus the adaptive readiness of veteran employees.

Stage 2: The Window of Least Exposure

The behavior-based approach, on the other hand, continually engages these vet-eran employees for safety. Often they are some of the most knowledgeable peo-ple at a site, serving with distinction as safety steering committee Members and as observers gathering hard, behavioral data and giving their peers both verbal and charted feedback on performance. In other words, behavior-based safety finds a way to help veterans move regularly back into Stage 2 activities. In Stage 2, people exhibit maximum adaptive readiness for safety because

- their subjective discomfort about hazards is falling, and since
- their knowledge and skills level is rising, and with increasing experience
- their adaptive readiness is high because it is *sharply focused.*

During Stage 2, as employees are trained and spend time acquiring and refin-ing skills, they may become more knowledgeable about the hazards that surround the job. Because they are able to recognize and respond to these hazards, their level of subjective discomfort falls. It is in Stage 2 that individuals exhibit their maximum adaptive readiness and are best equipped to work without routinely performing at-risk behaviors. Stage 2 is the window of least exposure to risk for the individual.

The Old Model Ignores the Stage 2 Window of Least Exposure

In traditional safety efforts the important properties of Stage 2 are not identified and harnessed for continuous improvement. Various individual employees enter and pass at random through the Stage 2 window of least exposure, while other employees are either passing through the high exposure of Stage 1 or are taking out a lease on the high exposure of Stage 3. Since this transition is natural, it is remarkable that facilities ever break free from the Accident Cycle.

Under the circumstances it would not be surprising if more companies did not just rest on their laurels, giving up the attempt to make the step change to contin-uous improvement in safety. To their credit, however, most facilities do want to achieve continuous improvement and their performance plateau is very frustrating to them. Not surprisingly, they do what many frustrated amateur athletes do—they throw money and equipment at the problem, and they try harder. In their willingness to experiment, they run through numerous off-the-shelf programs. By their own accounts, the companies that have gone on these safety shopping sprees often have little to show for their efforts except the old give-aways and gimmicks.

Ongoing Process versus Off-the-Shelf Program

It is not the focus on safety that is wrong—that is both admirable and right. The trouble is that off-the-shelf programs do not help a particular facility to sharpen and sustain maximum levels of individual and workgroup adaptive readiness. By definition, off-the-shelf programs have been developed somewhere else by some-one else. When a facility merely buys and adopts a program, it is pretty much in the position of the self-taught tennis player who is trying to improve a weak backhand by buying a new racquet.

The racquet is not the problem. Equipment fixes are not the remedy. Nor is try-ing harder—which means doing more and more of the same old thing. What is needed is a system of improvement—a process designed to maximize employee adaptive readiness. For performance improvement there is no substitute for an ongoing process that identifies behaviors critical to success and then supplies feedback on how well we are performing those critical behaviors. This moves the performance back into the mode of adaptive readiness. That is what the helpful tennis coach does. Where safety performance is at issue, this requires a system-atic way of identifying and counteracting cultural forces that build and sustain bad safety habits.

Optimizing the Window of Least Exposure

In the course of implementing behavior-based safety, a facility takes the follow-ing steps toward maximum adaptive readiness for safety. Personnel must

1. identify the hazards that are characteristic of their jobs
2. know exactly which behaviors put them at risk and which behaviors are critical to their continued well-being throughout their working lives
3. give and receive workgroup-based, peer-to-peer feedback on these behav-iors, and
4. make continuous improvement in their safety performance—constantly identifying new and emerging behaviors that are critical to safety at their facility as time goes by, and using observation data to remove barriers to safety

Points 1 through 4 are addressed in an integrated way, establishing ongoing safety measurement and feedback procedures by peer review and buy-in, and using the resulting data for problem-solving and continuous improvement.

In addition, this procedure sharpens and sustains the adaptive safety readiness of an entire workgroup or facility, enlarging the *Window of Least Exposure* for both rookies and veterans.

Figure 15.2 shows the modifications brought to the Stages of Task Familiarization. New employees move much more readily into adaptive readiness for safety. This is because their on-the-job training now includes the facility's inventory of critical, operationally defined behaviors. This inventory objectively pinpoints the critical at-risk behaviors that characterize the workplace. On the basis of this same inventory, new employees are regularly given performance feedback by peers who are specially trained observers. Contrary to the haphazard methods of attitude-based approaches, rookies introduced to their new tasks using behavior-based principles find that

- their subjective discomfort level falls rapidly and stays low
- their knowledge and skills level rises rapidly
- their ability to respond to safety challenges improves rapidly

Consider also the differences for veterans. Instead of experiencing complacency and a corresponding decline in their adaptive readiness, their ability to respond appropriately to safety challenges stays at a high, effective level. To achieve this kind performance for both new employees and veterans, there is no substitute for the behavior-based approach. The old attitude-based methods focused on heightening awareness and raising consciousness cannot succeed. The reason is that adaptive readiness is not the same thing as awareness.

Adaptive Readiness Is Not the Same as Awareness

Many facilities have been misled into thinking that the solution lies in making people more conscious of safety. The problem, however, is not the level of awareness at any given moment but the level of adaptive readiness. For instance, a person can be aware of many things and still not be responsive to them. Conversely, a person may be on *automatic pilot* or unaware and still respond very appropriately. Think of the many times any one of us has driven home from work *on automatic*. We may not be able to give a detailed account of the drive home, even though we have just made the drive, and yet we drove safely without performing at-risk behaviors. This is an example of safe habituation—we could call it Stage 3 driving.

Adaptive readiness is the manifest ability to respond appropriately to safety challenges as they arise. Workgroups that make the step-change to continuous improvement foster and exercise this capacity for adaptive readiness. There is nothing wrong with being habituated to do the right thing. This is the way that pilots follow a rote check-out procedure in preparation for take-off. The important thing is that they are responsive to wrong signals. If a gauge is wrong, pilots move immediately from the Habituation of Fig. 15.2, Stage 3 back into Fig. 15.2, Stage 2 maximum adaptive readiness. This flexibility results from being fluent in an objectively defined checklist that is designed to be compatible with adaptive readiness. In behavior-based safety the inventory of critical behaviors serves this function. Employees get ongoing input that is important to them from their peers. Doing a behavioral observation is like running through a checklist of important factors. This kind of external input brings flexibility even to a workgroup made up primarily of veterans. Instead of becoming more and more rigid in their work practices, the entire workgroup behaves the way pilots do—they follow their habitual procedures, and when a safety challenge arises they respond appropriately. Habituation only poses a problem when one loses the flexibility to move readily from Stage 3 to Stage 2.

Barriers to Flexibility

In most facilities there are barriers to flexible movement back and forth between Stage 3 Habituation and Stage 2 adaptive readiness. Rigidity is a primary source of these barriers. Company culture may be rigid. This is the case at facilities where wage-roll personnel know that they are not supposed to engage in the kind of workplace problem-solving that happens during adaptive readiness for safety. The culture has rigidly defined that kind of problem-solving as a management function. Or the work routines themselves might be very rigid, allowing no leeway for adaptive readiness. Or even if the culture and work routines happen to be more flexible, the informal habits of the facility may not offer a way to interrupt standard operating procedures for periodic review. Finally, individuals may be rigid in their approach to their work practices.

Taken by itself, any one of these sources of rigidity poses an important barrier to flexible return to Stage 2 adaptive readiness. Usually where one of these barriers is operating, the others will be at work, too. It is crucial therefore to have a safety strategy that is able to address any combination of these barriers at the same time.

Rigid Culture

Behavior-based safety is built on employee involvement. Wage-roll personnel are active at every phase and every level of the assessment and implementation effort at a facility. This approach addresses and dissolves the idea that wage-roll personnel have no need to exercise problem solving and adaptive readiness for safety.

Rigid Work Routines

A behavioral approach systematically identifies, analyzes, and develops action plans to solve problems related to work routines. It builds a computerized data base specifically designed for this purpose. For instance, if any work routine shows up as either the antecedent or consequence of an at-risk behavior, it will be targeted for improvement by workgroup action plans.

Interruption of Rote Practices

Using the inventory of critical behaviors, observers sample workplace practices in an ongoing feedback and data collection effort. The observers of a facility therefore act to interrupt established practices. Their inventory observation datasheet incorporates insights gleaned from facility incidents, and in addition to using that resource, observers typically also engage in situation-centered observation. This kind of observation looks afresh at rote practices, analyzing them for at-risk elements.

Rigid Individual

Resistance to change is a part of human nature. Rather than wishing it away or denying its influence, a behavioral approach acknowledges resistance to change and works with it. An individual's willingness to change varies from time to time, and some individuals are normally more rigid than others. Nevertheless, even resistant individuals gradually shift as their workgroup changes and as specific techniques are engaged to make change easier.

Things that decrease rigidity and increase flexibility include

- communication
- cooperation
- interruption that is relevant and that calls attention to the important safety issues

Behavior-based safety is strong on communication, cooperation, and behavioral observation is a kind of formal interruption of routine practices.

Communication

Safety communication is a clearly defined function of the ongoing safety initiative. observers regularly communicate with their peers to provide feedback on the behaviors they have observed. The accumulating observer data is also communicated on posted charts. Furthermore, the observation data is computer analyzed in safety meetings for safety problem solving. Action plans that result from workgroup problem-solving are communicated back to the steering committee and the observers for follow-up. This kind of communication fosters flexibility in the safety culture of a site.

Cooperation

Another significant achievement of the behavior-based approach is that it helps facilities reformulate safety as an non-adversarial field for action. Side by side with plant managers, union presidents support this process. Typically the line organization and wage-roll personnel serve together on steering committees. Cooperation of this kind encourages flexibility in work routines.

Relevant Interruptions

Behavioral observation is both situation-centered and inventory-centered. This means that even veterans are regularly observed in their work habits. An observer who notes the beginnings of complacency about the items on the inventory, gives feedback that *interrupts* the at-risk behavior in question. This feedback moves rookies *forward* and veterans b*ack* into adaptive readiness, Fig. 15.2, Stage 2. The movement increases flexibility of response.

The act of observation also *interrupts* the observer. Behavior-based observation is a highly skilled activity, a craft. When people put on their observer *hats* they see their own behavior in new ways, too. Practices and procedures that they may have previously taken for granted out of past habituation, they re-think in light of their site-specific inventory. This activity moves them back into adaptive readiness, Fig. 15.2, Stage 2.

SHARPENING WORKGROUP ADAPTIVE READINESS

Even veteran employees learn from the behavior-based perspective. The behavior-based process approach to safety offers uniquely apt ways of recognizing the hazards at a facility. One of the first tasks undertaken by the steering committee at a facility is the development and review of an inventory of behaviors critical to accident prevention at the site (Chapter 7). In the author's experience, even the people most keenly interested in safety at a site are usually mistaken about the cluster of behaviors that are the final common pathway of the majority of their incidents. Anecdotes and hunches have proved to be misleading in all cases we have observed. This is a remarkable state of affairs. People who voice skepticism about the value of doing a thorough behavioral analysis of accident reports almost always feel very sure that they can predict what the critical behaviors are from their own experience, from anecdotal evidence—in effect, from their memory and their *common sense.*

A combined group of managers and veteran wage-roll employees are typically the best source of knowledge about these behaviors. Wage-roll employees often serve with distinction on the steering committee that conducts a behavioral review of facility accident reports to produce an inventory of critical behaviors. Their contribution to this important safety resource for their workplace is one of the more important instances of employee involvement in the safety process. During review meetings, the steering committee presents the first draft of the facility's inventory of critical behaviors, getting peer input and buy-in for the process approach, and also using the occasion to improve site-wide recognition of operative hazards significantly impacting workgroup safety performance.

During an effectively facilitated inventory review meeting, the participants are continually asked to consider the impact of the behaviors in the inventory. The guiding question throughout the meeting is, "Will we be safer if we stop performing the at-risk behaviors listed on the inventory?" One important consequence of this focus is that during inventory review meetings critical safety-related behaviors are sharpened and defined for workgroup problem-solving. Until then, employees may never have considered the importance of the many seemingly mundane behaviors that have actually injured them over the years and which continue to put them at-risk of injury.

However, as important as this training is in sharpening workgroup adaptive readiness, sustaining readiness and changing behavior requires workgroup-based, peer-to-peer behavioral observation and feedback. Because of the natural sequence of habituation shown in Fig. 15.1, such readiness cannot be sustained from inside the individual as an act of will or as a consequence of insight. Human nature is such that the automatic pilot is supposed to take over. Attitude-based programs aimed at inducing in the employees a kind of constant hypervigilance or super awareness are contrary to nature, and are therefore destined to fail. The challenge is not to confront our nature but to work with it. This is the behavior-based approach. For instance, resistance to change is characteristic of human nature. This means that both rookies and veterans exhibit resistance to change. In terms of safety, resistance to change shows up as subjective discomfort in new situations and as habituation in routine situations. The behavior-based safety strategy effectively addresses both of these at the same time.

For Rookies

Knowing that rookies naturally experience an unproductive period of generalized subjective discomfort, behavior-based safety makes sure that their developing habits are sharpened and attuned to site-specific factors. This approach dramatically decreases the time that new employees spend in Stage 1, quickly *graduating* them to Stage 2, thus widening the Stage 2 window on its *leading edge*.

For Veterans

Knowing that Stage 3 *automatic pilot* takes over any routine function, behavior-based safety sustains adaptive readiness in veterans through ongoing observation and feedback on their performance, and by increasing the culture's flexibility through systematically identifying and solving problems that push people into bad habits. This strategy promotes in veterans a flexible return to Stage 2 problem-solving, thus widening the Stage 2 Window on is *trailing edge.*

The overall effect is to widen Stage 2 for all employees and to maintain a higher level of adaptive readiness throughout Stage 3, thus expanding the Window of Least Exposure into Stage 3, see Fig. 15.3.

SUSTAINING WORKGROUP ADAPTIVE READINESS

Ongoing Behavior-Based Observation and Feedback

Regular behavioral observation is the activity that promotes ongoing workgroup learning and knowledge about the hazards recognized in the facility's inventory of critical behaviors (Chapter 8.) The result is an ongoing safety mechanism that is proactive, data-driven, and focused on continuous improvement in safety performance. The mechanism brings both the Rookie and the Veteran into Stage 2. In this way the entire workgroup regularly interacts with its own members so as to sharpen its knowledge of hazards and to sustain its practice of safe behaviors (Flow Chart, Fig. 15.4.)

As systematic behavioral observation becomes routine, the workgroup begins to receive regular feedback in both verbal and charted form. At this point most workgroups make fairly steady progress on a number of behavioral inventory items as they *clean up* areas of their performance that are relatively easy for them to address. As this performance improvement gains momentum, most workgroups also discover that they have some performance areas that stubbornly resist improvement. These are the *barriers to safety* at the site.

Addressing Barriers to Safety

Barriers to safety are the aspects of the safety culture that impede improvement, or send the message that at-risk behavior is acceptable or even expected. These organizational habits are what people refer to when they shrug and say, "That's just how we do things around here." Sometimes these workplace forces or elements are so overwhelming to the individual that he cannot perform the behavior safely. A barrier either makes it impossible or it so discourages workers from doing it safely that, in spite of the fact that they are sharply aware of the behavior, they don't even try.

The answer of effective safety initiatives therefore is to put these barriers into the problem-solving loop of both the management and the employees. But this can only be done when there is a systematic method for gathering and analyzing behavioral data to identify these barriers to safe performance. When this is done, observation and feedback become even more powerful. The result is that even the cultural barriers to safety are open to analysis, problem solving, and action planning. This expands the employees' sphere of adaptive readiness, in effect widening Stage 2, Fig. 15.2. When the safety initiative has this kind of management involvement and support, employee support is a natural consequence. That is because the commitment to continuous improvement has become embedded in the routines of the safety culture itself. This is when continuous improvement becomes *ordinary,* flexibility becomes habitual, and alertness is *institutionalized.*

SUMMARY

By means of the behavior-based employee selection, safety training, and incident investigation, many companies have made solid gains in their performance. Part IV of this book presents the case histories and results of some of those companies.

Part IV

Results and Case Histories

16

Results: An Outcome Study of Incidence Rates and Workers' Compensation Costs

HISTORICAL BACKGROUND

In the late 1970s and early 1980s, three factors occurred independently that led to the development of behavior-based safety:

1. Academic psychologists started research on the use of behavioral techniques for accident prevention. Komaki et al. (1978) were among the first researchers to apply behavioral techniques to industrial safety when they used a behavioral approach to improve worker safety in manufacturing environments. Their studies developed and used operational definitions of safety-related behaviors to observe and record behavior, and to give feedback. Results showed that identified behaviors improved when feedback was given. With generally positive findings, academic research has continued in the use of behavioral strategies to improve safe behavior in the workplace.

2. Procter and Gamble developed a behavior-based system for managing safety on a corporation-wide basis.

3. In 1979, the author and Dr. John Hidley, a physician, developed an applied behavioral approach to industrial safety based in part on Komaki's research. In the course of the next several years, they expanded and refined behavior-based methods for use in industrial settings, with emphasis on the practical issues facing the managers who wished to implement this approach. The author and his associates discovered that verbal feedback was most effective in an industrial setting. They developed a standardized

Kristen Van Zee contributed to the development of this chapter.

method for extracting relevant operational definitions of behaviors (Krause, Hidley, and Lareau, 1984) from incident reports. They also developed procedures for site assessment and for implementing a behavior-based safety system.

In 1985, the author and his associates worked with chemical industry clients who were heavily involved in Total Quality Management / TQM. The behavioral approach proved compatible with TQM, relying on similar scientific principles. At those companies significant change occurred in the implementation roles and responsibilities. Instead of being supervisor-driven, implementations were employee-driven. This change solved a problem previously unaddressed; namely, the division created when supervisors attempted to *change the behavior* of the workers reporting to them. In the new model, workers at the first level were engaged in the process of upgrading their own standards.

The result of this shift to employee-driven implementations was that companies previously caught on the accident cycle (Fig. 16.1) or stalled on a performance plateau (Fig. 16.2) were able to make the step-change to continuous improvement. By 1986, the combined elements had evolved into a highly sophisticated and practical methodology.

PRELIMINARY CLASSIFICATION

In August of 1994, demographic and outcome data were collected from sites that had implemented the employee-driven behavioral process between 1986 and 1994 with the support of the author and his associates. Among this pool of 181 sites, 60 implemented after August, 1993, and 25 were expected to implement

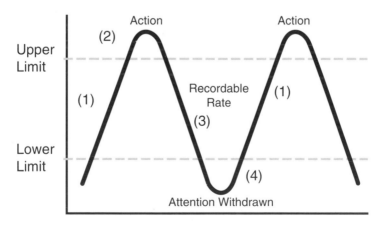

FIGURE 16.1 The accident cycle.

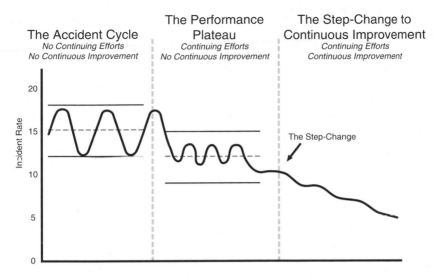

FIGURE 16.2   The three phases of safety performance.

before December, 1994. Based on assessments by the author and his colleagues, the remaining 96 client sites were grouped into four categories:

1. Inactive
   - Not making behavioral observations
2. Regular Success
   - Site currently active in the behavior-based approach, Making observations
   - Overall, the company regards the project as successful
   - Site achieves decreases in accident rates
3. Model Success, i.e., site meets criteria for Regular Success, and in addition:
   - Significant decrease in incident frequency—usually the incident variable is total OSHA recordables, but other variables are considered.
   - There is an active oversight process in place. This may be an entire steering committee, a single individual, or an organization of team leaders.
   - The author and his colleagues feel that the behavior-based safety process will last over the long term even if circumstances at the site change.
4. Unclassifiable
   - Any company not in the implementation phase for at least one year at the time of the study
   - Any company that was still making observations but did not view the process as successful

- Companies no longer in operation were categorized as unclassifiable, even where they had achieved significant reductions in injuries during operation.
- Companies for whom data was not available.

Of 181 client sites active at the time of the study, 86 were analyzable because they had been working with behavior-based safety for at least a year. Of the 86, 42 were rated Regular Successes, 36 were Model Successes, and 8 were Not Successful, Fig. 16.3.

STATISTICAL TESTING

As an independent check of success classification, injury data was collected whenever possible. Testable data was supplied by 23 sites. Of those, 19 had been rated as model successes—ratings were confirmed in each case by statistically significant reductions in injury rates at each site. More than 50 companies sent data in one form or another. These data were screened using the following criteria:

- The site had been using the behavioral process for at least one year.
- The data covered a minimum of two time periods before implementation and two subsequent time periods.
- Data did not violate statistical independence.

The 23 data sets that met these criteria and were therefore included in the study represented the following industries:

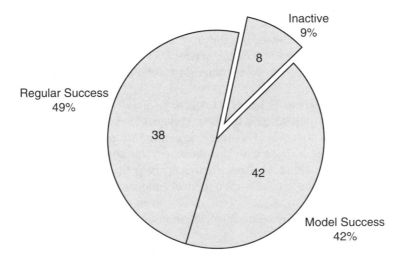

FIGURE 16.3   The overall success rate is over 90 percent.

- electronics industry—2 sites
- metals—3 sites
- paper—3 sites
- petroleum—4 sites
- chemicals—11 sites

These proportions are roughly representative of the different industries in the population of companies who have implemented employee-driven behavioral safety systems.

Summary of Findings—Incidents

Comparisons of pre-implementation incident levels to post-implementation incident levels revealed consistent and substantial decreases in incidents following implementation. Twenty-two companies achieved either significant or highly significant reductions in accidents, while one company's reduction approached significance, Fig. 16.4. Figure 16.5 shows that ranging from one to four years after implementation, the average reduction from baseline increases from 34 to 71 percent. Individual results are presented in Fig. 16.6 though Fig. 16.28.

Chemical Companies

Figures 16.6 through 16.16 show significant and highly significant improvements across 11 chemical companies. These sites are from various regions of the U.S.,

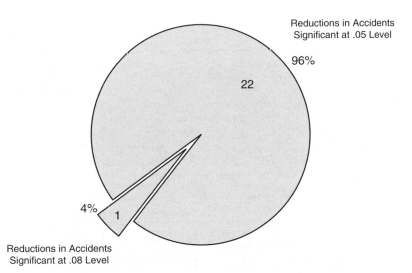

FIGURE 16.4 All 23 fully supported implementations tested showed substantial accident reduction.

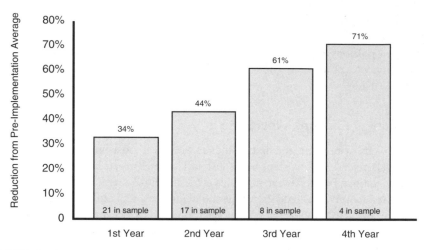

FIGURE 16.5   Average reductions in incident frequencies 1 through 4 years after implementations of behavior-based safety.

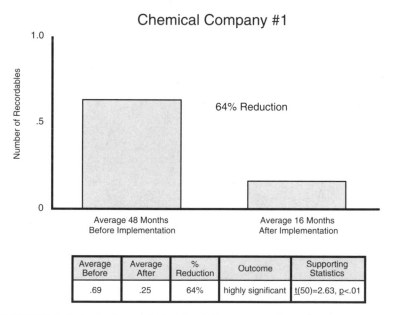

Average Before	Average After	% Reduction	Outcome	Supporting Statistics
.69	.25	64%	highly significant	$t(50)=2.63$, $p<.01$

FIGURE 16.6   Reduction in recordables, chemical company no. 1.

from Rhode Island to California, by way of Ohio, Virginia, Florida, Tennessee, Arkansas, Mississippi, Louisiana, and Texas. The typical products of these sites range from bulk alkali and acid stocks for the petroleum and natural gas industries, to specialty plastics and resins for computer consoles, surgical equipment, films, fibers, and emulsions. These sites have both union and non-union workforces. Where unions are present, shop stewards and other union officials are very active in the site's behavior-based safety initiatives.

In the 16 months after implementing behavior-based safety, chemical company no. 1 (Fig. 16.6), already a safety leader with a 0.69 recordable rate, achieved a highly significant 64 percent reduction to a 0.25 recordable rate.

At chemical company no. 2 (Fig. 16.7), in the 15 months after implementation the incident rate fell 45 percent to an incident rate of 3.55, relative to the 6.48 rate of the preceding 12-month period.

Coming off a performance plateau of a 15.32 total injury rate, chemical company no. 3 (Fig. 16.8) began the step-change to continuous improvement with a highly significant 20 percent reduction to a total injury rate of 12.21.

Chemical company no. 4 (Fig. 16.9) reported its improvement in the number of accidents versus accident rates. The 36 percent improvement of the site, from 39.16 to 25.25 accidents per quarter, means that in the four quarters following implementation the workforce experienced 55 fewer accidents than in the year preceding (39.16 minus 25.25 = 13.91, and 13.91 × 4 = 55.64).

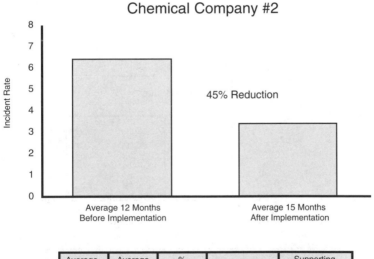

Average Before	Average After	% Reduction	Outcome	Supporting Statistics
6.48	3.55	45%	highly significant	$t(25)=8.55$, $p<.01$

FIGURE 16.7   Reduction in recordables, chemical company no. 2.

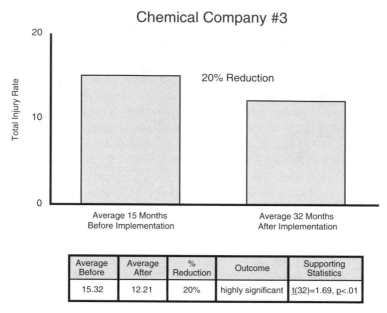

Average Before	Average After	% Reduction	Outcome	Supporting Statistics
15.32	12.21	20%	highly significant	$t(32)=1.69$, $p<.01$

FIGURE 16.8   Reduction in total injury rate, chemical company no. 3.

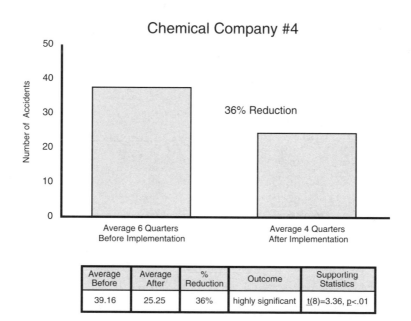

Average Before	Average After	% Reduction	Outcome	Supporting Statistics
39.16	25.25	36%	highly significant	$t(8)=3.36$, $p<.01$

FIGURE 16.9   Reduction in number of accidents, chemical company no. 4.

Chemical company no. 5 (Fig. 16.10) did even better, with a 61 percent reduction in its injury rate in the three years after implementation relative to the three years before implementation. Down from 17.31 to 6.8, this improvement in the site's injury rate represents significant savings in both direct and indirect costs.

Chemical company no. 6 (Fig. 16.11) illustrates another aspect of continuous improvement using behavior-based safety. This site's injury rate is sufficiently low that they have begun to measure their performance by their first aid cases. This is a common trend in successful employee-driven behavioral initiatives. As both the severity and frequency of incidents decreases, the site's workgroups manage their performance by less severe events such as first aid cases.

Chemical companies no. 7 through 11 (Figs. 16.12 through 16.16) show gains ranging from 19 to 84 percent improvement.

Electronics Companies

Specializing in the manufacture and repair of electrical motors and generators, and in the production of inductive ballast for fluorescent lighting, electronic companies 1 and 2 were experiencing serious ergonomics problems along with their other safety challenges. By tailoring their respective behavior-based safety initiatives to their need for ergonomics safety, both sites made significant gains.

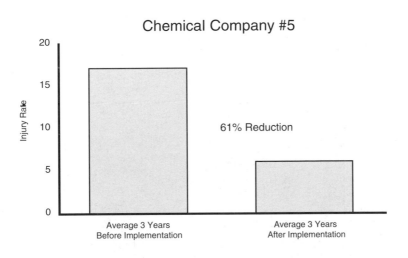

Average Before	Average After	% Reduction	Outcome	Supporting Statistics
17.31	6.8	61%	highly significant	$t(4)=3.43, p<.01$

FIGURE 16.10 Reduction in injury rate, chemical company no. 5.

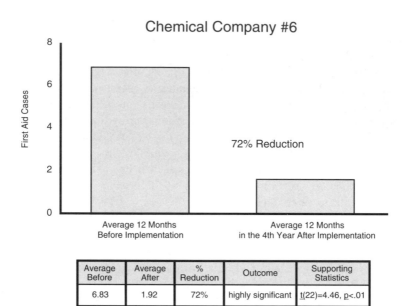

FIGURE 16.11 Reduction in first aid cases, chemical company no. 6.

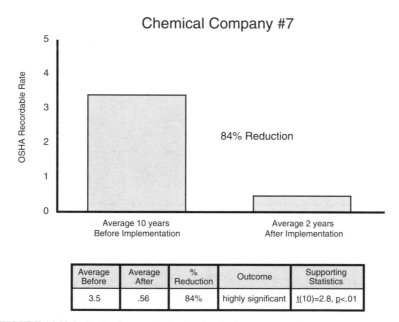

FIGURE 16.12 Reduction in recordable rate, chemical company no. 7.

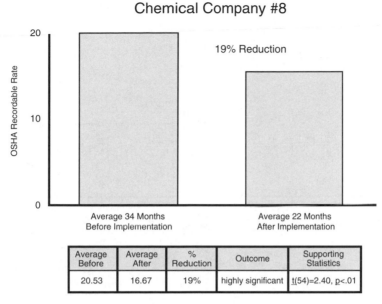

FIGURE 16.13 Reduction in recordable rate, chemical company no. 8

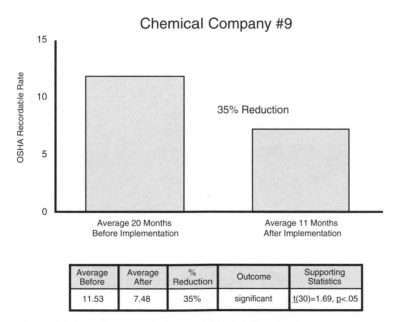

FIGURE 16.14 Reduction in recordable rate, chemical company no. 9.

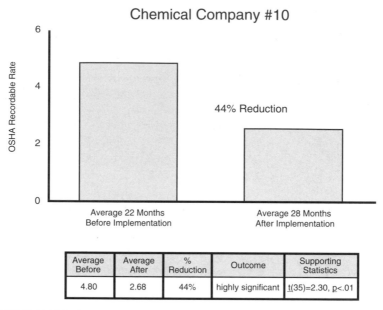

Average Before	Average After	% Reduction	Outcome	Supporting Statistics
4.80	2.68	44%	highly significant	t(35)=2.30, p<.01

FIGURE 16.15 Reduction in recordable rate, chemical company no. 10.

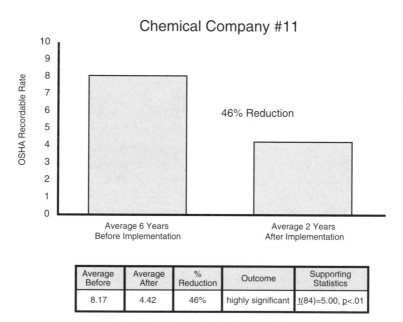

Average Before	Average After	% Reduction	Outcome	Supporting Statistics
8.17	4.42	46%	highly significant	t(84)=5.00, p<.01

FIGURE 16.16 Reduction in recordable rate, chemical company no. 11.

At company no. 2 (Fig. 16.18), the incident rate was down 35 percent over the three years after implementation, and the record was even better at the sister site (Fig. 16.17)—down an impressive 68 percent.

Metals Companies

The three metals companies represented here are all producers of aluminum. Located in the mid-West, Texas, and California, the three sites each include heat treatment equipment if not smelters, and the working hazards are numerous. Each of these sites cut its injury rate by more than half:

- metals company no. 1 (Fig. 16.19)—66 percent reduction in the lost time accident rate
- metals company no. 2 (Fig. 16.20)—59 percent reduction in OSHA record-ables
- metals company no. 3 (Fig. 16.21)—52 percent reduction in the serious injury rate

Paper Companies

Once again, the paper companies represented here are from very different regions of the U.S.—Washington state, Louisiana, and Minnesota. Working daily with huge rolls of product, paper workers are notorious for their lost fingers and

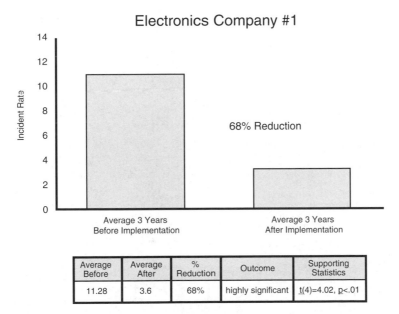

Average Before	Average After	% Reduction	Outcome	Supporting Statistics
11.28	3.6	68%	highly significant	$t(4)=4.02$, $p<.01$

FIGURE 16.17 Reduction in incident rate, electronics company no. 1.

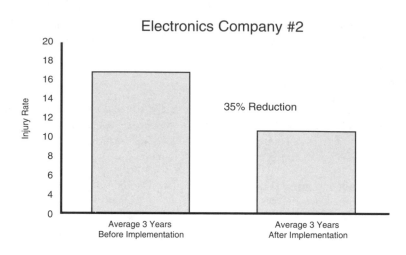

Average Before	Average After	% Reduction	Outcome	Supporting Statistics
17.13	11.13	35%	significant	$t(4)=2.30$, $p<.05$

FIGURE 16.18 Reduction in injury rate, electronics company no. 2.

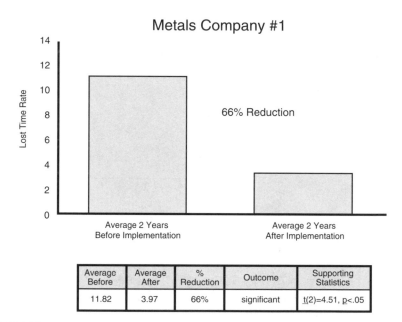

Average Before	Average After	% Reduction	Outcome	Supporting Statistics
11.82	3.97	66%	significant	$t(2)=4.51$, $p<.05$

FIGURE 16.19 Reduction in lost time accidents, metals company no. 1.

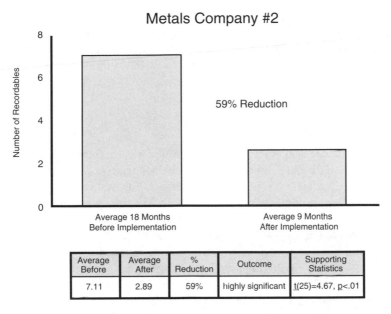

FIGURE 16.20 Reduction in recordables, metals company no. 2.

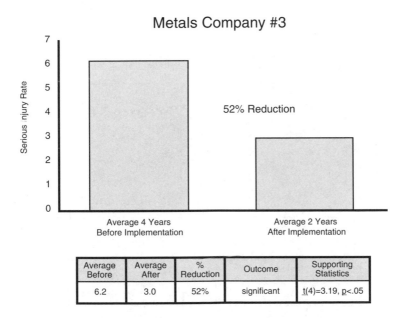

FIGURE 16.21 Reduction in serious injury rate, metals company no. 3.

thumbs. By using operational definitions of safe and at-risk behaviors, the safety initiatives at these three sites (Fig. 16.22 through Fig. 16.24) have been able to key on the behaviors that preserve the safety and well-being of the workforce. With significant reductions in their incident rates, these three sites have seen improvements ranging from 18 percent (Fig. 16.22) to 38 percent (Fig. 16.23) or 35 percent (Fig. 16.24).

Petroleum Companies

In another instance of geographic diversity, petroleum companies from the North Slope of Alaska to the Gulf of Mexico have used behavior-based safety to make remarkable gains in their OSHA recordable rates. With before-implementation rates below 10.0, each of these sites was a safety leader to begin with, as is apparent in the case of company no. 1 (Fig. 16.25). Their 6-month recordable rate before implementation was a low 1.5, and they went on to improve by 67 percent, achieving a 0.5 rate in the six months following implementation.

Company no. 2 (Fig. 16.26) improved its performance by 37 percent, dropping from a 4.56 rate to 2.88, and company no. 3 (Fig. 16.27) achieved a 52 percent reduction over three years, from a 5.36 recordable rate to a rate of 2.56.

In the case of company no. 4 (Fig. 16.28), we see the number of recordables. Their 48 percent reduction translates to a significant number of accidents that were prevented from happening.

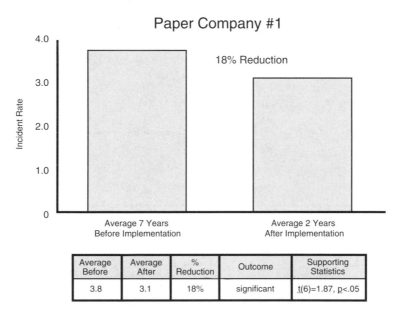

Average Before	Average After	% Reduction	Outcome	Supporting Statistics
3.8	3.1	18%	significant	$\underline{t}(6)=1.87$, $\underline{p}<.05$

FIGURE 16.22 Reduction in incident rate, paper company no. 1.

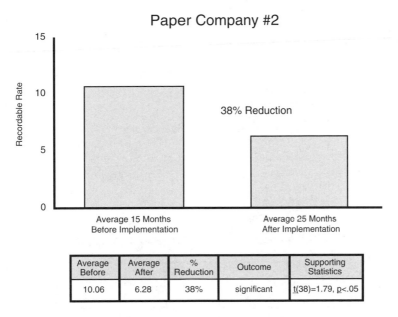

FIGURE 16.23 Reduction in recordable rate, paper company no. 2.

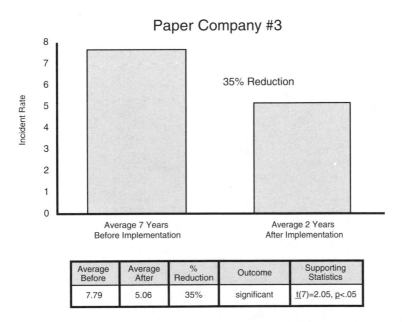

FIGURE 16.24 Reduction in incident rate, paper company no. 3.

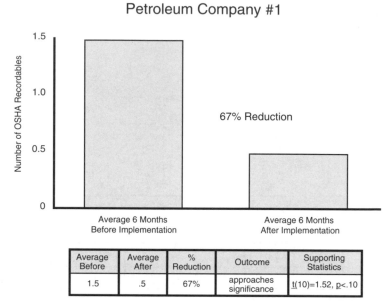

FIGURE 16.25 Reduction in recordable rate, petroleum company no. 1.

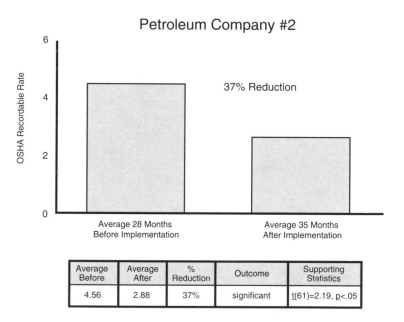

FIGURE 16.26 Reduction in recordable rate, petroleum company no. 2.

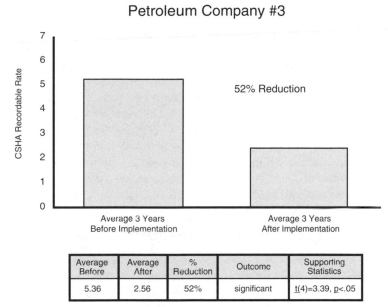

FIGURE 16.27 Reduction in recordable rate, petroleum company no. 3.

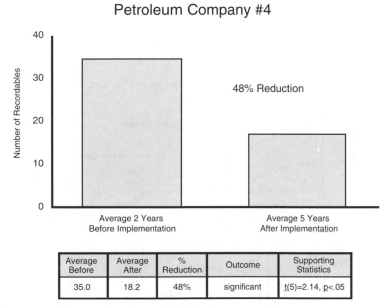

FIGURE 16.28 Reduction in recordable rate, petroleum company no. 4.

Summary of Findings—Workers' Compensation

Five companies provided workers' compensation data. In all five cases, workers' compensation variables dropped an average of 50 percent following implementation of behavior-based safety initiatives. Workers' compensation data is highly variable in its own right, which makes it extremely difficult to detect changes in the system affecting workers' compensation costs. In statistical terms, there is very little power to detect changes, even when the changes are very large—in this case, as large as 71 percent. Of the four cases with testable data, a 22 percent drop in a claims rate was not significant, and a 55 percent reduction in the number of claims approached significance. A 41 percent reduction in claims was statistically significant and a 61 percent reduction in dollars spent was statistically significant. These findings are illustrated in Fig. 16.29 through Fig. 16.33.

Discussion and Directions for Future Research

This study provides powerful evidence supporting the effectiveness of the employee-driven behavioral safety systems. In every case studied, incidents and costs decreased following implementation. In almost every case, the reductions were statistically significant. The strengths of this study come from the large number and variety of companies who participated. Because statistically signifi-

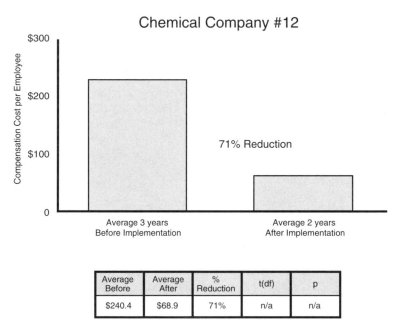

Average Before	Average After	% Reduction	t(df)	p
$240.4	$68.9	71%	n/a	n/a

FIGURE 16.29 Reduction in workers' compensation costs, chemical company no. 12.

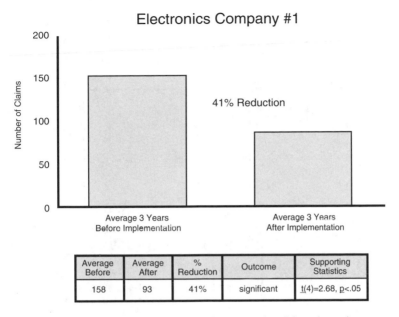

FIGURE 16.30 Reduction in number of workers' compensation claims, electronics company no. 1.

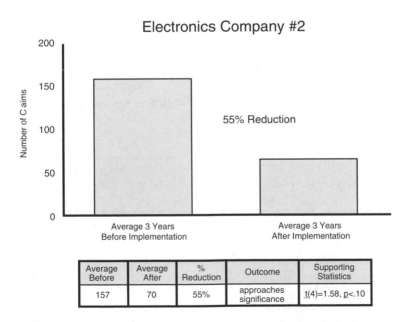

FIGURE 16.31 Reduction in number of workers' compensation claims, electronics company no. 2.

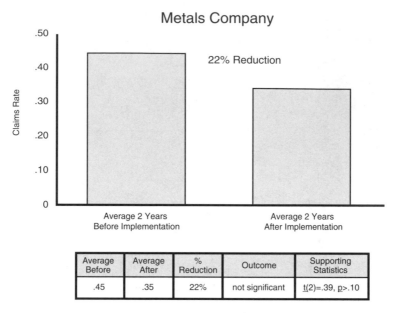

Average Before	Average After	% Reduction	Outcome	Supporting Statistics
.45	.35	22%	not significant	$\underline{t}(2)=.39, \underline{p}>.10$

FIGURE 16.32 Reduction in rate of workers' compensation claims, metals company.

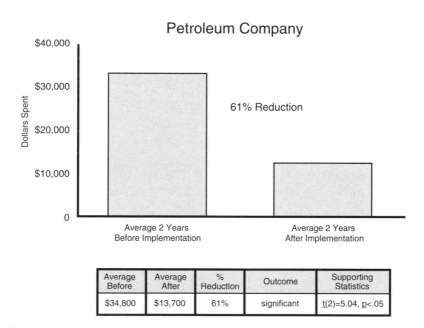

Average Before	Average After	% Reduction	Outcome	Supporting Statistics
$34,800	$13,700	61%	significant	$\underline{t}(2)=5.04, \underline{p}<.05$

FIGURE 16.33 Reduction in workers' compensation dollars spent, petroleum company.

cant reductions were demonstrated at various times, in different settings, and for different industries, problems of local history that would normally confound these findings are diminished. Another strength comes from the time periods covered. Because the patterns of incidents were assessed over long periods before and after implementation, this study gains protection from confounding due to regression, maturation, and instrumentation.

17

Case Histories

Before reviewing case histories, some observations on current trends in industrial safety, and some lessons from numerous site-level implementations are presented.

INTRODUCTION

Consultants and trainers from the author's firm have worked closely with companies from the United States and Canada, and with companies in Jamaica, Australia, and Britain. Moving toward the year 2000, three trends of the 1980s seem to be here to stay, shaping the way that business gets done, including the safety *business*.

Trend 1—More Employee Responsibility

One of the signs of greater and greater employee involvement is that many companies are moving away from the term *employee* in favor of titles such as associate, technician, operator, and so on. This shift reflects the trend toward greater expectations for employees and the greater acceptance of responsibility by employees. This is all part of the ongoing pressure favoring

- a leaner workforce

In addition to Jim Spigener of BST, the contributors to the development of this chapter include: Paul Villane and Glen Reddish of Monsanto Company; Tom Durbin and Roger Corley of PPG Industries Inc.; Jeff Johnston, Curtis Modisette, and John Ellis of Eastman Chemical Company; Bob Jones, Ron Griffin, Terry Ward, and Eddie Rhea of Boise Cascade; Carl Pederson, Randall Dover, Jerry Flynt, Sid Thomas, Jimmy Snow, and Ray Ward of the Chevron Pascagoula Refinery; Marc Swartz, Jackie Vanderpool, and Jim Mendenhall of Hill's Pet Nutrition; Manfred Kling and Ron Walts of the Canadian Department of National Defence; and Jim Marcombe, retired from Monsanto Co. and currently with BST.

- flatter organizations
- changing roles

Trend 2—Higher Costs

The costs of unplanned events is higher than it was just five years ago, and five years from now it will be higher yet. Human error is perhaps more expensive now than it has ever been. This fact of life in the industrial world shows up in various ways, from litigation to workers' compensation costs.

Trend 3—Greater Rigor

Economizing, downsizing, re-engineering, and even quality, these things bring a call for more rigor in business life. There is a growing willingness to go after the hard data of any situation, whether in safety, productivity, or quality. On the whole, this is a welcome development, but it does bring with it the expectation that safety efforts have to be able to justify themselves, and to distinguish the useful from the non-useful.

FIVE LESSONS FROM OVER 180 IMPLEMENTATIONS

The author and his colleagues have learned many lessons from each company they have worked with, but five big lessons stand out and they can be summarized as: the continuous improvement cycle, forthrightness about issues, slower is faster, perceptions predict results, and enthusiasm isn't enough.

The Continuous Improvement Cycle

Most companies that implement behavioral safety go through a predictable cycle, the continuous improvement cycle (see Fig. 17.1). Perhaps the most important stage of the cycle is step 5, *struggle*. Struggle is necessary. It prepares the way for the generalization of results that leads to continuous improvement. The behavior-based approach is a significant organizational change initiative. Since resistance to change is natural, the necessity for struggle can hardly be avoided. The key issue is how the organization deal deals with struggle. The continuous improvement cycle is presented in greater depth below.

Willingness to Address Issues

One might think that companies with fewer issues would be more successful with the employee-driven approach to safety improvement, and in some cases this is

1. Vision   2. Evaluation

7. Generalization   3. Assessment

6. Renewal   4. Implementation

5. Struggle

FIGURE 17.1   The continuous improvement cycle.

true, but not always. Some of the companies that have been especially successful with behavior-based safety started with a whole menu of seeming difficulties such as low trust between levels and areas, poor communications, skepticism about measurement, and low levels of supervisor involvement.

It turned out that what distinguished those companies and contributed to their success was their willingness to work through the issues that they identified. Companies with fewer initial difficulties but an unwillingness to work with them fared poorly by comparison. This is evidence of the importance of working with issues rather than ignoring them.

Slower is Faster

Hasten slowly has probably been good advice since the world began. It has certainly proved itself with behavior-based safety implementations. The irony is that companies especially impatient for good results (Trend 3), are sometimes the ones that take longest to get there. In the end it is faster to adapt rather than to adopt, building for the future.

Perceptions Predict Success

In 1993 the author began to analyze the correlations between implementation outcomes and the perception surveys that are part of the diagnostic behavioral safety assessment. The safety survey used has nine scales, each of which is related to a facet of the safety culture. Results on the *safety-related maintenance* scale show a significant correlation with implementation success (see Fig. 17.2). This is the scale that measures the degree to which site personnel believe that safety related maintenance is adequate at their facilities. Throughout the 1980s and early 1990s, the great majority of the companies interested in the behavioral

Safety-Related Maintenance

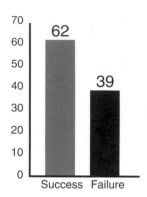

FIGURE 17.2   Safety-related maintenance is a good predictor of success.

approach scored high on that scale and went on to have successful implementations. Those companies who scored low did not do as well. This is a very interesting finding in view of the common management perception that, "things are not getting our people hurt." This is usually true; nevertheless, the willingness of employees to get involved may hinge on their perception that the "things" that affect safety are indeed getting fixed in a timely manner. An alternative explanation for this finding is that the high level of management ability involved in implementing safety-related maintenance systems is also required for implementing employee-driven safety.

Enthusiasm Isn't Enough

The fifth and final big lesson is that although enthusiasm for safety is necessary, it is not enough all by itself. This is the difference between merely *feel good* exercises and initiatives that deliver the goods. It is interesting to note that although people who favor hardware and engineering fixes sometimes mistake the behavioral approach as being *too soft*. There is a great deal of hard-headed accountability built into employee-driven safety; and all of it is there because it has shown its necessity.

In the end, the crucial difference is not enthusiasm but a commitment to the implementation of the behavioral mechanisms described in this book.

THE CONTINUOUS IMPROVEMENT CYCLE

Struggle is a stage that many sites go through while implementing an organizational initiative of significance such as a behavioral safety process. That process is geared to continuous improvement and struggle is the defining stage in an improvement initiative. In the author's experience, most of the effective employee-driven safety initiatives go through seven stages:

1. vision
2. evaluation
3. assessment
4. implementation
5. struggle
6. renewal
7. generalization

They then return to stage 1 with a new vision (see Fig. 17.3).

SEVEN STAGES OF THE CONTINUOUS IMPROVEMENT CYCLE

1. *Vision.*   A new vision for safety is the genuine starting point of an effective improvement process. One way to describe this new vision is "managing involvement for an injury-free culture."

2. *Evaluation.*   Having a vision of an injury-free environment or culture, companies evaluate themselves, usually much more carefully than anyone else does. They take stock with honesty, asking "What can we do to realize our safety vision of accident prevention?"

3. *Assessment.*   This stage shows companies their internal safety barriers and their safety assets.

4. *Implementation.*   This is the stage where most companies expend nearly all of their energy.

5. *Struggle.*   In most instances, struggle is unavoidable. Seeing this, effective companies approach this struggle as an opportunity to manage resistance to change and to regard it as a positive indicator that a process of genuine improvement is underway.

6. *Renewal.*   Companies that come through the struggle learn the most powerful lesson of all: "It works! We can do it! Accident prevention is in our power!"

7. *Generalization.*   This term refers to the spread of a great idea to other areas. Successful inventions are applied this way. People first learned to motorize pumps and lifts for the mining industry, then "generalized" their success to trains and ships. With renewal, the same generalization happens with employee-driven performance improvement. Then, on the basis of wider and wider generalization of the improvement process, the foundation is laid for a new vision.

1. *Vision.*   Back to stage 1, where "back to" really means forward to continuous improvement. The cycle lifts off and becomes a spiral. Past achievements point to new improvement possibilities.

FIGURE 17.3   The seven stages of the continuous improvement cycle.

Struggle

Implementation, stage 4, is where change efforts expend almost all of their energy. That is not surprising; there is so much to accomplish here. However, the trouble is that implementation is only stage 4—just before stage 5, struggle. Some facilities bypass this stage, but not many. Concerning struggle, the important questions are

- How long does it last?
- How successfully is it managed?

The crucial issue here is

- What is the best measure of the success of an implementation effort?

Uncertainty and complacency are common during the struggle stage of a behavioral change effort. Since facilities are not clear about how to measure success, they may glide unknowingly past some very important risk indicators. For instance, a facility may allow its behavioral observation frequency to fall off, but not be concerned because, for no good reason, it also happens to experience a decline in its accident frequency.

Using a Wider Perspective

Navigating a course of improvement requires having an overview of the arc or reach of all seven stages of a continuous improvement cycle. And perhaps most important is a proper appreciation of the storms that sometimes rock the boat during struggle, stage 5. Oftentimes facility personnel are so close to a problem that they begin to think of it as *our problem*—as though only their facility were wrestling with issues of observation frequency and quality, resistance to change, or supervisor buy-in. Each of those issues is serious. However, the quality of the attention given to problem-solving efforts depends very much on achieving an arm's length perspective on *our problems.* Lacking the compass of a wider perspective, site personnel begin to think that their problems are unique and that the continuous improvement cycle is mysterious. This is a set-up for defeatist thinking.

A very common version of the *Our Problem* approach is the *Our Region* approach. During the past 10 years of working throughout the U.S. and Canada, and in Australia, Jamaica, and Britain, the author and his colleagues have heard some version of the following statements many times: "Northerners don't like to be observed." "Southerners don't like to be observed." "The British don't like to be observed." Some people say, "Our unionized workforce doesn't like to be observed." Of course other people say, "Our non-unionized workforce doesn't like to be observed." By keeping the proper distance, by maintaining a wider perspective, problem-solving teams keep the whole forest in view, realizing that

- The continuous improvement cycle is not mysterious.
- The stage they are in now is predictable.
- Everybody engaged in this work has times like this.
- Observation is a positive process, but it is resisted until the positive aspect is demonstrated.

Stage 1—Spelling Out a Vision of Continuous Improvement

During stage 1, excitement is high, there is a very positive feeling, and expectations are very high. This is because site personnel charged with the implementation have arrived at a new vision for their safety performance, continuous improvement. Before adapting the principles of the employee-driven safety process, many sites have broken free of the accident cycle only to see their performance level-off as though trapped on a plateau—their continuing efforts do not bring continuous improvement. Seeing their efforts stall is very frustrating for them. Many of them have achieved continuous improvement in their products and services and they want it in safety, too. That is their vision for themselves—continuous improvement in safety performance.

Behavior-based safety shows them a way to do this. They see that behavior is the issue. Through their new understanding of behavior as the final common pathway of incidents, they see a path forward, a way out of the on-again, off-again wanderings of the Accident Cycle. Once they see this they are ready to consider how best to get there. This leads on to evaluation.

Stage 2—Evaluation

During evaluation there is still high energy; the positive feeling continues, and expectations remain high. The issue here for the site is what is the best method? What resources are needed? The most important resource here is other companies who are using the behavioral approach. Companies deciding that the behavior-based approach is right for them then move on to assessment.

Stages 3 and 4—Assessment and Implementation

During the assessment stage people begin to ask, "What are we in for?" This is the planning stage for implementation. During the implementation stage high energy is expended, positive feeling encounters resistance, and expectations are tempered by resistance. Important changes are initiated with the development of the inventory of critical behaviors, observer training, and so forth. Implementation personnel are thinking about the following issues:

- Is the training quality good enough?
- Can we get management support?
- Are we credible enough?
- How well is the steering committee functioning?

Stage 5—Struggle

During the struggle stage often there is uncertainty about the initiative; complacency takes over after some early success. This happened recently at a facility. Throughout 1992 their accident frequency was down, and they allowed their observation frequency to drop to inadequate levels. They seemed to be doing just fine.

However, in the first weeks of 1993, they had a rash of seven injuries. When they contacted the author to analyze their behavioral observation data, the following patterns emerged:

- Five of their seven incidents fell within a single behavioral category.
- The behavioral data sheets gave that category a score of 90 percent safe.
- Observation frequency was below 50 percent of target.

Given the low observation frequency, this meant that in 1992 there were some 3500 events/occurrences of the at-risk behavior that provided the final common pathway of those five out of seven incidents in 1993. This is a case where complacency missed an opportunity. Proper rates of behavioral observation would have registered the high rate of those at-risk behaviors. Proper use of the observation data would have triggered problem-solving to address those behaviors.

Stage 6—Renewal

During the renewal stage there is a justified sense of security and a justified sense of confidence. The energy level is sustainable, and expectations have matured and are both high and reasonable. A wider perspective is established in procedures. Renewal is the dawn after the night, the hard-earned calm after the struggle. At this stage a facility's efforts are truly rewarded—not the short-term fix, but the long-term sustainable *management* of safety performance. This is the stage of fluency in the continuous improvement cycle itself. The facility has moved from first acquaintance with the employee-driven process during evaluation and assessment, to familiarity with the process during implementation, to fluency in the process. Since they understand how every part of the process relates to every other part, they are poised to generalize their gains to other areas.

Stages 7 and 1—Generalization and a New Vision

During these stages there are mature expectations, and sustained energy and justified confidence. Facilities at this stage of the continuous improvement cycle apply their fluency to new applications. They consolidate and simply their efforts on a number of fronts by, for example:

- using behavior-based coaching for skills development throughout their training program
- unifying their safety and quality initiatives
- applying operational definitions wherever performance is an issue
- using sampling and data analysis techniques more widely
- incorporating data analysis into all problem solving and action planning

Although generalization first pays off as a way of realizing greater economies both of effort and of scale, it goes on to set the stage for an even more important gain—it primes the workforce for the next level of vision and wider perspective.

At this point the engine of *continuous* improvement runs steadily. Performance is characterized by adaptive readiness to safety and other emerging challenges. The workforce is engaged in ongoing, flexible direction-holding. They have a new vision. One of the projects they may turn to is that of re-engineering their safety system itself.

RE-ENGINEERING THE SAFETY SYSTEM

Each organization is living not only in the present but also in the past, and is also looking to the future. Organizations are still doing many things as they did them in the 1990s, such things perhaps as hiring, bookkeeping, and inventory control. Other things are very 1990s, such as the widespread move currently to more participatory management. However, some of the things that companies have begun to do represent a leap beyond even current paradigms and into the future, into new leading-edge paradigms. Behavioral safety is one of those *future* things. This fact has a number of important consequences for any behavior-based initiative. In each case there is a natural tension between the organization and the behavioral safety implementation that has jumped out in front, so to speak. Relative to the behavioral safety effort, the organization as a whole is large and its inertia is an important fact of life.

As a future paradigm, behavioral safety is out in front, but it is as though it were on a rubber band. It is still tethered to the organization. This tension between the known and the new is uncomfortable, and the organization has two ways to relieve it. The organization can go out and join behavioral safety, or the organization can pull behavioral safety back into itself (see Fig. 17.4). Re-engi-

What We Know

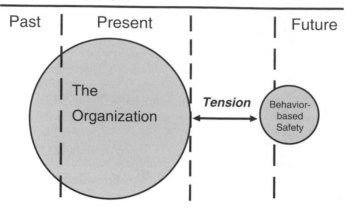

FIGURE 17.4 Harnessing the tension between the organization and a new behavior-based safety initiative.

neering the current safety system is an important priority because in the organization as a whole, the safety system is one of the stronger pulls on behavioral safety, trying to reformulate it in terms of older paradigms.

At first there is at least some duplication of effort between behavioral safety and older practices. For instance, a site that is still doing traditional housekeeping audits is very likely duplicating the behavioral safety observation data sheet. In some cases those older audits can be dropped altogether, freeing up important resources.

Some sites may still be spending time and resources on the old-style monthly, top-down, 15-minute, supervisor presentation done just to comply with some directive or other. Or their safety training still primarily *compliance* training. This may be *doing the minimum*, but it is a wasteful minimum when it is time spent simply re-watching the same old safety videos.

Accident investigations offer a very powerful opportunity to re-engineer the safety system. Some sites may still have an accident investigation system that is completely separate from their behavioral safety initiatives. Accident investigation needs to be a function of the behavioral process since at-risk behavior is the final common pathway in accidents. Before the safety system is re-engineered, accidents may be investigated in the traditional way only to be re-investigated by the behavioral safety team charged with incorporating accident findings into the site's inventory of critical behaviors. Therefore, as a function, accident investigation needs to be integrated into the employee-driven process (see Fig. 17.5).

Safety accountability offers another important opportunity for re-engineering. Accountability systems need to look exactly like behavioral safety—identify and define the behaviors that produce excellent performance, then measure those

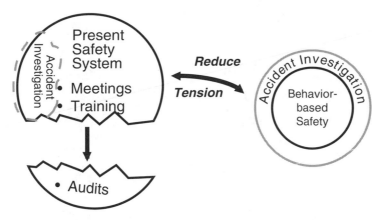

FIGURE 17.5   Re-engineering the safety system.

behaviors and give feedback on them. This is the only way to make *accountability* a positive, fair, and welcome factor in performance ratings. In addition to meetings, training, investigations, and accountability there are new challenges on the horizon that are best handled within behavioral safety. Among these are the OSHA ergonomics and process safety management (PSM) standards being formulated as this book goes to press.

As sketched here, re-engineering the safety system involves three related strategies:

1. Identify what no longer works and drop it.
2. Identify duplicate effort and integrate it into behavioral safety.
3. Proactively employ behavioral safety to meet new challenges.

Strategies 1 and 2 reduce the mass and inertia of the older approaches. Strategies 2 and 3 increase the momentum of behavioral safety, turning it into an ever more effective force for continuous improvement in the total safety system, and in the organization as a whole.

Re-engineering the Organization

Safety leaders fluent in the behavior-based paradigm for performance management have begun to look to generalize the success of behavioral safety to other areas of their organizations (see Fig. 17.6).

Environmental

Environmental concerns offer a natural area of overlap with the inventory of critical behaviors, in this case the behaviors that put environmental performance at

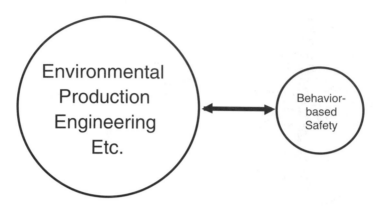

FIGURE 17.6   Re-engineering the organization.

risk. Behavior is often the final common pathway to those releases and spills, and to those occasions when substances are mishandled.

Engineering

From the outset the new designs and modifications of the engineering department need to be compatible with the site's behavioral inventory. Otherwise the new equipment may well be a barrier to safety because its operation/use requires at-risk behavior from the workforce.

SUCCESS RATES IN IMPLEMENTATION PROJECTS

Since 1988, the author and his associates have been engaged in a follow-up project. The effort has been to track results of each employee-driven implementation for which full consulting and training support was provided. For a detailed account of outcomes, see Chapter 16. In the U.S. the number of implementations has risen steadily since the late 1980s. These implementation projects are at sites throughout the U.S, and across industries. Thus far roughly 60 percent of the implementations have involved workgroup populations in the 0–500 range, with a fourth of them in the 500–1000 range. Oftentimes these groups represent subsets of a larger site population.

As this book goes to press, the successes have kept pace with the implementations, and a five-year evaluation shows 90 percent successful—42 percent Model Success and 49 percent Regular Success (Fig. 17.7). Another important measure is success rate by year of implementation (Fig. 17.8). Sites implementing behavior-based safety have consistently higher success rates than typical human

All 23 Fully Supported Clients Tested Experienced Substantial Reductions in Accidents

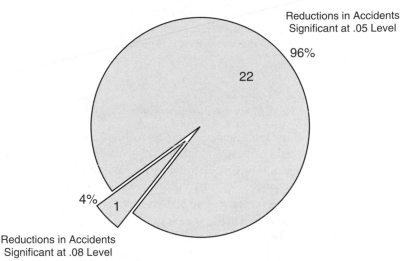

FIGURE 17.7 Overall success rate is over 90%.

Average Reductions in Incidence Frequencies 1, 2, 3, and 4 Years after Implementations of Behavior-Based Safety

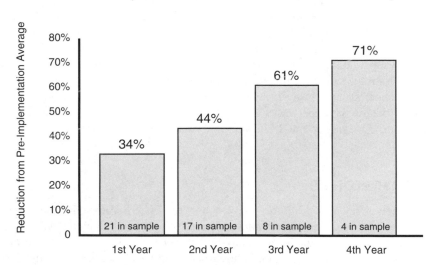

FIGURE 17.8 Average reductions in incidence frequencies.

resources (HR) initiatives or quality efforts. Five years after their 1989 kickoff, over 70 percent of those initiatives are going strong. Workgroups are tracking and analyzing their own behavioral data for use in action plans that achieve results like those presented above. It is very rare for a human resources initiative to even survive five years, let alone to flourish and become part of the site culture as these have done. The difference is that employee-driven safety is a process approach, not a program.

A Leadership Role for Safety Professionals

This represents a highly significant opportunity for the safety professional to assume a role of leadership in making employee involvement a reality. Traditionally, management has been slow to look to safety for leading-edge developments but that is beginning to change. The reason is that at companies using employee-driven safety, upper management is seeing bottom-line results that are better than with any of their other initiatives. The cause is not far to seek. Safety is a natural for strong employee involvement and behavior-based safety is framed so that employees can make it their own. Safety fits so naturally with employee involvement because the ongoing benefits of safety are immediately obvious to everyone. Some organizational resistance to change is always to be expected, but because productive well-being is the foundation of livelihood, genuine collaboration is perhaps easier to begin in safety than anywhere else. The author and his associates have seen this pump-priming effect happen numerous times. Even at sites where there is an adversarial relationship between management and labor, for instance, once the employee-driven safety initiative begins to take hold it provides the pattern for other collaborative efforts in quality and production. The report from successful sites is that by implementing employee-driven safety they learned how to undertake other important change efforts. In those companies it is common for the safety facilitators to be called to give presentations to quality and management groups, instead of the other way around. The next section of this chapter details the experiences of some of the sites where safety professionals and others have moved into leadership roles in their organizations.

CASE HISTORIES

This section reviews a number of case histories where companies have used behavioral methods, paying attention to the lessons learned along the way. Most companies that fully support their employee-driven safety initiatives achieve success. However, there is variation in how successful they have been, and the failures are instructive as well.

It is important to emphasize that success requires a collaborative effort between the consultant providing support and the facility responsible for implementation. Two kinds of possibilities exist for error in this relationship:

1. The consultant takes on too much ownership of the effort.
2. The implementing location is too rigid in its desire to control the implementation process.

A balance is needed, one in which each party plays an important role.

Often the location compromises its opportunities for success talking as though the consultant or the *program* were the solution to its problems, "We've got that covered—we're bringing in XYZ to handle the safety problem." Ultimately the site's own employees determine the success or failure of a behavior-based safety initiative. The *answer* to local problems is always home-grown, so relying too heavily on outsiders is a trap that successful sites avoid. An inexperienced consultant may collude with the site personnel in this mistake, wanting to show abilities and to take credit, "Our consulting organization can do XYZ for you." Interestingly, the success rates of the author and his associated consultants show very little variation between consultants, indicating that

- when consultants are uniformly well selected and trained, and
- they have adequate support (materials, software, etc.), then
- the success of implementation projects is more related to the characteristics of the implementing organization than those of the consultant.

The factors within the implementing organizations that distinguish success from failure are

- commitment from management
- ability to manage employee involvement
- willingness to address trust issues
- understanding of the process / realistic expectations

Not surprisingly, there is also a strong overlap with the major elements that make for success in quality initiatives. These successful safety initiatives also feature

- employee involvement
- data-driven, ongoing problem-solving efforts
- upstream measurement
- proper distinction between common cause and special cause

The following case histories illustrate the four elements listed above.

MONSANTO COMPANY

Maintenance and Engineering Safety Performance

Monsanto's Pensacola, Florida, facility is a chemical and nylon manufacturing plant with 2500 employees. During the early 1980s the recordable injury frequency rate of this plant ranged between 10.0 and 8.0. Those rates were within the normal range for the industry and the parent organization as a whole. Nonetheless, by 1985–86 safety results had plateaued, and in the Maintenance and Engineering Department there was a recognition that safety performance needed a step-change reduction. Past experience had shown that the program approach to safety gave only short-lived success at best. So there was agreement that what the department needed was an evergreen, long-term safety process.

Another factor contributing to the organizational awareness of a need for change was the fact that in the previous year the departmental workforce had been downsized. This meant that the department had fewer first-line supervisors—the very people who were traditionally the driving force behind the safety program.

The department was looking for a positive process approach to safety. The goal was to identify and implement a safety effort that would fit into and strengthen Monsanto's existing total quality management approach and its central philosophy known as the Plant of the '90s. At Monsanto the "plant of the '90s" meant total employee involvement and self-motivated work teams, teams that could manage, measure, and predict their performance in both quality and safety. The foundation blocks for the plant of the '90s were cost, team building, quality, and safety—with total employee involvement in all four areas. By implementing the employee-driven process Monsanto Pensacola was able to achieve just such a step-change in its performance (see Fig. 17.9).

Replacing Programs with a Process

After researching several possibilities, Monsanto Pensacola decided to implement the behavioral approach. The maintenance and engineering department and the yarn operations department, the two largest departments in the facility, took on the project of implementing the behavior-based approach to safety. The yarn operations unit numbered about 1000 employees. The maintenance and engineering department numbered about 650 employees. Both areas were successful, and this account focuses on the maintenance and engineering group.

During the assessment in late 1986, and before the decision was made to implement, the author provided an introduction of the basic behavioral concepts and procedures to a cross-section of approximately two hundred employees. This

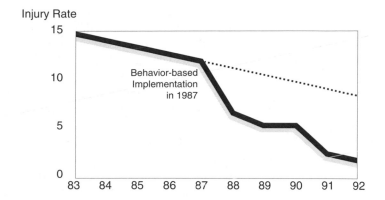

FIGURE 17.9 Chemical plant decline in overall injury rate.

introductory training took place over the course of one month. Employees were asked whether the behavior-based approach to safety was a method that they could support. This issue was debated and discussed in considerable detail. Early in the assessment effort an informal steering committee was formed. The members of this informal committee included the consultant and key facility personnel drawn from managerial and hourly ranks. The purpose of this steering committee was to guide the decision-making process and to provide leadership so that employees would be well informed and would feel supported and reassured as they considered the matter before them. Concerns were expressed and recorded, and the general feeling of the group of two hundred employees was that it was a good idea to pursue the employee-driven approach provided that

- management would commit to seeing it through in the long term; realizing that
- the behavior-based process would require support and patience, because
- behaviors take time to change.

The informal steering committee also considered organizational issues such as how to be sure that key facility leaders understood and endorsed the behavioral process, support that would prove crucial later in keeping the implementation effort on track. Working closely with the consultant, this informal steering committee was critical to the very high level of success of the assessment effort.

Implementing the Process

Following the decision to pursue implementation, a formal implementation steering committee was set up for the maintenance and engineering department. Eight of its ten members were hourly employees; the other two were salaried. The implementation committee members were selected for their credibility with their co-workers and for their commitment to safety. In addition, the department General Superintendent and safety engineer also attended the committee meetings as resources.

The steering committee was given adequate time to meet as a group and talk about issues involved in implementation. In good order the steering committee launched the safety process, calling it the Monsanto Accident Prevention Process, or MAPP for short (see Fig. 17.10). The steering committee members were trained by the consultant in how to train other hourly employees in behavior-based observation or sampling techniques. The implementation committee also received behavior-based coaching in how to train supervisors and managers in the core concepts, measures, and instruments of the developing Monsanto Accident Prevention Process.

In late 1986 and early 1987 the site began to put MAPP into action. In the course of the behavior-based analysis of the incident reports the steering committee developed an inventory of critical behaviors (Chapter 8). The steering committee carefully identified these and related critical behaviors and listed their operational definitions. The committee then conducted departmental inventory review meetings to inform its peers and to engage their input and buy-in for the behavior-based approach. Using a safety sampler inventory sheet keyed to these critical behaviors, the committee explained that observers drawn from hourly ranks could sample workforce performance and environment, and give the crews high quality feedback. The idea was to target areas for improvement, reduce the frequency of the identified behaviors, and thereby prevent accidents and injuries.

As it turned out the maintenance and engineering department steering committee jelled very early and took on a significant commitment to see the implementation effort through. The committee members were engaged and dedicated. They had strong support from their fellow workers and from management, and they

FIGURE 17.10 Logo for the Monsanto Accident Prevention Process (MAPP).

became very enthusiastic about making the behavioral process work. Management clearly proved its support of the implementation effort by sponsoring a full-time steering committee facilitator.

This challenge included development of the behavioral inventory, observer training, interpretation of observation data, and outreach, publicity and communication. The steering committee established quarterly review meetings attended by a rotating group of one-fourth of the department hourly workforce. That way during the course of each year, every hourly employee had input on departmental quarterly safety results.

Significant Results from the Start

The maintenance and engineering department implementation effort was a substantial success from the beginning. It had very high levels of support and involvement from employees throughout the organization. It achieved a significant reduction of injury frequency during the first and the second year (over 75 percent combined), and the effort continues to improve at this writing, eight years later.

This implementation effort was also characterized by a very important change in the safety culture of the department, a cultural change in which a much higher significance was accorded to safety performance. There were also many side benefits for the department organization—generally improved communications, teamwork, and working relationships. After the implementation effort was well launched, the steering committee branched off to form eight subcommittees, each of which took on a variety of new tasks. One subcommittee re-evaluated the safety incentive system in order to improve it by

- recognizing groups and individuals for safety efforts rather than focusing only on injuries, and
- getting away from gimmicks and prizes, and moving toward social reinforcement for significant contributions to the safety effort.

Another subcommittee investigated off-the-job safety. Another focused on department communications and procedures, and another on employee wellness, turning a nearly unused company gymnasium into a bustling and active health spa.

Continuous Improvement

With the behavior-based process well in place, they realized that continuous improvement would require each workgroup to identify its own targets, and use ongoing problem solving to keep the Inventory and its related Sampling Sheets responsive to new performance goals.

In addition to this commitment to continuous improvement in MAPP, a special steering committee was formed to foster employee involvement and empowerment actively. This committee was composed of wage-roll representatives from all maintenance disciplines within the department. In itself this development was a significant step-change in the management strategy of the Monsanto safety process. During 1990–91 the new steering committee implemented six important initiatives aimed at empowering each group to manage its safety performance:

1. Each workgroup was empowered to form an internal safety team to foster continuous safety efforts. The team also developed group safety goals which were prominently displayed in each shop.
2. A representative group was formed to develop an employee safety index/commitment system to reflect individual contributions to the safety efforts.
3. A subcommittee for recognition, publicity, and incentives developed a system for acknowledgment of individual, group, and departmental milestones.
4. A subcommittee was created to formulate and implement an internal inspection/audit system related to shop safety and housekeeping improvement.
5. Another subcommittee developed and implemented training for hourly Leaders in facilitating work group safety meetings. In addition, further training was planned to comply with all of the relevant OSHA Standards.
6. A subcommittee was formed to interact with the employees of contract-labor firms—the site's partners in safety, so as to actively exchange safety-related goals and efforts with them.

A Safety Mechanism In Place

Based on their solid achievements, Monsanto departmental hourly personnel formed the goal of becoming "The Best of the Best." This phrase reflected the fact that Monsanto was already an industry leader in safety, and that the Pensacola site had very good performance within Monsanto itself. An organization can only dedicate itself to becoming "The Best of the Best" when it moves from the standard, downstream *fix-it* approach to the proactive, upstream behavior-based safety process.

Monsanto Pensacola set itself the goal of installing and maintaining an ever-green safety mechanism. With their continuing emphasis on involvement, one group of 259 employees in the central maintenance and engineering department are making a reality out of Plant of the '90s. They are achieving an Injury-Free Workplace. In 1994 a number of work groups were in the 3.5–7 year levels of injury-free performance.

In the meantime the benefits of increased safety performance were felt not only in the Maintenance and Engineering Department, but in other key operations as well.

Business Results. Safety performance at current levels results in significant cost improvements.

Corporate Recognition. Monsanto Pensacola's safety performance earned recognition from OSHA, contributing to the plant's Star Status in OSHA's Volunteer Protection Program. In addition, the site has been awarded Monsanto's President's Safety Award for 1992, '93, and '94.

Plant Culture. Finally, performance of this level of excellence challenges the plant culture as a whole to strive for similar achievements.

PPG INDUSTRIES INC., GLASS BUSINESS

In 1989, in an important initiative for safety at PPG Industries, glass business senior management charged safety professionals to rethink safety in terms of accident prevention. Up to that time PPG's approach to safety was fairly traditional. The primary emphasis was on improved hardware and equipment, and on top-down development of requirements by the management group. PPG's glass business has about 17,000 employees in locations in North America, Europe, South America, and Southeast Asia. Relative to the glass industry, PPG's safety performance was quite respectable, but a comparison with a broader array of companies in the U.S. showed opportunities for improvement. The company committed itself to an accident prevention goal of zero injuries; and on the analogy of zero injuries = zero defects, senior management asked PPG safety professionals to apply TQM principles to the company's safety efforts.

Safety and Quality

By applying Crosby's four Absolutes of Quality to safety, the glass business found some very helpful parallels. Absolute no. 1 is *definition of requirements.* There is a natural fit between safety and quality on this point. To be safe, an organization must define the way to perform the task. Safe work practices, appropriate personal protective equipment, proper tools and equipment, and so on— these must be defined. Absolute no. 2 is *system.* Like defect prevention, accident prevention can only happen (conformance to requirements) within a proactive system. Most traditional safety systems are reactive. They emphasize inspections, tests, and audits that find and fix accidents after the fact.

Although prevention does require a new orientation, it does not have to be difficult. Communication of the requirements and training activities are two important ingredients in the quest to achieve safety Absolute no. 2. Performance standards are Absolute no. 3. PPG's performance standard is zero defects/zero accidents. The common phrase, "It won't happen to me," indicates that people take chances, that nonconformance to safety requirements is tolerated, or even expected. The company realized that it needed a performance standard that would be clear to everyone—zero accidents, 100 percent conformance to requirements.

Finally, upstream measurement is Absolute no. 4. PPG takes as its upstream measure of safety performance the frequency of conformance or nonconformance as measured against all identifiable safety practices and conditions. An individual either conforms to requirements (safe) or does not (at-risk).

A New Direction

This consideration of Crosby's Four Absolutes helped change PPG's approach to safety. Instead of thinking of a cluster of individual remedies, programs, and procedures, the glass business saw that they needed to develop a process dedicated to

- continuous improvement
- integrated safety measures
- employee involvement
- excellence

The company began to be bold in its goal setting (see Fig. 17.11). By *excellence* they meant that they wanted to be the best. By involvement they meant everybody—wage-roll, supervisors, engineers, and managers—and they knew that to be successful, the new safety measures would have to be integrated into the day-to-day work activities of the operating teams. With the help of the author and associates, glass business personnel developed inventories of critical behaviors and began the effort of implementing the behavior-based approach to accident prevention. It was clear to them that they were embarking on an important new course, one that deserved to be taken seriously from the outset. The company began by reconsidering its safety efforts from the ground up, an exercise that led them to redefine safety at PPG. The result was a new, total approach that they call the Worker Protection Process. Along the way they identified the conditions of success for this total approach.

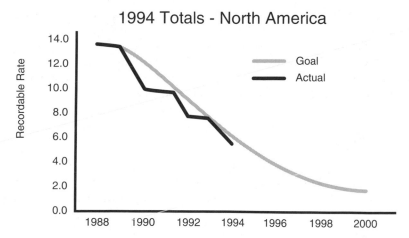

FIGURE 17.11 PPG Glass goals and performance recordable case incidence rate.

Conditions of Success

The following are some of the conditions of success that they identified:

- leadership and vision of senior management in the quest for an injury-free workplace
- operating teams responsible for their own safety
- long-term targets and strategies for achieving them
- objectively defined safety requirements
- statistical process control (SPC) techniques of safety measurement.

Leadership and Vision

The leadership vision and commitment of PPG's senior management has been crucial to success thus far. Management vision was there in the initial challenge to be the best in safety. It took vision to see the possible application of quality principles and techniques to safety. The connection between zero defects and zero injuries is one that needs to be made and sustained at the highest levels of an organization. Continuing leadership has been demonstrated in the commitment of resources and support for the total approach of the Worker Protection Process.

Operating Teams Responsible for Safety

The Crestline, Ohio, fabricating plant illustrates the commitment of PPG's glass business to safety measures that are integrated into the daily work activities of the operating teams. At the Crestline plant every work order now includes safety specifications along with the customer's product specifications and PPG's packing and shipping instructions, and the safety requirement has equal status on the work order. This means that the proper handling of an order of glass requires the wearing of prescribed personal protective equipment. An order that is produced, packed, and shipped consistent with the specifications will include worker conformance to the personal protective equipment requirements.

Long-Term Targets

In addition to identifying long-term targets, an important condition of success is specifying the strategies to reach those targets. At PPG there is now the recognition that success is a long-term phenomenon. The company doesn't want to be distracted by the short-term, either as gains or as setbacks. The company's eyes are on the longer arc. This, too, is a part of management vision.

On the way to the long-term target of sustained injury-free performance, they have important intermediate milestones through the year 2000 (see Fig. 17.16). Supporting the company on its way to its milestones there have been important ongoing activities. The benchmarking that they have done has brought them into contact with safety efforts of many other companies around the country. In addition to this safety networking about the long-term dynamics of accident prevention, they continually train the glass business workforce in the objectively defined safety requirements developed at their respective facilities.

The company undertook these and related activities because it knew that "long-term" is just a slogan if it is not backed up by strategies that facilitate continuity of effort and achievement on the way to identified targets. Another of the important strategies for long-term achievement is ongoing, measured conformance to objectively defined safety requirements.

SPC Measures of Safety Conformance

PPG's glass business is adapting the behavior-based approach to writing safety requirements. Behavioral analysis of the company's accident reports allowed them to generate an inventory of behaviors critical to safety at a specific facility. This basic SPC exercise for safety was a real eye-opener for them. As with the quality process, anecdotes, hunches, and intuition are almost always off the mark. There is a solid sense of achievement in working toward a reliable inventory of the small cluster of behaviors that are the final common pathway for most of the accidents at a facility. The development of objectively observable definitions of safety requirements follows, and provides the basis for measurement of workforce levels of either safe or at-risk behaviors. PPG also uses SPC control charts to track recordable case incident rates. The safety process is judged to be *in con-*

trol or *out of control* based on monthly performance rates and their relation to upper and lower control limits. Using the charts helps reduce the natural tendency to overreact when the rate moves up slightly, or to be overly optimistic when the rate drops slightly.

The Total Approach

As PPG's glass business launched this new total initiative, they realized that the traditional concept of safety did not convey enough of the new approach they were developing. The traditional safety approach focused too narrowly on acute trauma cases resulting from the one-time, sudden event; but the new record-keeping requirements were both broader and more rigorous than that (see Fig. 17.12).

For instance, in addition to occupational injuries, OSHA requires record-keeping for occupational illnesses. And this category has continued to expand, encompassing back sprains and strains (1987), ergonomics concerns (1992), and hearing loss (1993). PPG's glass business is proud of the fact that their recordable rate continues to drop (Fig. 17.11) even while OSHA requires stricter reporting of a wider array of possible recordables. They take it as an important signature of this new total approach that by using it they have, so to speak, stayed in front of the curve of OSHA concerns and requirements. In short, this feels like continuous improvement in safety performance. The company has begun to achieve this kind of improvement by defining and managing a wide range of actual practices that are predictive of safety in the workplace—proactively addressing in a unified strategy OSHA's emerging concerns, and beyond. This reflects PPG's commitment to a culture of worker well-being—the Worker Protection Process.

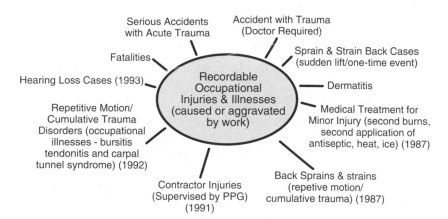

FIGURE 17.12 PPG Glass goals and performance recordable case incidence rate.

The Worker Protection Process

The Worker Protection Process for PPG's glass business is total in its charter and in its scope. Under the traditional safety charter, it counts as a safe day when someone works all day without an injury. But one may perform many at-risk behaviors in the course of performing an assigned task and happen not to be injured. Deming often referred to this situation as one where everyone is doing the best he can. When this level of behavior is reinforced as a "job well done," the employee thinks the job met the requirements even though his performance was marginal (that is, he did not happen to have an injury.) Total safety is expressed in an alternative charter more in line with the quality process. A worker protection process with a target of zero injuries defines a safe day as one when the worker works safely all day. Total scope is important too. By referring to the new safety initiative as the Worker Protection Process, PPG intends to convey the sense of a system of prevention of all injuries and illnesses.

This new total approach brings together many areas of concern that the company used to think of and manage quite separately, including soft tissue injuries and illnesses such as sprains, strains, carpal tunnel syndrome and others. It also includes occupational health issues such as hearing loss, dermatitis, and a host of others. This total approach addresses the entire productive lifetime of the worker, protecting against the onset of any occupational illness, however gradual. PPG has found a natural synergy between their quality initiatives and their new safety procedures. Since they implemented their SPC-related Worker Protection Process in 1989, their experience demonstrates that performance improvement can occur through the consistent application of these new techniques. The company intends to continue pursuing a safety process that is comprehensive in scope and charter, one which fosters employee involvement to achieve statistically valid continuous improvement in safety performance.

TEXAS EASTMAN DIVISION, EASTMAN CHEMICAL COMPANY

In the fall of 1990, safety professionals at the Texas Eastman Division of Eastman Chemical Co. in Longview, Texas, were curious when OSHA formed a Petrochemical Special Emphasis Program. From the procedures it looked like there could be anywhere from 10 to 30 OSHA inspectors on-site for upwards of 60 days. In 1989 the Polypropylene/Eastobond and Shops and Maintenance (S&M) divisions had launched behavior-based safety initiatives. The company had been stalled on a performance plateau since 1987 (Fig. 17.13), and their primary goal was to get off that plateau. The S&M division was not thinking about satisfying OSHA's Petrochemical Special Emphasis Program, let alone of qualifying for the

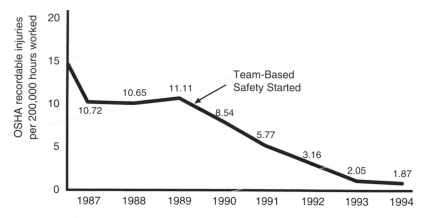

FIGURE 17.13 Texas Eastman Shops and Maintenance Division incidence rate.

agency's Voluntary Protection Programs (VPP). As it turned out, however, their team-based safety procedures helped them prepare for both of those things. The Shops and Maintenance division named its employee-driven safety initiative TIPP, short for Team Injury Prevention Process (see Fig. 17.14).

VPP Status

The Petrochemical Special Emphasis Program (PETROSEP) review mandates a number of areas for serious attention:

- training programs
- rules and regulations

FIGURE 17.14 Texas Eastman logo for its Team Injury Prevention Process (TIPP).

- process safety
- contractor management

Furthermore, the site's injury statistics not only have to be at or below the criterion threshold—they have to be improving.

Out of the momentum of doing the workup for a PETROSEP review, Texas Eastman turned its attention to the VPP application process. To some people, OSHA VPP qualification seemed like a dream, achievable at the earliest in two or three years' time. They assumed that the application process would require documentation they did not yet have. However, with the formation of a VPP Application Team, they took their first real look at the OSHA requirements. From the outset they noticed many overlaps between the VPP requirements and things they were already doing in their team-based safety initiative. Before they knew it, they had turned the corner. Texas Eastman was no longer wondering whether they could qualify, but how soon. The emerging consensus was, "Hey, we can do this—we're as good as VPP. Let's go for it now."

In October of 1991 the site submitted the application for VPP status. The VPP Review was conducted in July and August of 1992, and on February 24, 1993, the Department of Labor recognized Texas Eastman as a VPP Merit site.

Voluntary Protection Programs

There are three levels of VPP recognition: Star, Merit, and Demonstration. According to literature from the 1993 Ninth National VPP Participants' Association Conference, there are approximately 200 VPP sites: 180 Star, 19 Merit, and 1 Demonstration site. Of the 200 sites, 23 percent are union and 77 percent non-union.

Star recognition is for outstanding sites—their recordable injury rates run about 62 percent below national averages, steady since 1990. OSHA evaluates Star sites every three year.

Merit status is a stepping stone to Star. Merit sites have lost workday case rates 35 percent below national averages, and they are evaluated annually.

Demonstration status recognizes sites at which OSHA does not yet feel comfortable with its own knowledge of what systems and methods provide Star quality protection for workers there. The knowledge gained from such pilot sites is used to draft VPP Star requirements for other similar sites.

According to recent VPP Participants' Association figures, the industries most represented in VPP ranks are plastics (24 percent) and chemicals (21 percent). Next are manufacturing (16 percent), textiles (12 percent), and paper mills (6 percent). The VPP review covers

- management leadership and employee involvement
- training

- worksite analysis
- hazard prevention and control

The Shops and Maintenance team-based safety process was especially well-suited to addressing the first three VPP elements.

Peer-Based Safety—Shops and Maintenance Division

The 350 members of the Shops and Maintenance division work throughout the Texas Eastman facility. They perform a wide range of routine tasks, including mechanical maintenance, electrical and instrumentation maintenance, and plant turnarounds. In addition they handle a variety of special work orders, including nondestructive testing, crane work, and electrical troubleshooting.

From 1986 to 1989, Shops and Maintenance used a line-driven approach to safety. Supervisors measured workforce behaviors, and, for better or for worse, it was thought of as a supervisor audit program. People didn't like it. For one thing, the supervisor observation was often perceived as being negative both in its approach and its effect. The audits got results for a while, but then their performance leveled off in 1987 and even began to rise again in 1989. That was when they adapted the idea of sampling workforce behavior to a peer-based model focused on teams. The maintenance mechanics themselves began observing each other regularly, using a behavioral checklist they developed from incident reports. In addition, there was no secrecy about the peer-to-peer observations, just the opposite. And finally, the whole emphasis was positive, to let people know what they were doing right so they could make a habit of it and learn how not to expose themselves to injury.

Driving Out Fear

Shops and Maintenance managers realized that driving out fear is as important to safety excellence as it is to total quality management. With that in mind, the threat of disciplinary action was separated from team-based safety. Workforce performance is sampled not to assign blame but to gather data. The observers enter their own names on their data sheets, but no one else's. This lets the safety team track the frequency and quality of observer performance without compromising the confidentiality of the observations. This carefulness about confidentiality is no longer necessary to the credibility of the safety initiative, but at first it was the best way to assure the mechanics that this was not a "gotcha" program.

In the interest of complete data gathering, the safety team has encouraged their coworkers to be sure to report first-aids and near-misses. The campaign to maintain and even increase reporting levels has been successful. Since 1989 there has been steady improvement in the ratio of the all injury rate to the recordable rate (Fig. 17.15). This is the best sign that the improvement in the recordable rate is

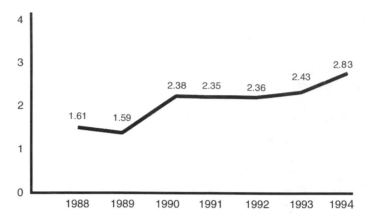

FIGURE 17.15 Texas Eastman Shops and Maintenance Division ratio of total injury rate to OSHA recordable rate.

not a result of underreporting. During 1993, crew members completed 8,347 behavioral safety observations.

Behavioral data was gathered and tracked during 1993. In response to these findings, 23 crews developed and completed 61 action plans. One crew working on path-of-travel brainstormed a list of areas in the plant where travel was a problem, then they worked with the operations department to improve the path of travel in many of the problem areas.

Satisfying the VPP Requirements

In 1991 when the VPP Application Team first looked at the OSHA requirements, they found significant areas of overlap with what they were already doing. The VPP application guideline lists eight elements, among which are

2. management commitment and planning
3. worksite analysis
4. hazard prevention control
5. safety and health training
6. employee involvement

VPP Categories 2 and 6—Management Commitment and Employee Involvement

The team-based safety process satisfied both categories 2 and 6. The entire effort is driven by employee involvement. They take part on steering teams, do safety observations and document results, and use those results in problem-solving meetings. In support of this ongoing effort, management commitment is substantial both in terms of time and resources. The site now has an OSHA Resources Office, which offers support of the following kinds throughout the plant:

- annual safety and health audits
- OSHA regulation monitoring
- coordination of safety and health training
- coordination of Texas Eastman's OSHA Process Safety Management (PSM) efforts

Category 3—Worksite Analysis

Under worksite analysis, the VPP application asks about, among other things, Job Hazard Analysis and Accident Investigations. The team-based data sheet has a comments section where observers regularly register at-risk conditions. Accident investigations are often conducted by the safety team. Using the team data sheet to review the accident, they extract the behaviors that put their coworker at risk, updating the data sheet where necessary to prevent future incidents.

Category 4—Hazard Prevention and Control

The team was already doing job analysis using the same data sheet, and team techniques of problem-solving were well established.

Category 5—Safety and Health Training

The Texas Eastman Health and Safety team members delivered the majority of the training for their coworkers. This training was extensive and ongoing. It covered such topics as

- emergency plans
- fire extinguishers
- lockout/tag-out procedures
- confined spaces
- fork lifts

Given these factors, they found that their version of employee involvement had prepared them well to apply for and achieve OSHA VPP status.

BOISE CASCADE—DERIDDER, LOUISIANA

Since 1989, personnel at Boise Cascade's Southern Operations in DeRidder, Louisiana, have been using the employee-driven approach to make gains not only in safety but also in employee involvement and in employee-management relations. Boise Cascade has seven paper mills and associated box plants, lumber mills, and office products locations throughout the United States and Canada. At Boise Cascade's DeRidder mill, which employs approximately 700 people, the workforce is represented by the United Paperworkers International Union.

SOAR

DeRidder personnel named their employee-driven process Safety observation And Reinforcement, or SOAR for short. Using SOAR along with several other safety performance processes, the DeRidder mill has won corporate safety awards as well as independent recognition from the American Paper Institute. These improvements in safety follow years of performance in which the DeRidder mill was already recognized as a safety leader.

Safety leaders are often attracted to the behavioral process to achieve a step-change in their safety efforts. They are looking for ways to develop an on-site mechanism that fosters continuous improvement in safety performance. And safety leaders are also aware of the important *side benefits* of the behavior-based approach, benefits of cooperation, involvement, and more open communication. According to the Southern Operations safety manager, the power of the SOAR safety effort is that it sends a clear and constant message to the workforce that the company is truly committed to safety. He says that the real plus for him as the safety manager is that with site-wide involvement in SOAR there are many more people looking out for safety concerns. Instead of thinking of safety as somebody else's business, now safety is understood as everyone's responsibility. The safety manager is equally impressed with the important side benefits of the behavior-based process approach to safety. He credits SOAR with furthering trust and cooperation between management and labor, because it is an activity where the workers get to show that they have good ideas and that they care. It is also an area where the workforce gets to make a difference that counts.

Since implementing SOAR, Boise Cascade, DeRidder, has introduced the behavior-based safety process to three sister mills—a project at the mill in Rumford, Maine, a pilot project in the Maintenance Dept. of the Boise Cascade Mill in International Falls, Minnesota, and mill-wide implementation at Boise Cascade, Tacoma, Washington. DeRidder has also hosted visits from several other Boise Cascade mills, as well as numerous visits from representatives of other companies. Visitors to the DeRidder site are impressed by the attitude of openness and straightforwardness about safety at the mill. In opening its doors to other companies interested in effective safety, Boise Cascade takes the commendable position that safety is so important that it goes beyond competition.

Employee Involvement

According to the woodyard SOAR facilitator, the union had reservations about behavior-based safety. He says that the idea of making observations of workforce safety behaviors sounded like it was going to be just another disciplinary program. On the other hand the union was genuinely interested in improving plant safety performance. The recordable incident rate had plateaued and there was widespread agreement among both management and labor that they wanted to do better. Throughout the mill there was a strong desire to achieve an incident-free environment. From the early wait-and-see position, the union became a strong supporter of SOAR. Union facilitators now say that SOAR is one of the best things that Boise Cascade has done in favor of employee involvement and open communication across departments and between the levels of the facility.

The Maintenance Department

The superintendent of maintenance services at DeRidder served as the management liaison on the maintenance department SOAR steering committee. The other fourteen members of the committee were Maintenance Mechanics who were skeptical about SOAR at first. When the maintenance department committee reviewed past incident reports, they discovered that the accident reports made little or no mention of the behaviors associated with the incidents in question. Using their years of combined experience the mechanics interpreted and reconstructed the reports, developing a truly accurate list of behaviors that are critical to maintenance department safety.

The superintendent says that in his experience the behavior-based approach to continuous improvement of safety is the most effective thing he has seen (see Fig. 17.16). He is convinced that if the site were a bit more consistent in doing their observations and action plans, they wouldn't have any recordable incidents. As it is, he says the response has been remarkable. People who were known for ignoring eye safety are conscientiously wearing safety glasses. The same is true for people working in the pipe racks—with no nagging or hassles or disciplinary action, they are using their safety belts and are tying off ladders.

In addition, the workforce has begun to rescrutinize many areas of work practice that they used to take for granted. People used to take it personally when changes were suggested, as though they were being criticized. Now everyone is much more willing to give the whole process a chance to uncover good ideas for improvement. There is very widespread appreciation of the fact that the bottom-line of this particular process is that everybody wins. A powerful sign of the new partnership for safety showed up when it came time to print the behavioral inventory data sheet. The maintenance department steering committee members wanted the instrument to bear the logo of the United Paperworkers International

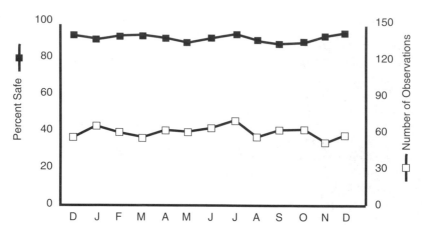

FIGURE 17.16 Comparing %safe and number of behavior-based observations at Boise Cascade's DeRidder, Louisiana, plant.

Union. They realized that the Boise Cascade logo would also be on the document. Since no precedent existed where the two logos appeared on the same document, permission to do this had to come from both management and the union.

As it turned out, no one found any reason not to just go ahead and do it. So there it is, the behavioral inventory arrived at through great challenge is out there on the shop floor. Across the middle of the data sheet is the emblem of the SOAR process, an eagle with its wings unfurled (see Fig. 17.17), keeping a keen eye for safety—in the upper left hand corner of the behavioral inventory sheet is the Boise Cascade logo and facing it top-right is the seal of the United Paperworkers International Union.

FIGURE 17.17 The Boise Cascade logo for its safety observation and reinforcement process (SOAR).

Employee Relations

To lay to rest the fears that the SOAR process would be used for disciplinary action, the maintenance steering committee implemented strong security measures. The completed SOAR observation data sheets went into a locked mailbox and only one person had a key. That person was the maintenance SOAR facilitator, himself a maintenance mechanic and union steward. Management respect for the SOAR process was so consistent that after the first year to eighteen months most people were no longer worried that it would be used for disciplinary action. In the beginning the maintenance facilitator was among the skeptics. He says that when he accepted the position of SOAR facilitator he went home and had a good long talk with himself. He discovered that when he just stayed with the central importance of safety, he could let safety be neutral ground.

From Neutral to Plus

As the SOAR initiative has gathered momentum at the DeRidder Mill, safety has moved from neutral ground to positive achievement, and word of their success has spread.

Boise Cascade's SOAR Facilitators are in demand as industry speakers and presenters, and at the May, 1992, annual meeting of the Southern Pulp and Safety Association in Williamsburg, Virginia, the DeRidder facilitators put on a one-hour presentation of their employee-driven safety process. The meeting's attendees included human resources managers, production managers, medical professionals, safety managers, and even a few facility directors. The audience was genuinely impressed, engaging the presenters in informative dialogue about management and labor union relations, and practical questions about design of the behavioral inventory.

CHEVRON—PASCAGOULA, MISSISSIPPI

In August of 1990, the refinery maintenance manager grew frustrated with their oscillating safety cycle and he asked for volunteers from the maintenance workforce to consider ways to stabilize and improve their safety performance. Sixty-three mechanics answered this call for volunteers, and from this group their Incident Prevention Steering Committee (IPSC) was formed.

The IPSC divided into a number of subcommittees to study various approaches to safety performance improvement. After hearing from the subcommittee studying the behavior-based approach, the IPSC elected to focus their safety improvement efforts on this format because the employee-driven process showed the most promise. At that time the IPSC was restructured to have twelve members—three from management and nine wage-roll employees. Also the group's name was changed to the S=AFE Process steering committee. S=AFE stands for Safe = Accident-Free Environment (see Fig. 17.18).

Behavioral Inventory Development and Review

The first order of business for the S=AFE steering committee was the development of their behavioral inventory. The committee reviewed accident reports and catalogued the at-risk behaviors that caused the accidents. In the summer of 1991, after the S=AFE committee completed a first draft of the behavioral inventory, groups of mechanics and management were brought in to review and critique the behavioral inventory. This was the committee's behavioral inventory buy-in program. In each group session the committee documented the recommendations by writing them down on large flip charts. This gave the employees positive feedback that their ideas were being considered, and it also gave the S=AFE committee documentation for review, and some good ideas to incorporate into the behavioral inventory and the observer data sheet.

Observer Training

In September of 1991, the S=AFE committee concentrated its efforts on training mechanics to be observers. The mechanics trained for three days—two in the classroom and one in the field.

FIGURE 17.18 The logo for the behavior-based safety process at Chevron U.S.A.'s Pascagoula, Mississippi, plant.

Day One

On the first day of training they studied the behavioral process—with discussion, review of behavioral inventory development and the data sheet, and behavioral analysis (ABC Analysis).

Day Two

The second day began with basic observer training. During this training the mechanics role-played the use of the data sheet and how to give positive and negative feedback. To give the observers practice, the second day they also saw a training video of three different crafts doing their jobs. The observers watched this video and practiced marking their data sheets to gain familiarity. This also allowed the trainers to review observer performance, getting their observation consistency as high as possible.

Day Three

The third day was spent practicing observations in the field. This reinforced the observer's newly acquired skills and gave the trainers a chance to give tips on feedback. At the conclusion of the third day, a senior member of management presented each newly trained observer with a folding portfolio with calculator. They were thanked for participating in observer training and the management spokesperson encouraged the new observers to become a significant part of the safety team.

Kickoff—October 1991

The S=AFE committee initially trained 40 mechanics as observers. Once that group was trained, it was time for the Kickoff, which was held in October of 1991. The entire workforce was shown the revised behavioral inventory and data sheet incorporating their suggested improvements.

Follow-Up Coaching for Observers

Approximately six months later, March–April 1992, the S=AFE committee started coaching their observers. Some of the steering committee members watched the observer do an observation, giving positive feedback to the observer and making notes on the negative aspects to be discussed at a later date. This was done to give the observers a morale boost and to reinforce their correct behaviors in an observation. The coaching helped the observers develop their feedback skills and also improved their consistency in filling out the data sheet properly.

This coaching also let the observers know that they had the support of the steering committee.

Action Plan Training

In May–June 1992, the steering committee concentrated its efforts on action plan training. Action plans are the culmination of a crew's safety efforts.

Monthly, each crew received feedback from the observers' data sheets in the form of computer-generated reports and charts from the behavioral observation software. Using these monthly computer reports for their area, each crew met to analyze its weak areas of safety. They also used any other source of safety data to discuss safety. Typically a crew focused its efforts on one to three items or concerns of safety, and formed action plans with a date for completion. When the agreed goal was reached, the crew members focused their efforts in another area of safety concern. This process repeats itself indefinitely, resulting in continuous improvement in safety.

Areas of Improvement

Early observations indicated that the facility could use improvement in the lock-out/tag-out of equipment prior to working on it. In this procedure, a refinery operator isolates equipment by chaining and locking valves, and by tagging the keys so that others will know not to return the equipment to service before maintenance work is completed.

Lock-Out/Tag-Out

The observations showed a general confusion concerning the lock-out/tag-out procedure. A review of the procedure indicated that it needed to be revised because it was difficult to understand.

The procedure has been shortened and simplified so that there is less room for interpretation. All operators and maintenance employees have been schooled on the changes. As a result, maintenance employees better understand that proper lock-out/tag-out of equipment improves their chance of performing a task safely.

Face Shields

Certain tasks performed with oxy/acetylene burning equipment can be better done while using full view face shields rather than with burning goggles. Early inquiries showed that their tinted face shields were not approved for use with oxy/acetylene equipment. As a result, the old face shields were phased out and the tool room now purchases only those tinted lenses for face shields that are ANSI approved for use with oxy/acetylene equipment.

Fall Protection

Gathering accurate, useful data requires that all observers are applying the same criteria to determine whether a task is being done safely. For that reason the observers asked whether the refinery had a policy concerning fall protection. The site discovered that it did not have such a policy. As a result, the refinery's safety department drafted a refinery instruction concerning fall protection. A refinery instruction is a formal document that states minimum refinery guidelines for performing a specific function.

Improved Access

Several minor changes tend to permit safer work. Since beginning their observations, individual crews have made safety equipment (ear plugs, mono-goggles, safety harnesses, ladders, and so on) readily accessible to the crew. This is important because people tend to use safety equipment if it is easy to obtain.

Safer Scaffolding

In the past, when scaffolding was required to do a job, the primary focus had been to get it built quickly and move on to the work that had to be done. Now site personnel also assure themselves that the scaffolding is constructed in a way that provides an easy and safe escape route.

Other Upgrades

There are several examples of physical changes. Wherever practical often-used tool air lines have been put on retracting reels. Davits have been placed above some equipment that requires repeated maintenance. Drive-through doors have been painted for increased visibility. The list is long and there are several other examples that could be mentioned.

Improved Credibility for Safety

Perhaps the greatest accomplishment thus far is a subtle change in the way that personnel view safety. Employees have begun to realize that someone will listen to their safety concerns. Management, supervision, and wage-roll employees are more open and sharing with their ideas. Everyone is willing to try doing tasks differently in order to be safer. The company is changing some of the culture that kept the workforce unaware that there might be a safer way to do its jobs. Implementation of the S=AFE Process has required mechanics and supervisors to work closely with one another, sharing opinions and ideas. This, in turn, has resulted in better understanding and respect for one another that can only be beneficial in the long run.

Learning from Missteps

Although the mistakes identified here were not critical, each of them slowed the site's progress toward improved safety performance. Each one has required additional time and effort to correct it.

Supervisor Involvement

Early in the history of the Chevron S=AFE process, three wage-roll employees (mechanics) and one supervisor were assigned to observer training. The supervisor became ill and was out of work for several weeks. He had to drop out and he was not replaced. One result was that they completed a year of observer training without a member of supervision doing active training. Because it was not recognized as a misstep at first the S=AFE committee unknowingly provided fuel for resistance. Their safety process is an employee-based process that should be beneficial to all employees, and all employees are encouraged to participate. By omitting supervision from their observer training team, they gave the appearance that S=AFE was a solely a mechanic's process.

Having recognized that misstep, all supervisory members of the steering committee have pledged themselves to be trainers. From that point on, they showed a unified front, both supervision and wage-roll employees working together to train new observers.

Communicating with the Workforce

Better continuous communication with the general workforce would have paid enormous benefits by reducing resistance and by minimizing the perception that the committee was somehow separate from the rest of the workforce. A team probably can't over-communicate. The company now encourage employees to attend S=AFE committee meetings, though they can only accommodate two or three per meeting. It should improve two-way communication and remove some of the appearance that the committee is isolated from the workforce. In that sense, the improved communication returns process ownership to the employees and restates the fact that the steering committee is acting as the employees' representative to direct the process.

Drafting Group Roles

Group roles should have been drawn up by representatives from those groups. For instance, supervisors should have written their own roles; mechanics should have written mechanics' roles; and so on. The steering committee's duty should have been to provide the guidelines for roles and to assist when asked. Supervisors more readily accept roles they have written for themselves. When they accept the roles, then they try harder to fulfill them. Acceptance of the process becomes easier when they accept their roles and are working to fulfill them. The same facts also apply to wage-roll employees.

A few helpful guidelines for writing roles:

1. Keep it simple.
2. Make it observable.
3. Know when you are finished and stop there.

HILL'S PET NUTRITION—RICHMOND, INDIANA

Featured in the October 1992 issue of Food Engineering magazine, the new Hill's Pet Nutrition site in Richmond, Indiana, is a state-of-the-art pet food manufacturing facility run by teams. In addition to managing quality and operations, Hill's work teams also manage safety at the plant. Headquartered in Topeka, Kansas, Hill's Pet Nutrition is a subsidiary of Colgate-Palmolive Company. In developing its new $80 million, 200,000 sq ft. Richmond facility, Hill's decided to address from the ground up the challenge of applying human-food standards to pet food manufacturing. The result is a showcase facility that incorporates many new design features—a *socio-tech* work environment built specifically for team management, computer-integrated manufacturing, human-food sanitation standards, flexible production lines for quick changeover, and just-in-time (JIT) production and shipment.

An Innovator for Decades

Only recently have food industry forecasters begun to talk about the coming of "neutriceuticals" or "pharmafoods"—food products formulated to prevent or manage specific diseases. However, Hill's has been producing such foods since 1948, for dogs and cats, that is. Distributed only through veterinarians, the company's Prescription Diet® brand pet foods are formulated to help manage life-threatening illnesses such as heart disease, diabetes, and gastrointestinal problems. Developed in the 1960s and marketed through pet shops, breeders, kennels, and veterinary hospitals, the Hill's Science Diet® brands are formulated to meet the needs of healthy pets at different stages of their lives.

Hill's Richmond produces both product lines in dry and canned form and distributes them across the U.S. and to over 30 nations throughout the world. The plant operates around the clock, seven days per week, with four shift workgroups organized into "cell teams." The total employment at the site is about 200 people.

Divided into two parallel operations, the canning (wet) process and the bagging (dry) process share a central area where their respective team centers are located. The center for each team has computer terminals for monitoring their production lines. There are also team learning centers equipped with technical libraries and with computer terminals for process simulations and training.

Highly Skilled Teams

The plant's computer-integrated manufacturing (CIM) system is driven by operational needs from the bottom up rather than by top-down management needs for business information. To assure quality, statistical process control (SPC) methods are used on-line by operators, who also have backup from a central QC laboratory and its at-line satellite labs. The batching and blending systems of the plant can handle as many as 25 different ingredients per product formulation. At the end of the dry process, special net-weigh scales gravity-fill bags with an accuracy measured in a few grams.

In April of 1991, the Hill's Richmond plant began commissioning its production lines. As start-up neared, plant personnel completed eight weeks of training in team building, communications, and an overview of the business as well as of specific job skills. However, they had not thought to seek out the state-of the art approach to safety. Although they had advanced processes in place to drive quality and production, none were in place for safety.

Team-Based Safety

In late 1991 Hill's Richmond personnel adapted a behavior-based approach to safety at their site, achieving important gains in their safety performance in 1992–1993 (see Fig. 17.19). In both its vision statement and its everyday practice, Hill's Richmond is committed to employee empowerment. Structured in just three levels—strategic, coordinating, and operating—the site organization is notably flat. And by relying on small, self-managed teams for all key functions, the organization is also quite lean. The leadership team has nine members and is led by the facility director. As its name indicates, the leadership team gives direction to the facility as a whole while providing liaison with customers, other Hill's plants, and with the business world at large. Hill's uses the term "socio-tech" to sum up its innovative effort at employee empowerment for highly-skilled self-managed teams. The "tech" side of socio-tech is present everywhere in the plant's highly computerized production and quality processes. The "socio" side of socio-tech has shaped everything from site architecture (Everyone at the facility comes and goes through the front door.) to the easy and constant collaboration of all three employee levels.

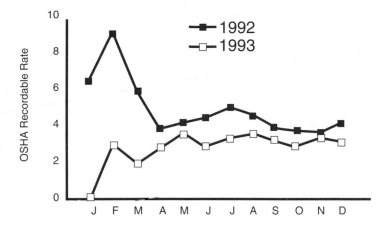

FIGURE 17.19 Incidence rates at Hill's Pet Nutrition (a Colgate Palmolive subsidiary) in Richmond, Indiana.

Coordinating and Operating Teams

The coordinating team acts as liaison between the operating teams and the leadership team, and is responsible for facilitating the daily operation of the production lines. Their duties also include regulatory compliance. There are 166 technicians divided among the various operating teams. They run the production lines, using statistical process control (SPC) measures to assure human-food standards. In addition to permanent teams for technical systems, continuous flow manufacturing, operations, manufacturing services, and quality, Hill's Richmond team members often form special, project specific teams to address particular problems.

A recent example of this in is the "Bottleneck Elimination Team," BET for short, formed by the Continuous Flow Manufacturing (CFM) Team to eliminate packaging bottlenecks associated with routine changes in volume and/or product line. The CFM Team did the preparatory time studies to identify the improvement needs, and then put out a site-wide flier addressed to anyone interested in participating on the new bottleneck team.

A Safety/Production Innovation

One special safety project was to improve the way that a specific ingredient flows through the production system. This team refers to itself as the Posse. The question of safety came up in connection with the flow of the ingredient because site personnel had been hand-dumping it from 50 lb bags into the batching equipment. Since the bags needed to be hoisted two stories overhead, this step offered various opportunities for improvement in both safety performance and in productivity. The Posse identified and evaluated several possibilities. High-volume ingredients enter the production process in three ways: from silos, from super sacks, and by hand-dumping from 50 lb bags. A super sack of eggs, say, weighs 2000 lb and it is handled by lifts and conveyors.

Of these three methods, the ingredient was being hand-dumped because of its consistency, which made it flow poorly from the silos. The Posse found that a high-density, granulated pharmaceutical grade of the ingredient would flow well from the silos but its cost was prohibitively high. With the silos ruled out and with hand-dumping in question, the team turned to super sacks as the other possibility. The problem was that at that time none of the site's vendors shipped this ingredient in super sacks. However, the Posse found a vendor who was willing to ship them an experimental super sack of the ingredient. Vanderpool says that although the sack weighed in at 750 lb rather than the standard 2000 lb, the Posse was nervous about that trial run, fearing that when they broke open the sack they would have to deal with a 750 lb brick. As it turned out that fear was unfounded, and plans are underway at both the vendor site and at Hill's Richmond to incorporate the new packaging for the ingredient.

Dancing with a Bear

Although problem-solving efforts of this kind are not always predictable and orderly, Hill's has no doubt of their high-energy value in both the near and the long term. At Hill's Richmond they have a saying that employee empowerment is like, "dancing with a bear—once you start, you don't get to stop just because it's tiring now and then."

CANADIAN DEPARTMENT OF NATIONAL DEFENCE SHIP REPAIR UNIT PACIFIC (SRUP), VICTORIA, BRITISH COLUMBIA

Roles of Ship Repair Unit Pacific (SRUP)

The primary role of the SRUP is to provide direct support to the Maritime Commander's forces operating in the Pacific Ocean. To this end, the site maintains the support skills and facilities to complete the entire range of repair and refit needs of a technologically advanced navy. SRUP's annual work effort of approximately 1.7 million personhours is spent principally in the repair and maintenance of over 85 naval and auxiliary vessels. The Unit also supports visiting warships, and other federal government departments including eighteen shore agencies. Workforce skills range from theoretical knowledge of integrated circuitry to tool and die making, and the management system is capable of planning and executing major refits involving as many as 800,000 personhours each.

To carry out its second-line maintenance duties, SRUP is an approved facility for the repair and overhaul of over 3800 line items of National Stock Inventory.

The Workforce

SRUP employs approximately 920 civilians and 12 military personnel. The Unit's production labor force is organized into eight groups by job specialization, which are further divided into 27 shops. The average level of experience is 13 years. At any given time there are approximately 90 apprentices in various stages of a four-year program. The SRUP apprenticeship programs cover 13 fields, ranging from boiler maker to refrigeration mechanic, from shipwright to sheet metal worker.

Behavior-Based Safety

In 1989 behavior-based safety was brought to this facility by the production officer. He saw the employee-driven safety process as having an important role to play at the Ship Repair Unit. At that site the behavior-based safety initiative is known as ACT (short for Action—Cooperation—Training). The first stage in developing the ACT safety process was dissatisfaction with the traditional, reactive approaches to safety. SRUP had safety data but there was no attempt to use that data to remove the root causes of incidents at the facility, nor to build on the basic safety assets of the facility. The production officer could see that something was missing but at first he did not quite know what it was. He was, however, very confident in some basic premises or principles:

- He wanted to see the facility move beyond the accident cycle.
- He believed in optimizing training of all kinds for all personnel.
- He was hoping for some new strategies that would build on the existing good relations between labor and management.

The Accident Cycle

For the SRUP production officer the most striking symptom of the ineffectiveness of the site's traditional approach was that the facility had a very evident accident cycle. Consequently when their safety numbers happened to be good, he couldn't get excited about it because he knew the performance numbers were sure to get worse in the near future. He also knew that the good numbers did not indicate that the site was doing something right. The safety system at the site was in control—in some quarters the numbers were up, in others down, but their baseline incident rate showed no improvement.

Contributing to the accident cycle at the site was a safety culture in which everyone thought of safety as just one specialty among others. This meant that for most workers safety was "someone else's job." They talked and acted as though safety could be departmentalized in the way that the maintenance or administrative function is departmentalized, "I don't have to protect myself because protecting me is the job of those guys over there in the safety department." Working with these questions about safety almost daily, and trusting the basic premises listed above, the production officer encountered the employee-driven safety process and he was impressed with the way it fit the situation at SRUP.

The behavioral process addressed the dynamic of the accident cycle. In addition, there was training for employee involvement to change the traditional departmentalized safety paradigm.

Training

The behavior-based approach offers unique training opportunities for a site. It is one thing to issue directives saying that from now on everyone is responsible for safety; it is quite another to actually provide workers with structured safety roles and responsibilities. I believe that this difference is crucial. The emphasis on coaching for skills development and on peer-to-peer behavioral observation and feedback obviously goes beyond the typical specialized training in welding, corrosion protection, electronics, or advanced weaponry, for instance.

This is one of the strengths of behavior-based safety training. It enhances everyone's observation and communication skills. It broadens the horizon of the workforce, acquainting them with concepts that they would not normally encounter. Without a solid, facility-wide grounding in new safety roles and responsibilities, it is not possible to launch and sustain a continuous improvement initiative. Continuous improvement means continuous change, and to sustain that kind of change management and labor need to trust each other in some new ways.

Management and Labor

For all its promise as a concept, employee involvement is just a fad or a buzzword without serious management involvement to assure success. Many of the gains achieved by SRUP's ACT safety process are due to the new organizational structures established by the behavior-based process. In its own way, this development parallels the move away from the departmentalized safety paradigm. By taking part in behavior-based training, all employees learn a new approach to their own safety roles and responsibilities. In a similar way, labor and management learn a new approach for sharing safety data-gathering, problem solving, and action planning.

It would be hard to overestimate the importance of this development. In addition to significant gains in safety, many other benefits flow from this new and mutual involvement of both management and labor. The behavior-based approach to safety can plant the seeds of this possibility because it is built on data-driven problem solving. This is accountable employee involvement, and it has the effect of moving the safety management function down into the workforce as a whole.

It is on this foundation that a facility can go on to address other big questions of quality and productivity. For instance, subsequent to ACT, SRUP set up its new quality council. At that time it was widely accepted that the quality council membership needed to include the labor union president. Before ACT it probably would not have occurred to either management or labor to work this closely together on quality.

CONCLUSION

The case histories covered in this chapter represent the broad sweep of what many companies are achieving with employee-driven safety performance. As site personnel adapt the TQM principles of the behavioral approach, they indicate their pride of ownership by giving their safety process a distinctive name. They then put in place a mechanism that helps them systematically prevent injuries through ongoing data gathering and analysis, and all of that communicated to the workforce through positive peer-to-peer observation and feedback. By integrating behavioral and statistical methodologies, this approach establishes employee-driven safety performance as the best all-around solution to some of the most important industrial challenges of the turn of the century. Quality, downsizing, environmental concerns, re-engineering, meeting challenges of this kind requires precisely the breakthrough that is taking place daily wherever employee-driven safety is practiced. The reason is that a workforce engaged in employee-driven safety grows fluent in new applications of basic science. Workforce engagement of this kind and degree is the necessary driving mechanism of continuous performance improvement.

Bibliography

Of General Interest

The Companion Volume

Krause, T. R., J. H. Hidley, and S. J. Hodson. 1990. *The Behavior-Based Safety Process*. New York: Van Nostrand Reinhold.

Articles

Krause, T. R., and J. B. Spigener. February 1994. "The Role of Training in Continuous Improvement." *MetalForming*.

Krause, T. R., J. H. Hidley, and G. W. Langston. January 1994. "Behavior-based Task Analysis Prompts Early Response to Ergonomic Problems."*Occupational Health & Safety*.

Krause, T. R., D. DiPiero, and T. Durbin. November 1993."Making Safety and Quality Work Together." *Occupational Hazards*.

Krause, T. R. April 1993. "Safety and Quality—Two Sides of the Same Coin." *Occupational Hazards*.

Krause, T. R. January 1993. "Attitude Alone is Not Enough." *Occupational Health & Safety*.

Krause, T. R., and J. H. Hidley. June 1992. "On Their Best Behavior." *Accident Prevention*.

Krause, T.R. 1991. "A Behavior-Based Safety Management Process." Chapter in *Applying Psychology in Business—The Handbook for Managers and Human Resource Professionals*. Jones, J.W., B. D. Steffy, D. W. Bray, editors. Lexington Books.

Krause, T. R., and J. H. Hidley. June 1991. "Measuring Safety Performance: The Process Approach." *Occupational Hazards*.

Krause, T. R., and J. H. Hidley. July 1990. "Broad-Based Changes in Behavior Key to Improving Safety Culture." *Occupational Health & Safety*.

Krause. T. R. December 1989. "Improving Safety Culture—The Critical-Mass Approach." *Insights Into Management*.

Krause. T. R. October 1989. "Improving Safety Culture—Behavior versus Attitude." *Insights Into Management.*

Krause. T. R. October 1989. "Behaviorally-based Safety Management: Parallels with the Quality Improvement Process." *Insights Into Management.*

Krause. T. R. August 1989. "Improving Safety Culture—Discipline isn't Enough." *Insights Into Management.*

Krause, T. R., J. H. Hidley, and S. J. Hodson. December 1988. "Behavioral Science in the Workplace: Techniques for Achieving an Injury-Free Environment." *Modern Job Safety and Health Guidelines.* Prentice Hall Information Services.

Krause, T. R., and J. H. Hidley. February 1988. "Managing Safety Means Focusing on Behavior." *PIMA Magazine.*

Other Books

Deming, W. E. 1986. *Out of the Crisis.* Massachusetts Institute of Technology.

International Business Machines Corporation. 1984. *Process Control, Capability and Improvement.* The Quality Institute.

McGuigan, F. J. 1968. *Experimental Psychology, A Methodological Approach.* Prentice-Hall, Inc.

Related Background Reading for Chapters 3 and 4

Ajzen, I., and T. J. Madden. 1986. "Prediction of Goal-Directed Behavior: Attitudes, Intentions and Perceived Behavioral Control." *Journal of Experimental Social Psychology,* Vol. 22, pp. 453–474.

Ajzen, I. 1989. "Attitude Structure and Behavior." Anthony R. Pratkanis, Steven J. Breckler, and Anthony G. Greenwald (Eds.) *Attitude Structure and Function.* Lawrence Earlbaum Associates.

Ajzen, I. 1985. "From intentions to actions: A Theory of planned behavior." J. Kuhl and J. Breckman (Eds.) *Action Control: From Cognition to Behavior,* pp. 11–39. Heidelberg: Springer.

Ajzen, I. and M. Fishbein. 1980. *Understanding Attitudes and Predicting Social Behavior.* Prentice-Hall, Inc.

Fishbein, M. and Ajzen, I. (1975). *Belief, Attitude, Intention and Behavior: An Introduction to Theory and Research.* Addison-Wesley.

Related Statistics Background Reading for Chapter 7

Koosis, D. J. 1985. *Statistics, Third Edition—A Self-Teaching Guide.* John Wiley & Sons, Inc.

Norusis, M. J. 1993. *SPSS® for Windows™, Base System User's Guide Release 6.0.* SPSS Inc.

Ott, L., F. L. Larson, and W. Mendenhall. 1987. *Statistics, A Tool for the Social Sciences.* PWS Publishers.

Phillips, J. L. Jr. 1992. *How to Think About Statistics,* Revised Edition. W. H. Freeman and Company.

Related Background Reading for Chapter 12

29 CFR Part 910—Ergonomic Safety and Health Management, Proposed Rule. Federal Register. Monday, August 3, 1992. Department of Labor, Occupational Safety and Health Administration.

California's Proposed Ergonomics Regulation. State of California, Department of Industrial Relations, Division of Occupational Safety & Health. San Francisco, CA. 415/703-4361.

Chaffin D., and G. Anderson. 1984. *Occupational Biomechanics.* John Wiley & Sons, Inc.

Ergonomics: A Practical Guide. National Safety Council, 1988

National Safety Council, 1994. *Accidents Facts.* Chicago—National Safety Council

The UAW Ford Ergonomics Process Job Improvement Guide. A publication of UAW—Ford National Joint Committee on Health and Safety, 1988. Regents of the University of Michigan.

U.S. Department of Labor. Occupational Safety and Health Administration, 1990. *OSHA 3123. Ergonomic Program Management Guidelines for Meatpacking Plants.*

Related Background Reading for Chapter 16

Komaki, J., K. D. Barwick, and L. R. Scott. 1978. "A behavioral approach to occupational safety: pinpointing and reinforcing safety performance in a food manufacturing plant." *Journal of Applied Psychology* 63(4): 434–45.

Komaki, J., A. T. Heinzmann, and L. Lawson. 1980. "Effect of training and feedback: component analysis of a behavioral safety program." *Journal of Applied Psychology* 65(3): 261–70.

Komaki, J., R. L. Collins, and P. Penn. 1982. "The role of performance antecedents and consequences in work motivation" *Journal of Applied Psychology* 67(3): 334–40.

Index